After leaving university, Clive Wright worked for over 30 years in the oil and chemical industries, principally in the UK but also in Africa, Europe and the USA. Since his early teens he has been a member of the Church of England. He has written and lectured widely on different aspects of the relationship between the Christian faith and the world of business.

The Business of Virtue

Clive Wright

First published in Great Britain in 2004 by
Society for Promoting Christian Knowledge
Holy Trinity Church
Marylebone Road
London NW1 4DU

British Library Cataloguing-in-Publication Data
A catalogue record for this book is available from the British Library.

ISBN 0-281-05426-6

1 3 5 7 9 10 8 6 4 2

Typeset by Avocet Typeset, Chilton, Aylesbury, Bucks
Printed in Great Britain by Antony Rowe Limited

To Kenneth Adams
friend, sage, fellow seeker

Contents

To the reader

This book is intended primarily (but by no means exclusively) for Christians who work in business. Christian teaching can offer much to help all business people.

In all walks of life faith poses questions. Countless Christians everywhere are engaged in business providing goods and services for their fellow human beings. For them the teachings of Jesus Christ present special challenges. The ideas and reflections in this book are intended to help meet those challenges, considered from the position of the practitioner.

Business people are generally more concerned with the practicalities of day-to-day work than with theorizing about it. I hope, nevertheless, that they will find the time to read chapters 1 to 5. Chapters 1 and 2 look briefly at an historical perspective, and chapters 3 and 4 consider aspects of the wealth creation process and offer some theological reflections about it. Chapter 5 addresses the present-day postmodern climate of uncertainty on matters of morality.

Chapters 6 to 10 seek to bring together insights from Christian moral thought and to look at how they help in addressing ethical issues that can arise during the conduct of business. These chapters are based upon practical experience in the workplace, not upon classroom theory. I hope they are helpful to all business people, Christians and non-Christians alike.

In the last chapter I set out a vision of hope in addressing critical issues surfacing in business today, especially those associated with globalization and conservation of the environment. The economic processes that dominate much of the world evolved in a culture shaped by Christian belief: it is right that there should be a Christian response to the concerns that materialize.

Acknowledgements

The origins of this book lie in discussions with many friends and contacts. I am particularly grateful for the fruits of debates conducted within the Christian Association of Business Executives, the Institute of Business Ethics, the Industrial Christian Fellowship, and the Ridley Hall Foundation, Cambridge. I also benefited greatly from the consultations held over the years at St George's House, Windsor Castle, and in the pages of *Faith in Business Quarterly*. I am indebted to all those who have contributed to those debates and I hope they will forgive my not mentioning any individuals by name.

Finally, my thanks to my wife for her patience and counsel as I wrestled with the pains of authorship.

Prologue

Economic considerations are present in virtually every aspect of daily life. Newspapers, journals, radio and television devote a great deal of coverage to matters relating to commerce and business. Activities which at one time were largely leisure pursuits, like sport and the arts, have become significant businesses in their own right. Nor is this concern with the economic dimension limited to the developed world; the importance of business is similarly evident across much of the underdeveloped and developing world, and the term 'globalization' has entered common usage in that context. For the Western world – Europe and North America – our unprecedented levels of wealth have not in any way reduced our interest in and concern about economic matters. Indeed, rising prosperity and wealth appear to have reinforced and increased a preoccupation with the process and the method by which it is brought about. Communism may be on the retreat but the view of Marx – that humankind is driven by economic considerations – seems to have acquired a different validity.

It is a reflection of the importance of the economic process, as an influence and determinant on the society in which we live, that we dedicate so much time and concern to that activity: to the businesses which produce the goods and services upon which we depend; to the successes and failures of companies and entrepreneurs; and to the general way in which the whole activity is conducted. The influence of the world of business is all-pervasive, shaping our behaviour, our thinking, the language we use.

To recognize the importance of the economic processes that shape our culture and our society is not to say that they meet with unqualified approval. On the contrary, an ambivalence and distrust towards business and towards the wealth it creates are marked features of our attitudes. This scepticism, not to say hostility, is not new. Warnings about excessive attachment to material things and to wealth in general, as well as critical assessments of the way in which the economic process is conducted, have been articulated in Western society since the writings of Plato.

Discomfort with the dominant Western capitalist model of wealth creation – indeed outright hostility to it – has been visibly manifested through public protests. Meetings of the World Trade Organization and its agenda to promote freer world trade have sparked violent and well-publicized demonstrations against the unfairnesses and deficiencies of the globalization of business. Likewise meetings of leaders of the more prosperous member nations of the Organization for Economic Co-operation and Development (OECD) have been the occasion for further vociferous rejection of those same perceived injustices and inadequacies of the world economic system. There is by no means unanimous approval of the dominant economic model.

Protest, fundamental and violent, is not confined to those living in countries where free-market capitalism has emerged as the most successful system. The fearful suicide attacks against the World Trade Center in New York on 11 September 2001 had many complex and interlinking causes. But undoubtedly, among these causes lay a fundamental and ideological disagreement with Western commercial culture, seen to be a threat to the very principles of Islamic societies and their way of life. It is tempting to dismiss such fears as 'fundamentalist' and the views of a fanatical minority. This would clearly be unduly simplistic and unwise. The very premises upon which the Western commercial system is predicated are challenged by a dissenting viewpoint that merits respect and serious attention – even though expression of dissent through acts of indiscriminate killing is to be condemned. That challenge demands an examination of the moral and even the practical credentials of the economic system that now pervades the world. If those who are prepared to live with the outcomes (both good and bad) of our wealth-creation system are to come to any form of accommodation with the voices of dissent and protest, they are bound inescapably to examine and address those critiques. One of those voices – the terrorist's – must be rejected, but the message must be understood and addressed.

Loud among the voices expressing profound unease with the whole subject of wealth creation has been that of the Christian religion, which is itself, of course, the great formative influence on the societies that have evolved in Europe and North America. Throughout Christian teaching and the prophetic witness of Christian thinkers, a clear note of reservation about wealth and riches is readily identified. The Bible contains many warnings on this subject. The 'option for the poor' – that special injunction laid upon Christians to care for those who have little share in the material things of this world – puts a particular emphasis upon the correct use of wealth. The dramatic renunciation of all material goods by St Francis of Assisi is perhaps the most extreme and challenging statement of Christian reservations about the creation and possession of worldly riches. The challenge of St Francis has coloured much Christian thinking and prophetic utterance over the last six centuries.

Thus, the unparalleled success of the economic systems that have developed in the West sits uncomfortably with some of the teachings of Christianity, which has shaped the culture in which those systems have evolved. Has this successful system emerged because of, in spite of, or independently of the Christian teaching within whose influence it began? Max Weber, in *The Protestant Ethic and the Spirit of Capitalism*, argued that religion has been the source of economic change.[1] R. H. Tawney, in *Religion and the Rise of Capitalism*, identified 'the secular and religious aspects of life . . . as parallel and independent provinces, governed by different laws, judged by different standards, and amenable to different authorities'.[2] In 1990 David Jeremy looked at the relationship between capitalism and religion in Britain over the period 1900 to 1960.[3] He concluded that the impact of business on the churches had been more substantial than the impact of the churches on business.

Examination of the relationship between Christian teaching and culture and the process of creating wealth has been a continuing subject of commentary. One theme explores discomfort with the very nature of the activity itself, asking the fundamental question whether it is compatible with Christian teaching about the dangers of undue attachment to riches and to material possessions. Another theme addresses the way in which wealth is created, the damaging social and environmental effects, and the imbalances of power and justice that may arise. The two themes are, of course, interlinked and became pronounced in Christian thinking from 1750 onwards. The Christian Socialist movement, which emerged in the late nineteenth century, articulated both strong warnings about the moral dangers of materialism and also severe criticism specifically of the free-market capitalist system, which – it warned – encourages materialism and produces social degradation and chronic injustice. It became difficult to distinguish between the theological admonitions about greed and materialism and condemnation of the political-economic system that dominates the Western world. Possibly because North America was much more strongly wedded to free-market capitalism than much of

Western Europe, the Christian critique of the business process was less forceful and strident there than in Europe.

However, towards the end of the twentieth century, as the failings and eventual collapse of communism became more apparent, political criticism of the free-market capitalist model became less vigorous. The success of that model in creating greater prosperity that was more widely spread throughout society led to a reassessment of the socialist–communist model. Questioning by many Christians of the hitherto assumed congruence between their religious beliefs and a socialist economy significantly changed the nature of the debate. Thus, Canon John Atherton, a British theologian who was strongly in the tradition of Christian socialism, made a major adaptation to the realities of the world following the collapse of communism. In his *Christianity and the Market*, he accepted that 'the churches had traditionally neither understood nor acknowledged the market as the *positively* least harmful way of operating a modern economy'.[4] He asserted that 'there is the requirement of the Churches in the West to be able to take seriously the framework and dynamic of [the] market ... it is increasingly unlikely that this can be developed by the existing mind-set of the established Churches'.[5]

Unsurprisingly, a robust Christian defence of the free-market capitalist model was set out in the United States. The Roman Catholic theologian Michael Novak expresses great confidence in the free-market capitalist system. His writings assert the positive value of creating wealth and see business as a worthy calling for Christians to pursue. He offers business as not just a morally serious vocation but as a morally noble one as well. In presenting his thesis Novak does not ignore the traditionally painful areas such as downsizing or the trade-offs to be faced between profits and human rights. For him, however, there is no equivocation: capitalism is better for the poor than is socialism or the traditional third world economy.[6]

Thus throughout these explorations, there is interplay between these two themes: a strand of discomfort with wealth itself, and an examination of the capitalist and socialist ways of generating wealth. It is difficult to look at one of these themes independently of the other. The debate is both conceptual (about the nature and desirability of wealth itself) and political (about the system by which it is created).

A notable feature of the literature on Christian belief and wealth creation is the relative absence of contributions by the practitioners themselves: that is to say by businessmen or businesswomen. By far the majority of contributions come from academics, teachers, clergymen or others not directly involved in the process whereby wealth itself is created. To make this observation is not to criticize or to seek to diminish these perspectives in any way. It is right that a detached and, one hopes, objective viewpoint is offered. Moreover, there is a long and regrettable tradition that businessmen are remarkably inarticulate – not to say silent – in offering justification or even explanation of the work they do. Even today when business activity, as we have already noted, has a much higher profile generally, it is still difficult to identify many leading businessmen who have tackled the challenge of talking intelligibly about what they do. As a breed they seem to prefer to talk in highly controlled situations and in ways that are not user-friendly for ordinary people. So it is perhaps hardly surprising that the thinking and writing about the congruence of the two major shaping forces in our culture – faith and the world of wealth creation – has contained only a modest contribution from the business community itself. As one distinguished businessman with whom I have worked expressed it, 'I am not really interested in talking about the job to be done: my concern is with getting on and doing it.' Perhaps this is a widespread approach shared by many businessmen and accounts for their apparent reluctance to join the debate about what they do.

It therefore seems appropriate to reflect upon these two great influences on our lives, Christianity and the Western model of free-market capitalism, and upon the ways in which they have interacted and may interact in the future. We can observe a number of significant changes and developments.

To begin with, as noted earlier, we are witnessing an unprecedented dominance of one particular model of wealth-creation activity – that which has emerged in the societies of Western Europe and North America. To recognize that dominance it is not necessary to subscribe to the famous statement made by Francis Fukuyama in his *The End of History*, where he makes the remarkable claim that 'the current liberal revolution . . . constitutes further evidence that there is a fundamental process at work that dictates a common evolutionary pattern for *all* human societies – in short something like a Universal History of Mankind in the direction of liberal democracy'.[7] Even if we reject this somewhat Hegelian view and reserve our position, it is hard to dispute the hegemony of that particular model at the present time. And, on its own terms, the model is highly successful. At no previous point in human history has one particular socio-economic system been so successful or so widely adopted.

As we have already noted, there has been a perceptible shift in attitudes towards the whole question of wealth creation. The cautious change in tone among Christians, adopting a less condemnatory view of the process of wealth creation in the thinking of Christians, is not an isolated phenomenon. There is now a general willingness across Western society to look at the operations of business in a more positive light. In part this may be due to recognition of the wider sharing of the material benefits which it has provided. It is less easy to condemn something of which one is the manifest beneficiary than it is to rail against a system from whose benefits one is excluded. Despite the affront of a gap between rich and poor in Britain at the beginning of the twenty-first century wider than at any time in the previous fifty years, it became impossible to deny or ignore the rise in living standards enjoyed by all the population over that time. This growth in prosperity for the West coincided with the weakening and eventual collapse of communism in the 1990s. Communism represented – at least in theory – a serious alternative socio-economic system. As long as the communist bloc remained in existence and most of us were largely unaware of the extent of its system's failure to deliver either economic well-being or social justice, there was the seductive hope that a viable, effective alternative to Western capitalism was available. It is no longer possible seriously to maintain the argument that communism is an acceptable alternative. Thus, while reservations remain about our economic system, the debate has moved on to the discussion of different approaches that might be adopted within it, rather than seeking a root-and-branch destruction and replacement of it.

The 1980s saw a different economic approach emerge in Britain and Western Europe which also extended to other economies. The role of the state as a provider of goods and services – the essential elements of wealth creation – was dramatically redefined. Large sections of economic activity, previously regarded as the exclusive domain of state control, were transferred to the private sector. To generations that had grown up with nationalization as a socio-economic goal, it was necessary to adjust to the reversal of that process: privatization. The wind of change that blew through traditional economic thinking brought with it a new awareness of economic activity itself. People became shareholders, had surplus money to invest and – for the first time – a generation emerged that inherited modest capital. They were the children of those who in the 1920s and 1930s had bought their own houses and bequeathed them to their children. These factors were among a number of developments that served to raise awareness of, and interest in, the economic processes of modern life. Greater numbers of people than ever before became aware of wealth, recognized that they were themselves possessors of wealth, and sought to educate themselves about the nature and creation of wealth.

The broader democratization of involvement in the world of wealth creation reflected a change in social attitudes. Over the centuries, a tradition of respect for the ownership of land as the most socially acceptable form of wealth had created a corresponding tendency to despise other forms of wealth creation, which were commonly dismissed as 'trade'. A social stigma became attached to the activities of industry and commerce – particularly in the nineteenth century. This attitude was reinforced in educational and social teaching in Victorian and Edwardian Britain. To the suspicion of wealth and riches, which, as we have seen, represented a strong strand in Christian thinking, was added a social dimension reinforcing the view that to work in 'trade' was an inferior activity and unworthy of a gentleman. An influential and well-known expression of these sentiments at their high point is to be found in Matthew Arnold's *Culture and Anarchy*, written in 1869, with its crushing condemnations of the philistinism of those who did not share his ideals.

The last two or three decades of the twentieth century saw a retreat from those attitudes. The creation and possession of wealth through business, industry and commerce no longer incurred social opprobrium and distaste. On the contrary, many modern role-models and heroes, representing a new classlessness, were those who rose through trade. The businessman came to be seen as a figure to respect and admire; successful businessmen were invited to bring their skills and talents to other walks of life, from government itself to public agencies of every kind. Business had become not only respectable, but even laudable. Western Europe made an important shift towards the North American model in its attitudes towards business.

At the same time as these shifts in attitudes occurred, major changes were taking place in the wealth-creation process itself. Until the last thirty years of the twentieth century, economic activity was dominated by manufacturing. The industrial revolution, which began in the middle of the eighteenth century, marked the transformation of an economy dominated by agriculture into one where the adoption of machine methods of producing goods (accompanied by a transport system that facilitated regional division of labour) became the principal economic activity. The pre-eminence of manufacturing, accompanied by a progressive decline in the importance of agriculture and the number of people employed on the land, persisted until the 1980s. Manufacturing is characterized by the exploitation of natural resources and the production of material things. It has often resulted in severe degradation and pollution of the natural environment, by rapid urbanization, and by wretched and unhealthy conditions both for work and for domestic life.

However, in the 1980s it became clear that, in the richer countries of the OECD, the balance of economic activity had swung from manufacturing to services. The proportion of the workforce in Britain engaged in manufacturing had shrunk, from around 40 per cent in 1900 to about half that level in the early 1990s. This change has been referred to as de-industrialization. In the 1980s the trend to services caused disquiet in the United States and in Britain. It was seen, and frequently referred to, as the export of jobs. In the 1990s it became clear that this change was more complex than that. It is obvious that a household can only use so many cars, television sets or dishwashers. What then happens is that a rising share of income goes on such things as holidays, leisure, fitness, and so on. Activity in these fields is not manufacturing.

Similarly, manufacturing itself has changed enormously. Many aspects of manufacturing – such as the design or marketing of products – really represent services. The traditional distinction between manufacturing and services now has less meaning. In all rich countries the manufacturing share of total output has shrunk: this is a repeat performance of the earlier decline of agriculture as the main component of those same economies. As an article in *The Economist* pointed out, the old definitions of manufacturing are no longer worth much.[8] If we take most everyday manufactures that feature in our lives – for example, cars, jeans, shoes – it is clear that great differences exist between different examples. A Mercedes is very different from a Trabant, although both are cars. For most manufactured goods, there is great differentiation by design, quality, durability etc. The material content of many goods is now a small proportion of their total value. For example, the metal of a compact disc is worth a few pence but when it carries a song cycle by Schubert or a number of pop hits, the disc is worth many times more.

This shift to the so-called weightless economy is dramatically reflected in the 'second economic revolution': the move to the information economy. On the basis of the rapid improvements in computer and telecommunications technology, coupled with equally rapid developments in software, new fields of economic activity and wealth creation continue to evolve. The 1990s, especially after 1995, saw the establishment and the development of the Internet, a process moving so fast and with such bewildering complexity that few would be willing to predict what will happen as the new millennium unfolds. What is quite clear, however, is that a new form of wealth creation had now emerged. And in the weightless economy the concern about addiction to material things may become a little less threatening. Certainly, this new kind of economic activity is less damaging to the environment, polluting less and consuming less of the globe's natural resources.

The second change in the wealth-creation process itself is closely related to the first. Just as the evolution of the weightless economy is intimately associated with rapid and profound changes in modern technology – particularly in the fields of information handling and telecommunications – so the second change, the globalization of business, is also closely linked to new technologies.

The dominance and effectiveness of the Western model for wealth creation – the democratic, free-market capitalist system – has encouraged two further developments. First, poorer, less developed countries seek to avail themselves of the benefits which this model delivers. Recent decades have seen the largely successful adoption of Western approaches by many countries, such as Thailand, South Korea, Malaysia, Taiwan and (with severe qualifications on some important points) mainland China. Second, the dynamic of the Western economic process has taken it into new, developing markets through the agency of international companies as they expand globally.

The term 'globalization' is used variously to describe the phenomenal increase in economic activity that has taken place throughout the whole world, the widespread adoption of the Western economic model, and the tendency towards a more uniform world culture. One feature of the global economy is the power and ubiquity of large multinational corporations such as Coca-Cola or Microsoft, whose goods or services are available in almost every country in the world. Modern communications and transport technologies make the process of globalization possible and speed it up. Globalization also means global competition. It is no longer possible for a company or a country indefinitely to protect itself from competing forces that may emanate from the other side of the world. This competitive drive is relentless in its demands. Quality must improve. Costs must be reduced. Productivity becomes a critical factor in performance. New technologies must be mastered and harnessed. Skills must be continuously honed and improved. Change is inescapable: there are no longer barriers to keep it at bay. Distinctive cultures and societies are exposed as never before to new external forces.

The drive to create wealth, and the economic processes that are associated with that drive, therefore present us with an old challenge in a new form. Humankind is the only species that lives everywhere across the globe, and our unique characteristics have enabled us to achieve unparalleled success and physical dominance over our surroundings. However, we have wrought terrible damage upon the natural environment, upon other species and upon ourselves. There is ample evidence to suggest that our technical capabilities may have outstripped our wisdom to deploy them properly. These capabilities are now put to the service of wealth-creation activity. How do we find the wisdom to ensure that this is done in a responsible way?

Part of the human heritage of wisdom lies in our accumulated moral understanding. This heritage is widely dispersed throughout the different cultures of the world. Much of it resides in the teachings of religion. In a pluralistic world pervaded by postmodern relativism, it is tempting to discard this heritage. It is a premiss of this volume that to do so would be imprudent.

It is at this point in our history that we should seek a congruence between two great determining forces of the Western world: the economic systems that have emerged in societies shaped by the Christian religion and by Christian thought, and the Christian religion itself. Religious beliefs and our creative energies have shaped the world in which we now live. The interaction between the two will greatly affect the way we conduct ourselves in the future.

As we have seen, Christian thinking has traditionally experienced discomfort with the process of wealth creation. Today, in Western Europe, business and commerce are mostly carried out with scant reference to Christianity. Yet the importance of wealth creation today poses a moral challenge: how is it to be conducted with due wisdom and responsibility? This book seeks to address that question from the perspective of the Christian working in business.

Notes

1. Max Weber, *The Protestant Ethic and the Spirit of Capitalism*, 1st publ. 1905.

2. R. H. Tawney, *Religion and the Rise of Capitalism*, revd edn (1937), repr. Penguin, 1990, p. 273.
3. David Jeremy, *Capitalists and Christians, 1900–1960*, Oxford University Press, 1990.
4. John Atherton, *Christianity and the Market: Christian Social Thought for Our Times*, SPCK, 1992, p. 273.
5. Ibid., p. 275.
6. See Michael Novak, *Business as a Calling: Work and the Examined Life*, Free Press, 1996.
7. Francis Fukuyama, *The End of History and the Last Man*, Hamish Hamilton, 1992, p. 48, his italics.
8. 'Post-industrial Manufacturing', in 'A Survey of Manufacturing', supplement to *The Economist*, 20 June 1998, p. 17.

♦ 1 ♦

Common good: private imperfection

As a gregarious species, human beings are constrained to behave in ways that serve the general well-being of all. An essential element of human nature is the capacity to live in some degree of harmony with our fellow human beings. Yet each of us is conscious of our own individuality and independence. There are times when even the most socially integrated and cooperative people act in ways that are selfish and disruptive for others. At a very fundamental level, there is a tension in human communities: the pressure to behave in ways that serve the community in order to safeguard its very survival versus our desires as individuals to pursue selfish and anti-social ends for personal gratification. Keeping these two conflicting forces in balance poses a challenge in almost every field of human activity, to which humankind devotes huge resources.

We can see this conflict in simple examples, such as a game of football. Eleven players must work together in order to beat the other eleven. Any player who wishes to show off skills at dribbling or kicking the ball huge distances must rein in his special attributes and tailor them to the needs of the team. He obeys a complex set of external and self-imposed constraints in order to achieve this end. Likewise, both teams know that the game of football has rules. There is always the temptation to cheat and to break the rules in order to secure an advantage. The referee and opponents (as well as the spectators) are on the lookout to prevent excessive breaking of the rules. But if all the players choose to ignore the rules the game breaks down: no winners; no losers; no game at all.

The game of football is a paradigm for most areas of human activity. And at the macro-level too we observe the tensions between cooperation and self-interest, when large groups of people, such as nation states or ethnic groups, come into contact and where conflicting interests arise. In our sane moments we recognize that armed conflict and war is a disastrous way in which to resolve disputes. Peaceful resolution of differences and opposing interests is incomparably preferable to the agonies of armed conflict. The common good of all should have primacy over the particular interests of some. Yet, as we know too well, resort to war is sadly a lot more frequent than the collapse of a game of football because the players decide to dispense with the rules. This all suggests that the tension between the common good and individual or particular group interest is one that may be inherent in the human condition and one that we may never fully resolve.

Business or commerce is one of the most widespread of human activities. There is virtually no human community in today's world that does not engage in some form of manufacture, trade, barter, exchange, buying and selling. And, as in other spheres, humankind's economic activities display the tensions between serving and supporting the community and the well-being of all, and the pursuit of selfish ends. It will be necessary at several points in our discussion to note that human business activities bring into play some of our less attractive attributes as a species, such as self-interest, acquisitiveness and competitiveness. Indeed, this phenomenon leads some commentators to point to business and commerce as full-blooded Darwinism in practice. David Hawkes put it in these words:

> It is ironic that both rational choice theory and evolutionary psychology claim to be strictly individualistic in procedure. They are united in their determination to exclude from consideration any phenomena wider than the desires and impulses of a single human being ... Biological imperatives have programmed us to be selfish, and we automatically fulfil these imperatives in our competitive economic activity. The concepts of agency or freewill are entirely lacking from such purportedly individualistic approaches, and this conception of the human subject is entirely objectified.[1]

So we indeed face a challenge. How can the common good be accommodated with this fact of selfish individual behaviour in the sphere of economic activity? If such an analysis is even partially true, what is to be done to tame the underlying viciousness that drives one of the most significant aspects of Western society?

As we shall see, the sphere of humankind's economic behaviour has, in the Western world, become secularized and to a large degree depersonalized. It is part of common wisdom that religions and their teachings have little or nothing useful to say about business and commerce. These business activities, it is argued, are independent of religion, conducted according to their own internal imperatives and rationale. It is our purpose in this study to question this assumption and to develop a serious case for the importance of dialogue and interaction between the Christian religion and the world of economic activity. We shall explore the validity of this proposition from several points of view. But we shall argue that there is a very particular and valuable contribution to be made within the traditions of Christendom by addressing the tension between the common good and private self-interest as it arises in the field of business. This tension, as we have seen, appears to be fundamental to the economic processes that create the wealth upon which we all depend. It is clear that the highly successful Western democratic capitalist model has the capability to create and sustain the means for great communal well-being – but that at the same time a vigorous and potentially damaging drive of self-interest lies at the very heart of that model.

The secularization of economics and the study of business and commerce may now be virtually complete in the Western world. But this has not always been the case. As we noted earlier, it is highly significant that the democratic capitalist form of wealth creation evolved in a culture shaped by the Christian religion. How, then, is it that the great wealth-creation machine which now dominates the globe emerged in Christendom but has come to be seen as a secular activity nevertheless?

The potential conflicts that arise between public and private interest do not occur in a society characterized by simple production methods (that is, methods requiring minimal specialist skills) and where property is held in common. Without private ownership the exchange of goods has little meaning. The absence of public–private conflict in a society where property is in common ownership and where production is simple enough for all to participate in has been the hallmark of a kind of utopia. The translation of this ideal concept into a political programme is the basis for most socialist-aligned thinking. However, the evidence seems fairly conclusive that without private ownership, the motivation needed for serious wealth creation does not materialize. Absence of private ownership may work on a small scale but not on a large one. We shall look at the nature of wealth creation more closely in Chapter 3, but the empirical evidence suggests that for it to happen on an effective scale, so that large numbers of people may be beneficiaries, certain conditions are prerequisites. These include a degree of private ownership of property and of process, and the division and specialization of labour, when we go beyond the point where the techniques involved are so simple that they can be practised by anyone. On the basis of what history and present experience teach us, these elements are a *sine qua non* for the creation of surplus and for rising above subsistence. Private interest seems to be an essential ingredient for the serious creation of wealth. The potential for conflict with the public good, therefore, may indeed be inherent in the process by which wealth is created.

The Judaic perspective on wealth

The society described in the Old Testament clearly had some of these features that are needed for the creation of wealth above minimal levels. We read of the private ownership of property and specialization in the work to be done. Goods are exchanged and money is used to facilitate that process. But, as we read the Old Testament, it is equally clear that these are not regarded as secular activities about which the religion of the Jews has nothing to say. Business in the market economy of the Old Testament is not secularized. However, tensions arising from economic activity have become apparent. Certain individuals accumulate wealth and become rich; others remain poor. There are early signs of the imperfections in the working of the market economy: unfairness and injustice; the intrusion of private interest to the detriment of the common good and the emergence of undesirable and anti-social behaviour, such as greed, addiction to the acquisition of material goods, and dishonesty in transactions with others. And we read of constraints built into the economic process to attempt to mitigate these damaging effects. The book of Leviticus is quite prescriptive about the ways in which business is to be conducted and famously sets out bases in chapter 25 for family ownership of land and the year of jubilee: 'And you shall hallow the fiftieth year, and proclaim liberty throughout the land to all its inhabitants; it shall be a jubilee for you, when each of you shall return to his property and each of you shall return to his family' (Leviticus 25.10). These prescriptions are accompanied throughout the Old Testament by prophetic judgements upon the iniquities arising from the commercial and business systems practised in Israel. But at no stage did those systems become secularized beyond the comment and correction of religious thinkers and leaders. Rather, they are regarded as part of a homogeneous system to be conducted in accordance with the will of God. This is not a free-standing, self-justifying market economy but one that is seen to be integrated into and conditioned by the religious and ethical teachings of Judaism.

Of course, the teachings of Old Testament Judaism on the conduct of economic life relate to a pre-industrial society. The complexity of modern business and commercial practice, and the loss of a separate identity and legal system for the Jewish people have to some degree affected the continuity of those teachings to the present day. But it is of considerable significance to our theme that there is nevertheless a distinctive Jewish framework that looks to the sanctification of everyday actions in this field. Its point of departure is that material welfare is a gift from God and is to be valued and prized on that account. All wealth is of divine origin and humankind has temporary ownership and stewardship of it. Thus in Deuteronomy 8.17–18 we read, 'Beware lest you say in your heart, "My power and the might of my hand have gotten me this wealth." You shall remember the Lord your God, for it is he who gives you power to get wealth'.

Meir Tamari, a writer and commentator on Jewish thought about business, to whom I am indebted for much of the background to my comments on this subject, points out that in the Pentateuch, the first five books of the Bible, there are no fewer than 613 commandments, of which some 100 relate to the sphere of economics.[2] This is the foundation for Jewish law and is regarded as being of divine inspiration. The additional written and oral law that has been developed subsequently is supplementary but based on the principle that economic desires are legitimate, and sanctified by God's commandments.

The Jewish community developed in Old Testament times and, as the canon of rabbinical teachings grew, governing boards were established which fixed wages, prices, weights and measures, and by-laws. The requirement to pay communal taxes was religious as well as social. Philanthropy was seen as an obligation, arising from the possession of wealth. The Jewish welfare state was not voluntary and contributions were demanded in proportion to means. Thus wealth creation was integrated into the values of Jewish society.

Rabbinical Judaism also demanded that the Jews make the fullest possible use of God's gifts and this evolved as a gospel of work, with economic progress based upon methodical problem-solving within a framework of law. The canon of teaching developed and became more complicated as new circumstances demanded. The scope of rabbinical teaching is today very wide, covering virtually every aspect of economic activity, including such areas as competition, prices, profits, wages and labour, money, banking and interest. For those who are practising Jews, the teaching has the full effect of law. It is contained in what is known as the *Halachah*, the collective literature of the rulings of Jewish written and oral law, as defined by and in accordance with the authoritative rabbinical rulings within the clearly defined principles of Jewish law.

Tamari identifies four principal areas under which Jewish law deals with economics: theft and exploitation; limitations on private wealth; economic justice; and patterns of consumption. The precepts set out in these groupings assume that the free market is an efficient and pragmatic way to secure the welfare of the community. Conflicts between market efficiency and social concerns are to be resolved according to the value structure of society. Judaism is prepared to put the efficiency of the market as secondary to its own values. It is this strand in Jewish teaching on economic behaviour which has remained central over the centuries and which maintains the warnings of the prophets of old. As we have seen, the starting point is that God's laws are laid down to enhance life and to bestow wisdom in a consistent, not a random, way. Underpinning the law, therefore, is the vision of people in harmony – with themselves, with their neighbours and with God. The tension between our good and our bad desires is resolved through our recognition that the law sets out the norms of conduct which we are to follow. The truly pious are encouraged to go beyond the law and to behave according to the promptings of conscience, a concept to which we shall return.

It is not within the scope of this book to explain in detail Jewish teachings on business life: writers like Tamari do so in considerable depth. We are here concerned with the significance of the continuity of that teaching, rooted firmly in the recognition that religion and economic activity are linked. Judaism has a theological basis for its endorsement of the world of business: that world has a purpose that is consistent with the divine will and that can be rationally translated into values that are essential to the proper conduct of business.

This continuity of thinking and of practice extends to Judaism today. It was reaffirmed by the Chief Rabbi, Dr Jonathan Sacks, in his lecture 'Morals and Markets', given in 1998. He points out that work is part of 'the essential dignity of the human condition. Animals *find* sustenance; only man *creates* it. As the thirteenth-century commentator Rabbenu Bachya put it, "The active participation of man in the creation of his own wealth is a sign of his spiritual greatness"'.[3] The world, says Dr Sacks, is God's creation; therefore it is good, and prosperity is a sign of God's blessing. But the wealth we create carries with it an obligation to use it for the benefit of the community as a whole.

Early Christian perspectives on wealth and its creation

Christianity, of course, has its roots in Judaism. Jesus himself was a Jew and so were his first followers. His teachings were in the tradition of the Old Testament prophets, who, as we have noted, were prepared to condemn unrighteous behaviour in economic activity. Jesus' message was one of emancipation for the poor – those who have lost out in the economic process. He condemns exploitation of the weak and the excessive accumulation of wealth.

However, there is a new, revolutionary element in the good news preached by Christ. He is speaking to the whole of humanity, not just to the oppressed or to the Jews, and he brings a message for the transformation of all human conduct on the basis of love and the redeeming power of God's love. Adherence to the law, Jesus teaches, is not enough: we are called to go further than the law demands. The principles and ideals of a society transformed through love were not practised in the society in which Christianity developed, nor were the early followers of Jesus empowered to bring about its immediate transformation. For early Christians, many of whom were slaves, improvement in their material conditions was simply not possible. This may be one reason why they developed strongly the spiritual aspects of their religion. Moreover, the Judaic tradition from which Christianity emerged had not placed great emphasis upon life after death, whereas the resurrection of Christ made this a central element in Christian belief. Early Christianity was more concerned with the afterlife than with this life. And a significant strand in the teachings of Jesus often seemed to be opposed to the material concerns of society, from which some Christians accordingly felt called to withdraw completely, to the point of retiring to the solitary life of hermits in the desert.

The famous hermit Simeon Stylites lived on top of a column in order to withdraw from the world. It is commonly said that the clergy in the pulpit are six feet above contradiction. At the commencement of his 36-year elevation, Simon elected initially for nine feet but later rose to sixty feet to avoid the crowds. In the light of his motives and rejection of the world, it is interesting to pose the question 'Who made the column?' Someone in the desert must have had the necessary skills.

To the extent that the early Christian church formulated views on the economic life of society, they seem to have been utopian in nature. In Acts 2.44–5, we read about the sharing of resources by the first Christians: 'And all that believed were together, and had all things common; and sold their possessions and goods, and parted them to all men, as every man had need' (AV). In chapter 39 of his *Apology for Christianity*, Tertullian describes the same kind of community. These descriptions have been interpreted by some later commentators on Christian attitudes to business and commerce as endorsement of a socialist or communist model, where private ownership of property should disappear. The passage in Acts is notable, however, as being one of the relatively few New Testament references, outside the Gospels themselves, which is concerned with economic processes at all.

Although Christianity began within Judaism, its universal message and the inclusion of the Gentiles within the early Church led to a rupture: Judaism and Christianity separated and went their different ways. This split marks a loss within Christianity of continuity with the traditional teachings of the Judaic canon of the Torah, including those elements concerning the proper conduct of business in accordance with God's law. There is no comparable strand in early Christian teaching. The guidance in the Old Testament was, of course, available to Christians but it was no longer adapted and developed in the same way.

One interesting aspect of this discontinuity is to be found in the Epistle of James. We do not know for certain who James was but it is generally thought that the author of the epistle was James, the brother of Jesus. James became a Christian when he saw the risen Christ and he became the leader of the church in Jerusalem. He remained faithful to Jewish law, in which he was clearly well trained, as well as a follower of Jesus. He was prepared to accept Gentile converts who had never been Jews by religion. In James's epistle there is a strong emphasis upon the practical application of faith in everyday life: 'But be doers of the word and not hearers only, deceiving yourselves' (1.22). At several points in his letter James reveals how deeply he has absorbed the Judaic teachings that possession of wealth carries dangers (5.1–2) and responsibilities to the less fortunate (2.1–6). Faith demands action and the practical use of wealth for the common good (2.14–16). In this short epistle we see an ethical perspective on wealth, derived from deep understanding of Judaic teaching in the Old Testament, to which is added the universal dimension of Jesus' message. It is the traditional prophetic call to repentance and to care with regard to wealth, but couched in the very language that Jesus himself used. While James remains true to the Jewish acceptance that wealth creation is a worthy act, he exercises the prophetic role of warning about the abuse of wealth and he underpins the whole with Jesus' teaching of love for all humankind. The integrated view taken in this epistle illustrates how the rupture between Jews and Christians subsequently impaired for the Christian community the continuity of centuries of thinking about wealth in a world where religion and commerce had been linked.

The Gospels, the epistles and the writings of the early Christian fathers reveal a degree of discomfort with and even opposition to the possession of worldly goods. The activities of business and commerce may not always be condemned outright, but they are rarely affirmed. St Augustine, for example, considered that the pursuit of trade turned men from their search for God.[4] In a Christian intellectual climate that viewed commerce with a jaundiced, not to say hostile, eye the monastic community evolved as a structured withdrawal – a calling to a life of prayer and search for God apart from the everyday world. In concept these religious communities shared property and eschewed the accumulation of wealth. Communal activity provided for essential material needs but, in principle, not for the creation of wealth beyond that point. The work for the religious community was sanctified – *laborare est orare* – but the monastic fathers remained generally silent on the work performed outside the monastery to meet the needs and wants of the secular community. In some instances, religious communities did not rigorously follow rules of poverty and developed as important economic units in their own right, accumulating great wealth which was to become a major injection of capital into the secular world at the time of the Reformation. However, over the centuries important and sophisticated economic systems emerged in the secular world, of which a key feature was the possession of private property. In the world outside the monasteries communities grew up based on manufacture and on trade. This vital world of business and commerce could not be ignored by the Church. Later medieval Christianity was obliged to come to terms with the reality of that activity. To do so it looked not to the teachings of Judaism but to ancient Greece, notably to Aristotle.

The views of the ancient Greeks on business, commerce and trade crystallized into what we would today call an elitist model. In his examination of how society should best be governed Plato developed the concept of philosopher-kings, those who by virtue of education and proven capabilities had shown themselves the best equipped to rule everyone else. The rulers in Plato's *Republic* do not engage in business or trade, which Plato regarded as inferior activities, to be carried out by the lower classes.

Aristotle did not follow Plato's ideas in general but in his *Politics* he did perpetuate the elitist differentiation in his examination of economic life, with inferior beings assigned to the conduct of commercial activity. Aristotle also differentiated between 'proper' economy, which consists in the management of the household (Greek *oikonomike*, from which our term 'economics' is derived), and the less satisfactory activity of supply or exchange. Aristotle accepted the legitimacy of exchange when it served to meet the wants that arise within the 'proper' economy. He distinguished this legitimate form of exchange from the kind which is conducted primarily as a means of accumulation. Thus, for Aristotle goods may be used in exchange to meet natural wants, or secondarily for the purposes of exchange itself. He regarded this second activity as barren, from which it followed that money, the surrogate for real goods in an exchange, also became barren when used in this way, i.e. for usury. From this Aristotle proceeds to identify an ethical basis for commerce, with distinctions derived from the intentions and purposes of the transactions involved.

Aristotle also accepted private ownership of property. He did so because he recognized that it provided incentives. Private property will be better looked after – a recognition of productivity as a fact of economic life. Furthermore, private ownership avoids the complaints about those who take much but work little in communal systems (the 'free-rider' problem). Ownership is a source of pleasure. And the virtue of liberality requires property before it can be exercised.

When the medieval scholastics were forced by social and economic change to formulate views on trade and business, they turned largely to Aristotle, supplemented by Roman law and by the Bible. The premisses of the scholastics were rooted in divine and natural law and their conclusions were deliberately ethical on that account. They sought to advise on proper economic conduct, with ethics as their focal point. Clearly, it was not possible to justify private economic vice as a public virtue but they nevertheless had to take account of greed as an incentive. The incentive of greed was seen as the consequence of the fall of man, like the incentives that are derived from private ownership. It was necessary to come to terms with these realities and to accept them. The perfectibility of all people remained an aspiration but one qualified in the light of humankind's fallen state. Having accepted this situation the scholastics were able to discuss the economic process as it is, and not as an ideal. The end for humankind remains a spiritual and otherworldly one, but it requires a material basis in this world and this life is lived within society. Thus the focus shifts from the individual to society and we return yet again to the dilemma that troubles Christian thought: we need the social benefits that derive from avarice but we appeal to benevolence. For the scholastics this necessitated a loosening of the reins on a process that they sought to control.

St Thomas Aquinas was the supreme medieval thinker who explained and evaluated social phenomena such as economic activity and sought to define their part in God's plan for the world. He argued that wealth is not an end in itself, nor does it contribute to full holiness, but there is a less perfect kind of holiness attainable in this temporal existence as a reward for virtue. Since our bodily condition impairs our ability to attain virtue, material wealth is necessary to meet the needs of this existence. But too much wealth will impede the attainment of virtue. So Aquinas, like Aristotle, accepts the necessity for private property, but with qualifications: 'If every man took care of his own possessions only,' he says, 'there would be no one to serve the common welfare'.[5] This resonates with Judaic teaching.

St Thomas provided a comprehensive Christian examination of economic activity, presenting a vision of how humankind should deal with those activities that are needed to sustain us. Within his overall framework he addresses certain aspects at length. For example, the concept of the just price, although not spelt out precisely, seems to be based upon a kind of cost of production to be applied in determining exchange values. In a transaction there should be equal advantage to both parties, although exactly what these advantages are and how to measure them is not explained in detail. One of the scholastics, Albert the Great, a Dominican friar, defined the just price as that which 'the good sold can be valued at according to the estimation of the market at the time of the sale'[6] – or what we would today describe as the competitive market price.

The scholastics perceived usury as the worst form of gain, rejected in both the Old Testament ('If you lend money to any of my people with you who is poor, you shall not be to him as a creditor, and you shall not exact interest from him': Exodus 22.25) and the New ('But love your enemies and do good, and lend, expecting nothing in return': Luke 6.35), and condemned, as we noted earlier, by Aristotle. The Third Lateran Council of 1179 prohibited usury. But gradually there was a retreat from this position and Christendom was unable to sustain a clear and unqualified prohibition. Detailed prescription became untenable as the economy flourished, fuelled by the charging and taking of interest. It became legitimate in the eyes of the Church to treat the lending of money as an investment, albeit one that involved risk as well as gain.

In brief, the scholastics accepted that, despite the imperfections and dangers of economic activity, it was a necessary evil, as long as trade was not fully developed and was based largely upon a natural economy. Regulations were put in place and enforced through legislation such as that of the medieval guilds, all under the authority of the Church. In both the instances we have cited – the just price and the practice of usury – we can see a continuing slow compromise. The weakening of doctrine in the face of commercial developments continued throughout the late Middle Ages, and the power of the Church to regulate commercial life was further eroded.

It would be wrong to omit from my somewhat simplistic consideration of medieval thought on wealth and the economic process a reference to St Francis of Assisi, who represents, of course, an uncompromising rejection of wealth. He denied himself any right to hold property and goods because of the moral hazard entailed in doing so: material goods of any kind will be paid for with spiritual loss. St Francis represents in its purest and most unequivocal form a Christian rejection of wealth and, by extension, the economic process that creates it. Indeed he sees poverty as a desirable condition that allows total dedication to God. He takes literally Jesus' words: 'Look at the birds of the air: they neither sow nor reap nor gather into barns and yet your heavenly Father feeds them . . . Therefore do not be anxious about tomorrow, for tomorrow will be anxious for itself' (Matthew 6.26, 34). The message of St Francis had enormous impact in his own day and still resonates very strongly today. We shall return to the appeal of St Francis and his uncompromising stance. Suffice it to say at this point that it has commanded universal admiration but not universal emulation.

Christian responses to economic activity after the Reformation and the industrial revolution

In the sixteenth century, the Reformation challenged still further a consistent and enforceable teaching on commerce and business across Christendom. After the Reformation Christendom was no longer sufficiently structurally unified to provide a theological view on wealth creation. Two forces were now combining to weaken the impact of its teachings on economic matters: the divisions within Western Christendom and the rapid developments in economic practice itself. The failure of mainstream Christian teaching to cope with the evolving situation was already acute at the time that Protestantism emerged. Eric

Roll has described and summarized this collapse in somewhat stark terms:

> Canonist thought was essentially an ideology, in economic matters it was an illusory representation of reality. It was successful as long as the conflicts of reality had not become very acute. With the sharpening of these conflicts, the antithetical elements in this ideology were seized upon by the contending parties, and the original universal character was lost ... As the gulf between precept and practice widened, the foundation on which the precepts rested could only be saved by jettisoning the claim that they had a direct relevance to practical affairs ... Religion became something apart ... from those concerned with the mundane problems of wealth getting. Though attempts were again to be made to introduce ethical elements into the main stream of economic thought, it remains henceforth independent of religion.[7]

From the breakup of unified Catholic Christendom in Western Europe and the collapse of a coherent theological teaching on economics, progress to the present-day secularization of the world of business and commerce was rapid and virtually total. We can conclude this simplified and selective overview by considering three themes:

- the progressive retreat by the churches from offering ethical perspectives on economic matters;
- the great explosion of wealth creation and commercial activity that accompanied and followed the Reformation;
- the emergence of a secularized expression of Christianity as part of the political response to the emergence of dominant free-market capitalism.

It does not fall within the purpose of this book to describe the evolution of economic activity over the centuries that followed the Middle Ages, when feudalism declined and was succeeded by commercial capitalism and by industrial capitalism. What is significant for our thesis is to note how over this period Christian theologians progressively withdrew from commenting on these matters. The Reformation re-emphasized the value of the individual as a fundamental part of Christian doctrine. It was possibly this emphasis that brought about from the sixteenth century a concentration in Christian thought upon the responsibilities of the individual in the conduct of economic life, and a lessening of concern about the processes involved.

The vision of an integrated Christian theology on wealth creation faltered as its coherence was challenged by the ever-increasing diversity of economic activity itself. Markets became wider as trade outside Western Europe expanded. The emergence of banking as a distinct and necessary activity presented a new sphere for consideration. The explosion of ever more sophisticated tastes and fashions brought into play aspects of commercial life not previously considered.[8] The same Renaissance princes who had delighted so conspicuously in accumulated wealth became the heads of nation states, another phenomenon that added a spur to economic growth. Later, in the seventeenth and eighteenth centuries, industrial capitalism emerged. Just as the productive use of money had undermined theological injunctions against usury, so industrial capitalism (and the competitive environment produced by the entrepreneurs who thrived in it) represented individualism and the pursuit of individual wealth in a form that Christian theology had not previously addressed.

For Max Weber, whose seminal work *The Protestant Ethic and the Spirit of Capitalism* was published in 1905, the impulse for these later developments was to be found in the nature of the Reformation itself. He argued that the ascetic spirit of Protestantism, and the Calvinist doctrines which identified faith by its results and the elect by their works, were responsible for the spirit and form of capitalism: 'The Puritan idea of calling and the premium it placed on ascetic conduct was bound directly to influence the development of a capitalist way of life', he argued.[9] The Protestant ethic represents the pursuit of 'private profitableness', which gives a stamp of divine approval to the profit motive. Weber's thesis is open to challenge (though it has proved remarkably resilient) but he does point to one incontrovertible fact: capitalism emerged and began to flourish as Protestantism also emerged and became significant in Western Europe. We can debate which was the chicken and which the egg – but clearly some kind of accommodation between the form of Christian belief represented by Protestantism and industrial capitalism had been found. However, what is lacking in Protestant, as in Catholic, teaching is a systematic theology of wealth creation. The Protestant work ethic and its affirmation of labour and diligence is not a substitute for a deeper integration of a religion's ethical teachings on economics, such as we found in Judaism.

There is, however, an aspect of Protestantism and its role in business that merits further comment. In many European countries non-conformists were kept out of some of the more materially rewarding activities in society. Accordingly they sought to earn their living in those fields from which they were not excluded – such as trade, commerce and manufacture – and this undoubtedly shaped their attitudes towards wealth and how it should be created and used. Making and selling things was less frowned upon in non-conformist churches than in the established churches. John Wesley, founder of Methodism, exhorted his followers to gain all they could, save all they could, and give all they could.[10] The Huguenots became skilled weavers – skills that many of them took to new communities when persecutions drove them from France.

No account of Christian attitudes towards wealth and its creation would be complete without reference to the Society of Friends, the Quakers. The Society originated in the seventeenth century, its founding inspired by George Fox, who had been brought up as a Puritan. With their belief in the light of Christ in each and every person, Quakers abandoned any form of a separate, ordained ministry and in Britain came into sharp opposition with both Church and state. As dissenters they were debarred from many professions and they engaged primarily in industrial and commercial enterprise. They were particularly distinguished in banking (through such families as the Gurneys and the Barclays) but also by founding companies such as Fry's, Rowntree's, and Clark's. These firms became a byword for successful and humane management at periods when much of industry and commerce displayed very different attitudes towards employees.

It is not in the nature of Quakerism to formulate creeds or theological statements. Their adoption of pacifism is probably their most distinctive feature but it is not set out in any formal way. They emphasize that God makes himself known in the heart of all people and accordingly doctrinal statements and declarations are not needed. There is no written statement about Quaker attitudes towards wealth and its creation. But the successful and energetic participation of Quaker families like the Cadburys and the Rowntrees in nineteenth-century business manifested no discomfort with wealth creation as such. It was, however, accompanied by an acute social conscience and a drive towards social reform. Quaker firms were early exponents of paternalistic employment, a form of enlightened entrepreneurship that became less fashionable in the twentieth century – a shift occasioned to some degree because of the greater acceptance of the role of the state in matters of social welfare.

Although Quakers were reluctant to put into words a theology or doctrine of work, Quaker companies were noted not only for enlightened treatment of employees but also for high standards of honesty and integrity in the conduct of business. For Quakers, the world of work was not something to be rejected, but rather a field for humanitarian concern and proper conduct. This was manifested, for example, in the adoption of fixed pricing and guarantees of services to be provided. The influence of Quakers in the fields of commerce and industry has been out of all proportion to their numbers.

The role of Quakers in business became less marked in the twentieth century. Quakers are now as likely to be found in teaching or other professions as in business. But the Quakers do offer a startling and challenging example of committed Christians engaging wholeheartedly and honourably in economic activity.

As we have seen, at the heart of the tension in mainstream Christian thought about the proper conduct of economic life lies the recognition that it is an activity which can be, and often is, motivated by greed and acquisitiveness. In 1714 Bernard Mandeville explicitly recognized and approved the baser motives that are the driving force in economic activity in his poem 'The fable of the bees'. Mandeville was no theologian: he attacked the Christian ideals of self-denial and the suppression of private vices. Indeed, he went further: he argued that selfish gratification of our desires and the invention of new ones made a greater contribution to the welfare of human beings than did learning, personal righteousness or public-spiritedness. In 'The fable of the bees' Mandeville describes a hive of bees driven by viciousness:

> A spacious hive well stocked with bees
> That lived in luxury and ease
>
> .   .   .   .   .   .
>
> Millions endeavouring to supply
> Each other's lust and vanity
>
> .   .   .   .   .   .
>
> Thus every part was full of vice
> Yet the whole mass a paradise.[11]

The bees complain about the corruptions that are necessary for their comfortable circumstances. In response Jove reforms their manners and the bees go and live in simplicity – but with serious drawbacks:

Now mind the glorious hive, and see
How honesty and trade agree.
The show is gone, it thins apace
And looks with quite another face.
For 'twas not only that they went
By whom vast sums were yearly spent:
But multitudes that lived on them,
Were daily forced to do the same.
In vain to other trades they'd fly:
All were o'erstocked accordingly.[12]

This is a sad tale of huge bee redundancies, arising from the collapse of the market demand for luxury goods. Mandeville lived before the industrial revolution, but anticipated mass consumption before modern techniques showed how demand might be stimulated and technology showed how it could be satisfied.

Mandeville's poem is an interesting illustration of the degree to which Christian thinking had retreated in this field by the early eighteenth century. In what was still a Christian culture, Mandeville approved of greed and luxury as drivers of economic activity. The eighteenth century was, of course, a period of outright questioning of the tenets of formal Christianity, articulated by philosophers like David Hume and the *philosophes* in France. The Church and Christianity generally were put on the defensive by the rationalists of the Enlightenment, and it was this same recourse to reason that formed the basis for an upsurge in technical and scientific knowledge, which was to make possible dramatic advances in industrial processes. This is not the place to dwell upon the culture of the Enlightenment, but we should note that defensiveness against attacks on religious belief based on reason surely contributed to defensiveness regarding the new wealth-creation activity that was rooted in rational and methodical processes. The retreat from a coherent Christian theological approach to economic activity continued apace throughout the eighteenth century.

It was in the eighteenth century that economics emerged and developed as a serious science. The two foremost thinkers responsible for this were Adam Smith and David Ricardo. Smith's work is set out in his *An Enquiry into the Nature and Causes of the Wealth of Nations*, published in 1776. Underpinning this work is Smith's belief in the benevolence of the natural order, which is marred by the imperfection of human institutions. If these were removed 'the obvious and simple system of natural liberty' would re-emerge. We can hear echoes, albeit faint echoes, of the medieval scholastics and their concept of natural law.

Smith had previously written *The Theory of Moral Sentiments* (1759), which looks at the forces that motivate human behaviour. The basis for our behaviour, he says, is essentially self-interest, because nature commits us to self-preservation and to bettering our condition. In society, the desire to better our condition is related to class distinction and attributed to 'vanity' and the desire 'to be observed, to be attended to, to be taken notice of with sympathy, complacency and approbation'.[13] Coupled with this desire for approbation, Smith saw human conduct governed by a sense of propriety, the custom of labour and a propensity to trade (barter and exchange). If individuals naturally pursue their own interests, they should be allowed to do so, because in so doing they further the common good. Because, by natural law, human motivations are balanced, the benefit for the individual should not conflict with the common good. In an echo of Mandeville, Smith even suggests that the individual promotes societal interests more effectively by seeking personal advantage than if he or she sets out simply to pursue the public interest. Maximization of personal advantage contributes to maximization of common well-being. Herein lies a contrast with traditional Christianity, which saw self-interest as damaging to the individual, a barrier to virtue and in opposition to the common good.

The Theory of Moral Sentiments provides rules of natural order which, when applied in economic affairs, mean that a natural balance of motives ensures the greatest effectiveness. Thus, through division of labour the individual increases the productivity of his own efforts and, at the same time, is no longer independent of other people. *The Wealth of Nations* explores this happy symbiotic relationship, arguing for minimal state interference in the conduct of business. Smith is the champion of laissez-faire and provides a theoretical support for the interests of the business class. If we were to substitute the Church (or 'religion') for the state in Smith's analysis, it would be seen by him as another unnatural impediment to economic progress and the benefit of all. To quote Eric Roll again, 'In helping to create an economic structure in which alone enterprise could flourish, Adam Smith could rightly claim that he was furthering the welfare of the whole community.'[14] This concept of harmony bringing about social development remained for a long time a key element in classical economic thought and still forms an important contribution to present-day analysis and debate.

Smith did not completely deny any role for the state in economic

matters. He was pessimistic about the part the state could play in reducing privilege in business and commerce, which leads to monopolies and
other abuses. He was optimistic that it would be possible to sweep them
away, and the intervention of the state as well. However, the protection
of private property, a given for economic development, was for Smith
the responsibility of the state. Writing in 1776, Smith was naturally
unaware of the full consequences of the industrial revolution taking
place at that time. *The Wealth of Nations* does not deal in any depth
with the question of poverty or the differences in wealth between rich
and poor that were to arise from the transformation of society from
rural agricultural communities to crowded industrial towns. Nor could
he take into account the damaging social and environmental consequences that were soon to become so apparent. The Christian churches,
Catholic and Protestant alike, despite their failure to offer a coherent
Christian commentary in the field of economic affairs, were to be drawn
inescapably to comment upon the social and other consequences of its
most potent form: industrial free-market capitalism.

One of the early features of economic activity that offended the
Christian conscience as the eighteenth century matured was slavery.
Slavery was not the inevitable outcome of any particular form of business or trade. It had existed in ancient Greece without attracting disapproval from Aristotle. Likewise early Christians lived with slavery as
part of life in the Roman Empire, where Christianity first developed.
But the extent to which slavery formed an integral part of contemporary trade and commerce attracted increasingly strong condemnation
from Christian activists in the eighteenth and early nineteenth centuries,
reinforced by the emphases given to human dignity and to human
rights, as articulated by the thinkers of the Enlightenment. These views
were given clear expression with the Declaration of the Rights of Man
(1789) and, in milestone political form, with the American Declaration
of Independence (1776).

However, it was later, in the nineteenth century, that the Christian
voice spoke out with full force in its condemnation of the social and
physical conditions that resulted from the mass migrations of workers
from rural communities to the towns. The protests were certainly not
confined to those expressed by Christians. Indeed, as the nineteenth
century progressed, the demand for reform assumed a secular nature, in
the shape of political writing and political movements. It is at this period
that political expression harked back to the same utopian ideals that had
inspired some early Christians: the sharing of goods, the abandonment

of private property and the aspiration to a life lived communally in the simplest form. Socialist writers and thinkers, many of them Christians, assumed a significant role, first in political thought and then in political action. The evolution of socialist and eventually Marxist theories, offering solutions for social and material ills, accelerated in the second half of the nineteenth century and in practical terms had become a serious political force by the beginning of the twentieth. Christian social concern mirrored and, to some degree, was part of this evolution.

For the Christian conscience, the wretchedness of the conditions brought about by the upheavals of the industrial revolution prompted concern at many levels – housing, nourishment, health, working conditions, sanitation and so on – and the contribution of both individual Christians and Christian communities to tackling these problems has been exhaustively recorded and discussed. Because the general culture in Western European countries at that time was Christian, it was inevitable and natural that much of the reforming energy was provided by Christians and came from Christian institutions, such as the churches. As the problems became more apparent, the position of the churches shifted from indifference and acceptance at the beginning of the nineteenth century to concern and then action to correct the ills and abuses. But throughout the century, there was little strength in theological attempts to come to terms with the latest manifestations of economic life itself. While eventually an articulate and passionate Christian voice emerged calling for action to address social problems, the processes that were deemed to have brought it about were left largely to secular thinkers to analyse.

There are several outcomes of these developments that are of interest for our purposes. First, a strong, clear Christian expression of concern was established for social issues of practically every kind. In Britain, this social doctrine was to be found in all Christian denominations by the late nineteenth century, from Catholic to Quaker, from Anglican to Baptist. Christian social ideas and social action took a new and vigorous shape which has been a vital strand in theological thinking in the twentieth century. We shall look at this further in Chapter 2.

Second, the nineteenth and twentieth centuries witnessed a renewed Christian response to the issue of poverty. For many Christian commentators up to the nineteenth century, the state of poverty was a part of life that had to be accepted. Throughout most of the two thousand years of Christianity, poverty meant what we would today understand as destitution – the virtual absence of the basic necessities for survival, such as food, clothing and shelter. Philanthropy and charity were the traditional Christian response to poverty. The creation of wealth on a scale sufficient to raise *everyone* above poverty was just not considered feasible (as in practice it was not). The poor, as Jesus had said, were always with us. Wealth and comfort were, by contrast, the privileges of the few.

The industrial revolution, with the first mass production of ordinary goods and the availability of cheap energy, changed both perceptions and reality. For the first time, humankind began to glimpse the prospect of wealth and prosperity not just for a few, but for many and – possibly – for all. As the worst effects of deprivation that accompanied the first stages of the industrial revolution were addressed and slowly greater numbers of people became the beneficiaries of its wealth-creating capacity, the equation of poverty with destitution was regarded as unacceptable. Wealth creation was no longer a zero-sum game. Destitution could be eliminated. My possession of shoes did not mean that someone else had to go without; everyone could wear shoes. And so a distinctive Christian imperative, at one with Jesus' teachings, was articulated with ever growing emphasis: the option for the poor. It was not a new element in Christian teaching – but it was given a new urgency, a new strength and a new vision. We shall return to the option for the poor again.

The third outcome of industrial development by the end of the nineteenth century was the emergence of the Christian Socialist movement. As we have noted, socialist and communist political philosophies evolved most vigorously in the latter two-thirds of the nineteenth century. While there were many Christian contributions to the evolution of socialist prescriptions for the conduct of economic affairs and the social problems that were perceived to result from economic activity, socialism was primarily a secular political movement. In a Christian culture there was plenty of Christian commentary to support the concept of common ownership and communitarian solutions to problems. Both socialism and Christianity share utopian visions for humankind. But the goals of socialism are strictly for this world. Christian precepts form no part of socialist teaching. Socialism is essentially a secular movement. It evolved in a Christian culture, but it requires no assent to Christianity. Thus, by the second half of the nineteenth century, the secularization of economic life had reached a point where the solutions formulated to moderate its deficiencies were equally secular. To the extent that Christians supported socialism, the goals of Christian thought itself shifted to a secular agenda.

I do not intend to treat the subject of Christian Socialism at length.

The term itself describes it well. As we have already observed, the concept of a new economic and social order did not have its origins within organized Christianity. Indeed, socialism in its early days was viewed with suspicion by the institutional churches. For example, the Wesleyan movement was initially far from enthusiastic about it. The first Christians in Britain noted for looking sympathetically at socialism were Samuel Taylor Coleridge and Frederick Denison Maurice. Maurice was an ordained Anglican clergyman who wrote and taught widely on political and social problems and assumed great influence in the mid-nineteenth century, arguing that the true principles of socialism conformed to Christianity. Along with others he produced a series of *Tracts on Christian Socialism*. From these beginnings emerged some years later a considerable array of movements and initiatives, all designed to promote solutions for social and economic problems from a socialist perspective. The Christian Social Union, for example, was founded in 1875. Its first two stated aims were:

1. To claim for the Christian Law the ultimate authority to rule social practice.
2. To study in common how to apply the moral truths and principles of Christianity in the social and economic difficulties of the present time.

The Christian Socialist League was created in 1906 with an uncompromising political purpose, integrated with their observance of Christian duties such as prayer and participation in church life. These movements, and the growing importance of socialist political parties in which many Christians were active, grafted socialism into the Christian body corporate. Christian commentary upon the economic scene in the twentieth century became largely a commentary on social issues relating to economic life, but with little to offer about the processes themselves and how they should be conducted. We shall look at the twentieth-century Christian critique of economic life in more detail in Chapter 2.

The brief survey that we have conducted in this chapter charts how, having parted from the Judaic tradition of an integrated approach linking religious and economic life, Christianity progressively allowed the economic sphere to become secularized and dissociated from Christian insight. In his important work *Religion and the Rise of Capitalism* (1926) R. H. Tawney took as his point of departure Weber's thesis that the seeds of modern capitalism were to be found in the Reformation. He charted the secularization process in detail from the late Middle Ages to the beginning of the twentieth century. At that point, he believed, there was a complete separation of religion and economics. In the conclusion to his book he states,

> But the quality in modern societies, which is most sharply opposed to the teaching ascribed to the Founder of the Christian Faith, lies deeper than the exceptional failures and abnormal follies against which criticism is most commonly directed. It consists in the assumption . . . that the attainment of material riches is the supreme object of human endeavour and the final criterion of human success. Such a philosophy, plausible, militant, and not indisposed, when hard pressed, to silence criticism by persecution, may triumph or may decline. What is certain is that it is the negation of any system of thought or morals which, except by a metaphor, can be described as Christian. Compromise is as impossible between the Church of Christ and the idolatry of wealth, which is the practical religion of capitalist societies, as it was between the Church and the State idolatry of the Roman Empire.[15]

This is an uncompromising and stark statement: the capitalist system, as it had evolved by the time Tawney was writing, is dedicated to the idolatry of wealth and is incompatible with Christianity. The espousal of a political alternative – socialism – was seen by Tawney, the Christian Socialists and many of their Christian counterparts across Western Europe as the only solution for Christians. But it was a secular solution that placed emphasis upon the social consequences of an economic system (as perceived at that time), rather than upon a Christian theology of the activity of creating wealth. Had the economic process remained where it stood in the early twentieth century, the Christian case might well have rested at what Tawney had to say.

The intellectual shift in Christian thinking at the end of the nineteenth century towards the socialist model was not followed by all Christians, of course. The hostility to socialism at the beginning of the century persisted. Many middle-class Christians and indeed many working-class Christians viewed socialism with suspicion. At the same time, study of the impact of the Christian religion upon the working classes reveals a singular failure to engage them:

To the minds of at any rate the most articulate and class-conscious working men, the Christian missionary was a representative not only of a faith but of groups which were defending an unjust set of social arrangements . . . since there were no advantages to be gained from participating in the affairs of churches comparable with those to be derived from voting or belonging to trade unions, the appeal to attend worship was met simply by indifference.[16]

And so at the beginning of the twentieth century, Christianity had ceased to engage intellectually with the theology of wealth creation as currently conducted and had begun seriously to espouse a secular political philosophy opposed to the capitalist model, while failing at the same time to carry many middle-class Christians with it and equally failing to engage seriously with large sections of the industrialized working class. Not for the first time Christian thinkers were less than successful in relating to the realities of contemporary economic activity.

Notes

1. David Hawkes, review of John Dupré, *Human Nature and the Limits of Science*, *Times Literary Supplement*, 11 Jan. 2002, p. 6.
2. Meir Tamari, *With All Your Possessions: Jewish Ethics and Economic Life*, Free Press, 1987, p. 35.
3. Jonathan Sacks, *Morals and Markets*, Institute of Economic Affairs, 1999, p. 15, his italics.
4. Quoted in Eric Roll, *A History of Economic Thought*, 4th edn, Faber and Faber, 1973, p. 45.
5. Thomas Aquinas, *Summa contra gentiles*, III, 135, quoted in O. Langholm, *Economics in the Medieval Schools*, E. J. Brill, 1992, p. 216.
6. Aquinas, *Commentary on Aristotle's 'Politics'*, quoted ibid., p. 179.
7. Roll, *A History of Economic Thought*, p. 53.
8. Exhaustively described in Lisa Jardine, *Worldly Goods*, Macmillan, 1996.
9. Max Weber, *The Protestant Ethic and the Spirit of Capitalism*, trans. Talcott Parsons, George Allen & Unwin, 1930, p. 35.
10. Quoted ibid., p. 175.
11. Bernard Mandeville, 'The fable of the bees, or private vices, publick benefits' (1714 version), ll. 1–2, 33–4, 155–6.
12. Ibid., ll. 333–42.

13. Adam Smith, *The Theory of Moral Sentiments*, sect. 3, ch. 2 ('Of the Origin of Ambition, and the Distinction of Ranks'), ¶1.
14. Roll, *A History of Economic Thought*, p. 151.
15. R. H. Tawney, *Religion and the Rise of Capitalism*, revd edn (1937), repr. Penguin, 1990, p. 280.
16. K. S. Inglis, *Churches and the Working Classes in Victorian England*, Routledge and Kegan Paul, 1963, p. 355.

♦ 2 ♦

The twentieth-century perspective

As we saw in Chapter 1, the question of how economic life should be organized had, by the beginning of the twentieth century, become a serious political issue. On the one side stood the supporters of capitalism, free markets, the status quo; on the other side stood those who argued for socialist or communist systems, where private ownership was eliminated, where a benevolent state should ensure equity and well-being for all. The imperfections of free-market capitalism had demanded a response, the pursuit of a more egalitarian and less impersonal approach to the conduct of economic affairs. Socialism adopted a utopian vision where individual selfishness was subordinated to the benefit of the wider community through state ownership of the means of production and distribution. By the removal of private property and by the common ownership of production and distribution, socialism claims to guarantee an equitable distribution of wealth that would be unattainable by the free-market capitalist approach.

The Christian response to this politicization was divided. Having abandoned the attempt to formulate a realistic theology of wealth creation, Christian thinkers turned their concern more towards the social outcomes of the process. And with the potential now offered for the transformation of poverty from the inevitable to the avoidable, a priority emerged to tackle the issue of material prosperity. As the technical means for creating wealth for large numbers of people were developed, it became easier for Christians to worry less about how wealth was created and more about how it should be distributed. Christian socialists, unsurprisingly, found it difficult to separate the creation of wealth from its distribution.

At the same time, it should be noted that in Western Europe, the emergence of democratic societies as we now know them was at a relatively early stage. The key democratic characteristics of universal suffrage, the rule of law, respect for individual freedom and choice, the peaceful transition from governments of one persuasion to those of another and freely expressed opinions on all matters – these features were in their infancy in the opening decades of the twentieth century and it was only after the cataclysms of two world wars that they were to become generally and constitutionally widespread in Western Europe and to be taken for granted.[1] Before the Great War of 1914–18 freedom of choice, of movement, of expression, of association were by no means universally accepted, nor were other hallmarks of modern democratic societies, notably the peaceful transition from one government to another (the right 'to throw the rascals out'). It was, arguably, the catastrophe of that war which provoked some of the most important steps towards modern European concepts of democratically functioning societies, with the overthrow of the Russian, German and Austro-Hungarian empires.

These critical elements of political democracy were more easily to be found in the United States. Here the constitution was firmly rooted in the separation of powers and the maintenance of checks and balances between the different elements of government; in the Declaration of the Rights of Man and in freedom of choice and action by individuals. Free-market capitalism flourished in the United States, relatively unaffected by the socialist/communist critique that developed in Europe. The circumstances that brought this about are much more complex than I have suggested. But it nevertheless remains true that around the end of the nineteenth century, the United States seems to provide an example of a possible synergistic relationship between the freedoms of modern democracies and the ability to engage in serious wealth creation on a large scale. We shall return to this theme in a future chapter.

For the Christian commentator in Europe in the early twentieth century, there was a fundamental difficulty with wealth creation. Not only was the temptation of wealth and materialism something against which there were very severe warnings in much Christian teaching, but the process itself was driven by unattractive and even sinful behaviour: greed, selfishness, acquisitiveness, materialism and so on. Furthermore, the social outcomes of economic activity even at its most successful were not always attractive: environmental and physical degradation, social exclusion and damage, incitement to dishonest and anti-social behaviour.

Against this background Christian thinking in the twentieth century shows continuing uncertainty about the field of economic activity and – in many instances – a significant alienation from it. As the century progressed, emphasis grew upon facing the challenges posed by the outcomes of economic forces. With regard to the process itself, Christian thought followed in large measure the secular agenda and became politicized to a significant degree.

Roman Catholic social teaching in the twentieth century

Throughout the twentieth century the Roman Catholic Church, however, sought to develop a position which was neither an uncritical acceptance of capitalism nor the taking of refuge in the unrealistic rigidities of communism. Over a period of more than a hundred years Roman Catholic teaching on social issues has been set out in a series of papal encyclicals (pastoral letters), commencing with *Rerum Novarum*, written by Pope Leo XIII in 1891.[2]

This encyclical was the fully developed expression of Pope Leo's concern for social issues. Leo was not a young man when elected as pope and was pope for a long time (from 1878 to 1903, when he died at the age of 93). Earlier he had written another encyclical, *Quod Apostolicam Muneris – Against the Socialist Sects*. This earlier encyclical was strong stuff: in the opening sentence it called socialism 'a murderous pestilence' and went on to declare that the right of property was established by natural law. Like some other popes, however, Leo had a fertile old age and his eventual ascendancy among the workers won him the title of Father of the Workers and for *Rerum Novarum* that of the Magna Carta of Labour.

Rerum Novarum was a forthright condemnation of a situation in which the excesses of capitalism had reduced many workers to living in unacceptable conditions. It is a treatise on the rights of workers and the need to protect the worker 'from the brutality of those who make use of human beings as mere instruments for the unrestrained acquisition of profits' (¶43). *Rerum Novarum* does not, however, adopt a socialist point of view. At the time of its publication it was widely perceived as socialist in nature. But Pope Leo explicitly rejected such a view: 'when socialists endeavour to transfer privately-owned goods into common ownership they worsen the condition of all wage-earners. By taking away from them their freedom to dispose of their wages, they rob them of all hope and opportunity of increasing their possessions and bettering their conditions' (¶4); 'The dream of equality would become the reality of equal want and degradation for all' (¶12). So, while endorsing the creation of wealth through free-market capitalism, Pope Leo looks for equitable distribution of that wealth, asserting the primacy of people over things and of labour over capital.

At the very core of this thinking lies the notion of 'the common good', a concept which, as we have seen, reaches back to the teachings of St Thomas Aquinas. The common good respects the integrity of the individual as well as creating conditions for human cooperation and the achievement of shared objectives. Unlike Adam Smith, Pope Leo sees an important role for the state in safeguarding the common good. And similarly his notion of the common good is more complex than that of the utilitarians, who sought the greatest happiness for the greatest number. He writes of 'the common good in which one and all, in due proportion have a right to participate'. It is the responsibility of public authority 'to show proper concern for the worker, so that from what he contributes to the common good, he may receive what will enable him, housed, clothed, and secure, to live his life without hardship . . . Such solicitude is so far from injuring anyone, that it is destined rather to benefit all, because it is of absolute interest to the state that those citizens should not be miserable in every respect from whom such necessary goods proceed' (¶51).

The coherence of Roman Catholic teaching in the papal encyclicals that followed *Rerum Novarum* is based upon the concept of the common good, but as social and economic factors changed in the course of the following century, so new emphases were drawn out. *Quadragesimo Anno*, issued in 1931, reflects the proper and growing concern at that time for due respect for the individual. Pope Pius XI, who issued the encyclical, was concerned that the state should not usurp or arrogate to itself those things which individuals could do for themselves: 'It is gravely wrong to take from individuals what they can accomplish by their own initiative and industry and give it to the community' (¶79). In stressing this principle of subsidiarity (the notion that decisions should be taken at the lowest level compatible with good government) Pope Pius is addressing a familiar challenge: the reconciliation of economic freedom with the promotion of common values.

We noted in Chapter 1 that the industrial revolution dispelled the fear that humankind was for ever condemned to live with poverty. To rise above subsistence became attainable for many, not just a few. Poverty shifted from an absolute to a relative state. In the 1960s further encyclicals in the evolving Roman Catholic social teaching brought a new sharpness to Christian concern for the poor. *Gaudium et Spes*, issued in 1965 by Pope John XXIII, argued: 'there must be made available to all men and women everything necessary for leading a life truly human such as food, clothing and shelter; the right to choose a state of life freely and to found a family' (¶26.1). This encyclical marks a widening of the scope of Catholic social teaching: it addresses issues on a global scale, accepts the primacy of concern for the poor, and shows a greater recognition of the reality of the ordinary life of ordinary people.

These particular themes were progressively explored in subsequent encyclicals. *Populorum Progressio*, issued in 1967 by Pope Paul VI, not only made a strong criticism of capitalism but expressed more clearly the option for the poor: a Christian duty to care for those who are the victims of the world's inequalities. The critique of capitalism extends to the market itself: 'When two parties are in very unequal positions, their mutual consent does not alone guarantee a fair contract: the rule of free consent remains subservient to the demands of natural law' (¶6). One hundred years after *Rerum Novarum* Pope John Paul II issued *Centesimus Annus*, in which he raised serious questions about the operations of the market: 'there are many human needs which find no place on the market' (¶34). Arguing a step further, he states that 'society . . . demands that the market be appropriately controlled by the forces of society and by the state, so as to guarantee that the basic needs of the whole of society are satisfied' (¶35). At the end of *Centesimus Annus*, Pope John Paul identified problems and threats emerging in more advanced economies at the close of the twentieth century. Economic activity had moved from satisfying needs to responding to the demand for quality and this leads to the phenomenon of consumerism, as new needs arise and are defined. Consumerism calls for the responsible use of the power of choice: 'It is not wrong to want to live better; what is wrong is a style of life which is presumed to be better when it is directed towards "having" rather than "being", and which wants to have more, not in order to be more but in order to spend life in enjoyment as an end in itself' (¶36). Further concerns pointed out by Pope John Paul include the ecological question and the dangers of arbitrary use of the Earth by humankind with scant regard for future generations. Likewise, humankind has dangerously embarked upon a comparable destruction of the human environment. Economic freedom is only one element of human freedom: 'When it becomes autonomous, when man is seen more as a producer or consumer of goods than as a subject who produces and consumes in order to live, then economic freedom loses its necessary relationship to the human person and ends up by alienating and oppressing him' (¶39). We see in this critique a clear expression of the continuing Christian unease with the power and outcomes of economic processes.

The canon of Catholic social teaching as developed in the papal encyclicals issued since 1891 is a consistent exposition of a Christian response to the ever-growing importance of economic factors in human life. As Keynes helpfully put it, the political problem of humankind is to combine human efficiency, social justice and individual liberty. Catholic social teaching warns that the correct balance between these goals may have been lost. The search for economic efficiency has led to efficiency being regarded as the key criterion by which progress is judged. Further, an unhealthy desire for absolute freedom over our lives has led to individual choice itself becoming an absolute.

The papal encyclicals represent a robust and valuable Christian commentary upon some of the consequences of humankind's economic activities. A broad acceptance of the capitalist free-market system is heavily qualified on specific aspects, notably those expressed in *Centesimus Annus*. The world of economic activity is perceived as secular and the Christian critique is largely reserved for its outcomes, rather than the processes themselves. Pope John Paul II very properly warns that concern with economic efficiency and with individual freedom and choice threatens the harmony of social justice. Market freedoms, he argues, are means to an end, not ends in themselves. And individual freedom, the pursuit by *homo economicus* of personal wealth and well-being, has a seriously damaging effect upon the common good.

Catholic social teaching is noticeably lacking in commentary upon the operations of the money and capital markets, which are essential to the functioning of the modern economic system. It may be that this omission reflects yet again an unwillingness on the part of Christians to address the way the economic system operates – a further manifestation of a distancing and a discomfort that we have noted previously. Notwithstanding this distancing, the riches of Catholic social teaching represent a deep mine to be explored by the student of Christian attitudes to wealth.

Anglican attitudes

Anglican thought in the twentieth century regarding wealth creation and economic activity does not offer such a finely crafted approach as that of Catholic social teaching. As we have already observed, Christian socialism emerged as a potent and distinctive strand in Anglican thought towards the end of the nineteenth century and it remained important throughout the twentieth century. It seemed to reflect a general societal and cultural distaste for the whole business of trade and commerce which had come to characterize British society and academia throughout the nineteenth century. To illustrate this point, it is interesting to quote from a speech delivered by Winston Churchill in 1904 (shortly before he left the Conservative Party to join the Liberals, over the issue of free trade):

> No one seems to care about anything but money these days. Nothing is held of account except the bank accounts. Quality, education, civic distinction, public virtue seem each year to be valued less and less. Riches unadorned seem each year to be valued more and more. We have in London an important section of people who go about preaching the gospel of Mammon, advocating the 10% Commandments, who raise each day the inspiring prayer 'Give us cash in our time, O Lord'.[3]

As in the rest of Western Europe, the Great War of 1914–18 marked a cataclysmic change in British society and many ordinary people – in particular those who had fought and suffered as combatants – looked for a renewal and cleansing of society as life returned to normal in the 1920s. Britain, said Prime Minister Lloyd George, should be a land fit for heroes, by which he undoubtedly meant a society where economic benefits should be more widely and equitably distributed. But it was not to be. The 1920s and 1930s were decades of economic depression, of widespread unemployment and of social suffering caused by failures of the wealth-creation machine to deliver the benefits which everyone sought. Against this background of deprivation and failed economic performance, it was unsurprising that many people looked to systems other than the prevailing capitalist one.

Anglican thinking between the two world wars in the twentieth century reflected in large measure this widespread general disillusionment with the capitalist system and a desire for a fresh start. Throughout this period, the so-called Christendom Group was influential. Led by a group of senior Anglican clergy, of whom Canon V. A. Demant was one of the most vocal, the Christendom Group attempted to revive Christian judgement upon the structures of society, not only upon the behaviour of those within it. It was a group whose thinking was relevant to our theme, since it sought the return of Christendom and the hope of renewed Christian guidance in the secular sphere. It was set out in T. S. Eliot's *The Idea of a Christian Society*, published in 1939 and based upon lectures that Eliot had delivered that year. In the preface to the book Eliot wrote, 'what I am concerned with here is not spiritual institutions in their separated aspect, but in the organization of values, and a direction of religious thought which must inevitably proceed to a criticism of political and economic systems'.[4] While not contesting the view that humankind lives by spiritual institutions, political institutions and economic activities, he denies that it is possible to put trust in one of these alone, to the exclusion of the others. The Christendom Group argued that to isolate humankind's economic activity and judge it exclusively by its own 'laws' makes the economic process an end in itself, which it is not; for it and all its parts are primarily a means to something more than economics – the life of man. We find here an anticipation of the views expressed sixty years later by Pope John Paul. But the Christendom Group did not explore the economic process and its consequences in depth. It left that task to other groups.

The Industrial Christian Fellowship (ICF) was a body that represented the desire for a fresh approach to economic activity and the rejection of the failings of the current systems. Through such figures as the Reverend Geoffrey Studdert Kennedy and its General Secretary, Prebendary P. T. R. Kirk, ICF preached, wrote and argued about the social ills of the period that flowed from a flawed and unjust system. The Bishop of Manchester, William Temple, probably the leading churchman at the time, was a major supporter of the Christian Socialist movement. He was in some ways an unlikely candidate for a socialist prelate. His own father had been Archbishop of Canterbury; his own career had essentially been that of an academic. Yet he won a place of great affection in the hearts of ordinary working people in Britain. I can remember, when I was a small boy, the very real sadness and grief that was expressed throughout the nation at his early death.

In 1924 Temple chaired the Conference of Christian Politics, Economics and Citizenship (Copec). The conference ultimately envisaged a Christian corporate action programme that would pursue the necessary economic and social reforms to correct the evils of the day. In retrospect this appears as an adoption by the Christian community of a secular agenda indeed – the advocacy of a particular political stance.

Copec was followed by the more celebrated Malvern Conference, which was convened by the ICF in 1941, after the Second World War had begun. Temple, by this time Archbishop of York and shortly to become Archbishop of Canterbury, was again the chairman. The objects of the Malvern Conference were to reflect upon the economic and social reconstruction that would be required after the war ended and to offer a distinctive Christian contribution to the debate. Attended by more than four hundred delegates, including such distinguished Christian thinkers as Middleton Murry, T. S. Eliot and Dorothy Sayers, the Malvern Conference followed a strongly socialist line of thought (although it balked at endorsing the strongly held views of one of the leading participants, Sir Richard Acland, that common ownership was a matter of fundamental Christian principle). The outcome of Malvern was the publication of 26 propositions – drafted by Temple himself – which it commended to the whole Christian community. The Malvern Declaration struck a strongly prophetic note and while it is difficult to assess its precise impact, there can be little doubt that it contributed strongly to the immediate post-war climate in Britain, with its commitment to social welfare and reform and to the programme of socialist corrections to the injustices of capitalism.

Following World War II, reservations about wealth and economic activities became very much a hallmark of Western European Christian attitudes. We have seen how papal encyclicals emphasized social outcomes and drew attention to their adverse effects. The Anglican Church, rooted in a society that had been greatly changed by the post-war Labour government, strongly reflected that *Zeitgeist* and its acceptance of the socialist approach to the organization of affairs. For many Christians in the decades after 1945, socialism came to be seen as the practical application of Christian principles in the sphere of economics. Dr Edward Norman (himself no socialist sympathizer) stated in his 1978 Reith Lecture, 'Criticisms of capitalism are now the staple matter of much Christian social commentary.'[5] The influence of the Malvern Conference and its Declaration was perhaps demonstrated by that remark.

Two other significant developments in this period showed the orientation of Christian attitudes on economic matters. In the Roman Catholic Church, the worker priest experiment was launched. It captured public imagination in a way that was out of all proportion to the numbers of worker priests, of whom there were only about a hundred. The movement emerged in 1942 during the Second World War when France was occupied and some of the priests went to work in German labour camps. The worker priests – the *prêtres ouvriers* – represented a response by the hierarchy to the secularization of attitudes that accompanied industrialization and the urbanization of the working masses. Worker priests were trained specially for ministry in urban mission areas and the movement grew in size and influence after the end of the war. But the experiment was rapidly politicized and many worker priests became overtly communist. By the mid-1950s, the secularization of the worker priests had reached a level that prompted the hierarchy to terminate the experiment and to re-clericalize the priests. Since that time the Roman Catholic Church has maintained the integration of priests within the traditional parochial church structure, with no separate ministry identified for the sphere of industry.[6]

The Anglican Church engaged on a not dissimilar project: Industrial Mission. From the 1940s the Church of England established chaplaincies and missions to work outside the normal parish system. Their remit was to engage positively with the secular world of work, seeking to re-christianize the working masses through a variety of initiatives such as 'meal-break' meetings, discussion groups and attempted dialogue with management. But by the end of the twentieth century, Industrial Mission had lost much of its impetus. The reasons for this are diverse. Mission chaplaincies were outside the parochial structure and thus somewhat isolated and lacking in support. As full-time clergy, mission chaplains found integration into the work environment a major challenge. In common with their worker priest counterparts, many of them felt alienation from the Church itself and espoused radical left-wing views. Not only were Industrial Mission chaplains outside the main church structure; they were not integrated into the workplace either. Their role was not clearly definable.

The last years of the twentieth century therefore saw Industrial Mission dwindle. The ambiguity in the role of its chaplains, the lack of measurable impact and financial pressures on the Church all led to reduced emphasis and support. The difficulties were addressed in an appraisal produced by the Board for Social Responsibility in 1988, which clearly recognized that the work of Industrial Mission was under threat. The appraisal contains some interesting and revealing 'snapshots' of Industrial Mission on the ground: at Manchester airport chaplaincy, conversations with people 'ranging from senior management to cleaning staff and union convenor to baggage loaders raised huge issues about justice, with regard to privatization, new hard-line management styles, sub-contracted cleaning and catering services and the role of trade unions'.[7] In Liverpool 'a new member of the team described his job as being not a factory visitor but an economic missioner. His emphasis was, first, one of listening, analysis and research, with a view to understanding the economically dominant factors in his local borough; second, of challenging these from the Kingdom perspective; and third, of making recommendations to the Church for action'.[8] At the personal level I clearly recall attending a meeting at which the industrial missioner for one diocese made no secret of the fact that he saw destruction of the existing model of business as his primary goal. A somewhat distinctive interpretation of 'mission' perhaps.

It is perhaps significant that the Church of England employed the term 'Industrial *Mission*' in characterizing the attempt to engage with industry and commerce. The term has connotations of an endeavour to convert or transform an ungodly activity. It also implies engagement from outside, perhaps because the activity itself is uncongenial: an encapsulation of the Christian attitudes over the centuries that we have been examining in this and the previous chapter.

The post-communist experience

We are coming to the end of our historical sketch. The last decades of the twentieth century saw deep changes in attitudes in Western Europe towards business. In the early 1990s Soviet communism collapsed and revealed its singular failure effectively to create wealth, to meet the needs of its people, and to adapt to new technologies. The most public and enduring of socialist systems could be seen to have failed and – in so doing – to cast doubt upon the validity and effectiveness of many of the assumptions upon which it was based. At the same time there was serious questioning of some of the assumptions that had for many years dominated economic and social debate, centring on the key issues of public ownership, the role of competition in economic activity, and the liberation of 'market forces'. This questioning arose in large part from the deficiencies in performance of entities under state management, coupled with acute pressures on public finances and attempts to seek alternative additional resources from the private sector. Comparison of economic performance in Europe with that of the United States further prompted a degree of reappraisal. Thus the period saw a considerable degree of privatization, of stimulus to the economic process by the freeing of market forces, and recognition of the benefits brought by competition. The field of economic activity was transformed. Indeed so profound did these changes appear that Francis Fukuyama famously pronounced a paradigm shift: the end of history. Socialism was banished for ever, he claimed.[9] The adoption of free-market, liberal trading systems was, he argued, inevitable and the changes that had occurred were irreversible.

This dramatic change in economic thinking was, perhaps unsurprisingly, the stimulus to a degree of reassessment by Christian thinkers. Important in this field was the seminal work in Britain of Professor Brian Griffiths (now Lord Griffiths).[10] His work in the 1980s (before the collapse of communist systems and the other changes to which I have referred) was influential in restoring a biblical and Christian perspective on wealth creation as a serious alternative to capitalism or socialism. Griffiths returned to Old Testament fundamentals for a social ethic, enhanced and enriched by the teachings of Christ, not as a textbook reformer, but as a revelation of the establishment of the Kingdom that puts the material world in perspective. Jesus, argued Griffiths, did not condemn wealth as such but warned that its pursuit can numb spiritual realities. Crucially, in *Morality and the Market Place* he identified guidelines drawn from the Bible: a positive mandate to create wealth; private property as the Christian norm for society; each family should have a permanent stake in economic life; the requirement to remedy injustice arising from economic activity; a warning against materialism; accountability and judgement.[11] Wealth creation was thus, he argued, within the realm of Christian engagement, not an alien activity to be shunned by believers.

Griffiths' work anticipated a new interest among Christians in the world of work and the functioning and importance of business generally. The renewal of entrepreneurial activity in Britain prompted by the changes introduced by Prime Minister Thatcher had created a different climate. A greater sense of confidence in the value of business was also apparent in the United States, induced in part by Thatcher's kindred spirit, President Reagan. Much of the new thinking showed a preparedness to engage with and to understand the forces of free-market enterprise. Christians shared in this. In Britain a series of consultations at St George's House, Windsor Castle, in the 1980s explored wealth creation as part of God's plan. Somewhat later the Institute of Economic Affairs invited a series of thinkers to reflect upon the morality of the market place and produced a series of thoughtful papers on the subject.[12] A vigorous debate took place. Socialism retained its supporters despite the collapse of communism in Eastern and Central Europe. The case for state intervention rather than state ownership was argued as the way to counteract the inadequacies of market-led capitalism. Professor Ronald Preston, while perhaps sceptical of Christian socialist movements, wrote in support of this viewpoint and for the qualification of capitalism.[13] On the other hand, an unrepentant Christian apologetic for full-blooded capitalism was articulated by Professor Michael Novak, an American Roman Catholic.[14] He rejected the portrayal of capitalism as a system that condones selfishness, arguing that it channels self-interest into the service of others. He argued later that the work of the businessman should be regarded as a calling, with its own spiritual requirements and rewards.[15]

There is no call for us to consider the debate in detail, but I would like to touch on one or two contributions to give some flavour of its wide-ranging nature. We have already noted the revisionist work of Canon John Atherton, whose *Christianity and the Market* was published in 1992, and we saw how he recognized the need to come to terms with market forces. In the same year other works of interest to the student of Christian approaches to wealth and its creation were published.

Peter Sedgwick's *The Enterprise Culture*[16] is an academic examination of the enterprise culture that had been renewed in Britain, endeavouring to assess its implications for Christians. Sedgwick, it should be noted, refers briefly to the emergence of business ethics as a new area of study,[17] although significantly he offers no particular Christian input.[18] Sedgwick's contribution regarding enterprise is theoretical and third-hand, offering no serious new thinking. It is little more than a portrayal of some aspects of the new business-oriented culture that had emerged in Britain: it is reactive and offers no signposts to guide future discussion about how wealth should be created.

Bishop Richard Harries' book *Is There a Gospel for the Rich?* is a considered reflection for the Christian in a capitalist world: an in-depth examination from a theological standpoint of how Christians have tried to come to terms with riches. Harries finds difficulty with the successful delivery of wealth by the capitalist system: 'The main question which arises, however, is why the advocates of a capitalist system never place [the] goal [of the liberation of the poor] in the forefront of their objectives. Capitalism is seen as the system which best favours the interest of those who have the biggest material stake in society, those who own houses and shares.'[19] He is particularly exercised at the plight of the desperately poor in undeveloped countries. To address this he calls for a Christian 'intervention' to ameliorate the harshest outcomes of capitalism – such as the debt burden of developing countries. He looks to faith as the means whereby transformation can be effected to purify the operation of the wealth-creation machine. But his thoughts on doing this are, in practical terms, very unspecific. Overall Harries gives what turns out to be a reluctant and somewhat qualified Christian acceptance that wealth creation is here to stay. He pleads for Christians to work within the process 'with a conscience that is at once both easier and more troubled.'[20]

Works like those by Atherton, Sedgwick and Harries were written some years after Griffiths' work and followed a decade of changes brought about by the Thatcher government. Their reflections and conclusions can be seen as highly significant: an abandonment of the politicized stances adopted previously and characterized by a recognition that wealth creation and its associated activities can be seen as vital and dynamic elements in the developed world. The institutional churches, however, were generally less responsive to the changes that were taking place. The Roman Catholic Church's teachings express strong reservations about the social consequences of wealth and its creation within the frameworks of free-market capitalism. Two major Anglican initiatives in the 1980s – *Faith in the City* and *Faith in the Countryside*[21] – addressed chronic social issues that had arisen in town and country communities. Both reports show strong residual influences of thought along the old corporatist lines. *Faith in the City* was described as the last gasp of old socialism; *Faith in the Countryside*, however, offered a more biblical method of argumentation. Both reports, even as they were published, appeared somewhat out of touch with the *Zeitgeist*. Their impact on wider society as a distinctive Christian viewpoint was accordingly limited. These studies were to some extent characterized by a reluctance and even an unwillingness to come to terms with the realities of the contemporary system whereby wealth is created.

Much of the Christian commentary that we have considered is of an academic and theoretical nature – often deficient in practical proposals for addressing the difficulties that are found in free markets and the operations of democratic capitalism. Some fundamental misconceptions characterize much Christian discussion. For example, there is often an assumption that wealth is limited – that there is insufficient to go round. The lessons of the industrial revolution – harsh as they were – should have changed that perception. The ingenuity of humankind had pushed back the frontiers and opened up very different horizons of what is possible. Another misapprehension that is to be found underlying much Christian commentary, and which is linked to the first, is that wealth creation is a zero-sum game. Many commentators assume that one man's gain in wealth must be at the expense of someone else. The notion, for example, that because some people have shoes they somehow deprive others of shoes is a persistent fallacy implicit in much of the thought that we have considered. Yet another set of misunderstandings arises from the failure to understand that economic behaviour is one of continuous change. Failure to perceive this led many Christian commentators to offer views that were clearly out of date even as they made them. Thus in the 1980s much Christian comment referred to industrial manufacturing processes that were already being superseded by the application of new technology. The demand for manual human labour in heavy industry was rapidly reducing as technology and cheaper energy replaced it. Yet many Christians failed to see this change happening before their eyes. The lack of understanding about the nature of wealth and its creation has blunted the sharpness of much Christian commentary.

As the twentieth century drew to its close it was possible to identify critical issues and concerns that were crystallizing in the general sphere of economic activity and which were of great importance for Christian understanding. Sedgwick's reference to business ethics in 1992 picked up a major new dimension that had been identified in the United States in the 1970s and 1980s. Business ethics was about to become an important dimension of the business process. What was to be the Christian contribution? Would Christians yet again fail to offer any significant and distinctive perspective?

Our survey of Christian thought about wealth creation and the activities that sustain it has necessarily been selective. We have not examined any particular period or development in depth. The purpose of this overview has been to demonstrate the ambiguous and uneasy positions adopted by Christian thinkers over two millennia. We have noted underlying reasons for this discomfort which, despite debate and analysis, has never been satisfactorily resolved. The tension remains. For individual Christians, particularly those whose lives have been spent working in trade, industry or commerce, the ambiguities have been unsatisfactory. Many have been made to feel that they are indeed endeavouring to do the impossible, to serve two masters: God and mammon.

Unease about wealth is perhaps the most enduring aspect of Christian attitudes that we have considered. But the history of Christian examination of wealth and its creation reveals a number of other features. Over the centuries, as has been said, Christian commentators have been slow to comprehend the dynamic and ever-changing nature of the process.

The transformation of societies into rural communities did not disturb settled opinions. Since Christ had lived in a community shaped in large measure by agriculture this was not surprising. But other changes have gone largely unremarked. The emergence of banking in the Renaissance period evoked no Christian reaction. The implications of the industrial revolution were not understood until long after its full impact had occurred. Christian writers and teachers were very slow to address the issues of environmental conservation arising from humankind's economic activities. As developed-world modes of economic behaviour have spread across the globe, it has been hard to find a seriously informed Christian view about the phenomenon. Much of such commentary as there has been seems to be characterized by misunderstanding and ignorance about how business is conducted. The arrival of the weightless economy stimulated little Christian reflection. History suggests that Christian theology has been and remains ill equipped to address the issues that arise from one of humankind's most widespread and important activities. The gulf is most apparent in the secularization of the world of economics. It is almost as though the people who conduct economic affairs are perceived to be different from those who do anything else!

There is, of course, a kind of unreality about much of the examination of the subject by Christian thinkers. The arguments and counter-arguments over the centuries are, for most Christians, somewhat academic. Adam Smith believed that human beings are born with a propensity to trade and there is a great deal of evidence to support such a view. Certainly in those societies of which we have reliable records, we know that work and activities such as manufacture, trade and the provision of goods and services were essential features. To ask second-century farmers, or fourteenth-century clothiers, or nineteenth-century coal miners whether the work in which they engaged was compatible with God's will would most surely have provoked puzzlement if not incomprehension. It was by such activities that they and their communities lived. The niceties of theological and academic debate have been largely irrelevant to the ordinary person earning a living and seeking to improve his or her material state. Over the period we have considered, the majority of people have not seriously questioned the necessity for their regular toil in the fields, the workshop, the mine or the office. They just got on with it! So does this debate matter?

There are, I believe, several reasons why these issues should be addressed. As we have seen, views on economic practice became politicized during the twentieth century. The debate centred on whether free-market capitalism or socialist state control was more effective and benevolent. This political debate overlooks the essential nature of economics, and the polarization of much Christian comment along political lines has stood in the way of a full theological understanding of wealth creation. The political system to be adopted became more significant than its purpose. Alexander Pope wrote in his *Essay on Man*,

> For forms of government let fools contest;
> What'er is best administered is best.[22]

The wisdom of this aphorism is relevant to the debate about capitalism versus socialism. Whichever system is more benignly effective might be best. Or, as pragmatists would contend, perhaps there is validity in both systems. But I would argue that for Christians to adopt the secular agenda and to conduct the debate about economic life in terms of secular politics has been seriously misguided. The world of politics does not include the consideration of God's purpose. And so for Christians to exclude God from the world of wealth creation is to surrender the field to the secularists. This seems particularly strange when we consider that the wealth-creation system that dominates the present day arose, as we have seen, within a culture shaped and inspired by Christianity.

The processes that constitute the wealth-creation process are far from static. Over the centuries since the birth of Christ, the way in which humankind has invented and adapted the processes of manufacture and trade have changed continuously. We are all aware of major developments – the emergence of agriculture, the industrial revolution, the technological revolution – and within such great cycles there is a further process of change and adjustment in myriad smaller ways. This perpetual development is akin to the evolution that we observe in the natural world – a process of adaptation and modification, driven by humankind's limitless creativity and limitless desires. It seems a singular oversight to offer no attempt at a Christian theological understanding of something so dynamic and fundamental to our existence. It has been a recurring weakness of Christian thinkers that they have failed to come to terms with this energy and dynamism and to tease out the implications.

Most importantly – for the purposes of this book – it is necessary for Christians to be guided (and to help guide others) in the manner in which economic activity should be conducted. I am here referring not to a system (socialism, capitalism, or whatever) but to guidance for the decisions that have to be taken all the time in the conduct of business. As we looked at two thousand years of attempts by Christian thinkers to engage (or disengage) with the process of wealth creation, we observed occasions when the threads of Judaic practice and moral guidelines were taken up as points of reference. As economic activity became progressively more secularized, such endeavours had less and less impact and meaning. Christian promptings were directed at the outcomes of humankind's pursuit of wealth, rather than on how it was carried out. There were severe reservations about the ethical basis for such an activity. It was certainly rarely affirmed. By the same token and probably for that very reason, there has been little guidance on a Christian ethical approach to the conduct of business. Put bluntly, there has been difficulty in offering a Christian ethical perspective when much Christian commentary has had difficulty in affirming wealth creation as an inherently ethical activity in which to engage. That seems to have characterized much Christian response to the world of business. If Christianity is to offer an ethical framework for the conduct of business, there has to be a balanced Christian approach to the theology of wealth creation. In Chapters 3 and 4 we shall look at this issue.

Notes

1. For an interesting study of the status of democracy in twentieth-century Europe see Mark Mazower, *Dark Continent*, Penguin, 1998.
2. Apart from *Rerum Novarum*, the principal texts of Catholic social teaching are: *Quadragesima Anno* (1931); *Mater et Magistra* (1961); *Pacem in Terris* (1963); *Gaudium et Spes* (1965); *Populorum Progressio* (1967); *Octagesima Adveniens* (1971); *Justice in the World* (1971); *Evangelii Nuntiandi* (1975); *Redemptor Hominis* (1979); *Dives in Misericordia* (1980); *Laborem Exercens* (1981); *Sollicitudo Rei Socialis* (1987); *Centesimus Annus* (1991); *Tertio Millennio Adveniente* (1994); *Evangelium Vitae* (1995); and *Ethics in Advertising* (1997). For a comprehensive examination of Roman Catholic social teaching see Joseph Cardinal Höffner, *Christian Social Teaching*, Ordo Socialis, 1983, English edn trans. Stephen Wentworth-Arndt and Gerald Finan, 1996; and Paul Vallely (ed.), *The New Politics: Catholic Social Teaching for the Twentieth Century*, SCM Press, 1998.

3. Quoted in Roy Jenkins, *Churchill: A Biography*, Macmillan, 2001, p. 86.

4. T. S. Eliot, *The Idea of a Christian Society*, Faber and Faber, 1939, p. 6.

5. Edward Norman, *Christianity and the World Order*, Oxford University Press, 1979, p. 7.

6. For further reading on the worker priest movement see G. Siefer, *The Church and Industrial Society*, Darton, Longman & Todd, 1964.

7. General Synod Board of Social Responsibility, *Industrial Mission: An Appraisal*, XXX, 1988, p. 10.

8. Ibid., p. 11.

9. Francis Fukuyama, *The End of History and the Last Man*, Hamish Hamilton, 1992.

10. Brian Griffiths, *Morality and the Market Place*, Hodder and Stoughton, 1982; *The Creation of Wealth*, Hodder and Stoughton, 1984.

11. Griffiths, *Morality and the Market Place*, pp. 91–9.

12. Pamphlets published by the Institute of Economic Affairs on this topic include: Michael Novak, *Morality, Capitalism and Democracy* (1990); Jon Davies (ed.), *God and the Market Place* (1993); Michael Novak and Ronald Preston, *Christian Capitalism or Christian Socialism?* (1994); Revd Robert A. Sirico, *A Moral Basis for Liberty* (1994); Rabbi Jonathan Sacks, *Morals and Markets* (1999); and Brian Griffiths, Robert A. Sirico, Norman Barry and Frank Field, *Capitalism, Morality and Markets* (2001).

13. Ronald Preston, *Religion and the Persistence of Capitalism*, SCM Press, 1979; *Religion and the Ambiguity of Capitalism*, SCM Press, 1991.

14. See, for example, Michael Novak, *The Spirit of Democratic Capitalism*, Institute of Economic Affairs, 1991; and *The Catholic Ethic and the Spirit of Capitalism*, Maxwell Macmillan, 1993.

15. Michael Novak, *Business as a Calling: Work and the Examined Life*, Free Press, 1996.

16. Peter Sedgwick, *The Enterprise Culture*, SPCK, 1992.

17. Ibid., pp. 139–41.

18. 'Churches', he says, 'should remain in this area, criticizing where there is evidence of malpractice but more importantly commending the hopeful signs in employee participation and ethical concern', ibid., p. 141. So much for a Christian view on the importance of business ethics!

19. Richard Harries, *Is There a Gospel for the Rich? The Christian in a Capitalist World*, Mowbray, 1992, p. 102.
20. Ibid., p. 173.
21. Church of England Commission on Urban Priority Areas, *Faith in the City*, Church House Publishing, 1985; Archbishop's Commission on Rural Areas, *Faith in the Countryside*, Churchman Publishing, 1990.
22. Alexander Pope, *Essay on Man*, epistle 3 (1733), ll. 302–3.

♦ 3 ♦

Wealth

Any discussion of business, its purposes and the manner in which it is conducted must recognize at the outset that we are dealing with one of the most powerful forces that humankind has at its disposal. Over the centuries, few subjects have provoked as much debate as commerce, business and economic activity generally. Prejudices and misconceptions abound. The very terms that we use in this context carry highly emotive and often contradictory meanings.

In 1985 Richard Foster of Friends University, Kansas, wrote a book which was published under the alluring title *Money, Sex and Power*. He said that these three issues touch humanity profoundly and universally: 'No topics cause more controversy. No human realities have greater power to bless or curse. No three things have been more sought after or are more in need of a Christian response.'[1] Few Christians, one suspects, would disagree with these assertions.

The fact that Foster chose to write about 'money' is itself significant. Money is an integral component of the business process. It is a means of exchange and a measure of value in payment for goods and services, or in discharge of debts or obligations: a replacement for the clumsy process of bartering one commodity for another. Economists refer to 'money illusion', whereby money values are unconsciously treated as though they were true values. In these circumstances money is valued at its face value, not as the power to pay for goods and services. But money, of course, is a measure of value, not something of value in itself.

So money is more of a symbol than a reality, which makes Foster's assertion about its power a matter for special concern. Money has assumed a reality that it does not possess. People desire it for itself rather than for what it represents. This perhaps illustrates how any discussion of the processes of business and commerce rapidly finds itself in a welter of terminology which is both confusing and frequently highly emotive. We have a set of conscious and subconscious prejudices in this field and, whatever terms we use, sooner or later we stumble over those prejudices. It is therefore important to set out the meaning of some of the terms that will frequently be employed in our discussion.

Wealth creation

'Wealth creation' is a term that merits some clarification and explanation. 'Wealth' is one of those English words that has many near-equivalents and that itself carries a variety of meanings. 'Riches' and 'opulence' are perhaps the most common synonyms for wealth but a host of other terms come readily to mind: assets; money; property; possessions; estates; belongings; means; resources; the list is very long. The nineteenth-century philologist George Crabb identified three close synonyms for wealth: riches, affluence and opulence. Wealth, he pointed out, derives from the Middle English *weal*, meaning prosperity, and is allied to 'well'. It denotes having a considerable share of riches, outward possessions. For Crabb, wealth raises a man in the scale of society and contributes to his *weal* or well-being. This notion of well-being is important.

For the economist, wealth is represented by commodities and services that are capable of satisfying wants. This is clearly allied to the notion of well-being. If my needs and wants are satisfied, then a sense of well-being is induced; if they are not satisfied I have a reduced sense of well-being. The concept of wealth as that which satisfies needs and wants is fundamental to this book. We are defining *wealth creation* as the process whereby needs and wants are satisfied. It therefore follows that if I am not satisfying a need or a want, then I am not creating wealth. For example, I may create the most exquisite piece of jewellery, but if no one wants it I have not created wealth.

This is perhaps a concept with which some people have difficulty. But perhaps it will help if we think of the story of Midas. King Midas desired gold above all else. But when the water that he wanted to drink turned to gold as it touched his lips, it was no longer gold that he wanted. He wanted – he needed – water, not gold. At that moment gold did not give him well-being at all. As the story makes clear, at that point the gold was unwanted and therefore did not constitute wealth.

Taking this further, we can see how the nature of wealth can change over time. Communities grew wealthy by providing a particular commodity that was in great demand – that is, which many people wanted – such as spices in the eighteenth century, or coal in the nineteenth. But when tastes changed or when alternative sources of energy were preferred, those commodities declined in value and the wealth of the communities that supplied them was diminished.

Added value

It is useful to apply this understanding of the nature of wealth creation when considering another term that often causes confusion: that of *added value*. Goods or services are demanded because they have the power to serve human wants or needs. They have value in use. That value in use is also affected by the supply of the goods or services in question. Thus – to use an example employed by Adam Smith – water, being plentiful, has a lower value than diamonds, which are scarce. The want for diamonds is greater than that for water.

However, value can be added to a commodity if it can be put to a use for which there is greater demand (or where the want is greater). A simple example illustrates this. We walk past a lake of water but if we are thirsty we drink from a bottle of mineral water. Why do we do that? Lake water is free, but we pay for bottled water. We drink from the bottle for a variety of reasons: we believe that the water in it is cleaner and purer; the bottled water is more convenient to drink; it may be that the bottled water is fizzy and we prefer our water like that. The purity, the convenience and the fizziness of the water have all added to its value. They have led us to want it more than the water in the lake. All these additions of value stem from the same principle: value or wealth has been created by identifying and meeting more wants.

The capacity to add value is, it would seem, unique to the human species. By the stimulation of desire we are metaphorically, and almost literally, able to turn dross to gold. It is an act of creation. And it would appear to be of infinite potential. We shall return to this consideration later.

As an aside, I have often reflected upon the ingenuity of the French people in the art of adding value. If one takes some of those goods and services of which the French are considered to be leading purveyors, the degree of value added is frequently remarkable. Wine, water and food are generally produced at low cost, yet the French have succeeded in marketing them at greatly added value. In the field of taste and fashion, the French have for a long time persuaded people that perfume and design created in France have greatly added value. These are good illustrations of human creativity adding considerable value to base materials of low initial worth.

The importance of the wealth-creation process and what drives it is fundamental to understanding what business is about. Commercial and business activity is about serving people's needs and wants. The company or organization that does not do so goes out of business. This is a much more basic truth than is generally realized. It is frequently said that the purpose of business is to make a profit. It is more accurate and more meaningful to say that the purpose of business is to meet needs and wants and to do so profitably. The levels of profit earned are a measure of how effectively and how efficiently the company is meeting the wants of its customers.

Wants and needs

A critical eye will have noticed that the terms 'want' and 'need' have been used somewhat indiscriminately up to this point. There is, of course, a distinction. My needs are, generally speaking, more urgent than my wants. In normal usage we do not always take care to use these two words precisely. But 'needs' imply a necessity and a constraint in the natural constitution of things: an unavoidable law which prevails in the sphere of human action. So I need food, warmth, shelter because these are physical constraints upon human existence. I need them because I shall probably die without them. My wants are somewhat different. The word implies something that is desired but not necessarily essential. I want those things that I need, but I do not always need what I want.

Although I have suggested something inherent in our needs which stems from an unavoidable law and thus distinguishes them from our wants, this is not invariably the case. Wants can transmute into needs. My mother possessed a fridge only during the last few years of her life, because in her old age a great deal of food was sold that had to be kept refrigerated, in place of the fresh food she had bought before. The fridge had gradually changed from something she wanted into something she needed. It is not difficult to think of countless examples of modern arte-facts which are necessities for people in their jobs and at home but which fifty years ago had not been invented. So the frontier between wants and needs is a fluid one. Nevertheless, the distinction we have drawn is certainly important in one respect. If initially needs stem from natural constraints – as in the case of the need for food and drink, for example – wants can have a very different origin. Wants can be created and stimulated. A century ago no one in Britain wanted raspberry ripple ice cream. It was created and the desire for it was stimulated. People were prompted to want something that they had never possessed or even heard of previously. The prompting of new wants lies at the heart of the economic processes that dominate the lives of those in a modern economy. And as we know, many people have serious moral concerns about the endless stimulation of new wants. We shall look again at this issue.

The escape from subsistence levels and the creation of surplus

The creation of wealth is the meeting of needs and wants. We satisfy needs that are basic to the lives that we lead. We meet wants that are created and stimulated by that same economic process. We have developed a canon of knowledge about that economic process and how it has evolved. The father of economics – the dismal science – in the modern world is generally recognized to be Adam Smith, in his seminal book *An Inquiry into the Nature and Causes of the Wealth of Nations*. It is not our job to analyse this work in detail. But it is important to note some of the key steps that he identified in the evolution of the wealth-creation process.

The *Oxford English Dictionary* equates poverty with deficiency and scarcity. The most extreme state of poverty is that in which the means of supporting life itself are lacking. The earliest state of human society, known as 'subsistence level', is characterized by lack of food, clothing, protection and security – with attendant low levels of life expectancy. Through the dismal science of economics we have identified the processes by which humankind has been able to escape from mere subsistence. Since Adam Smith explained in the eighteenth century how we escape from an undeveloped standard of life to the high material standards of a modern industrialized society, the process has been analysed in depth.

The key to escaping from the subsistence economy is the creation of surplus. A *surplus* is that which is produced over and above what is required to support those who produce it. We recognize that division of labour by product and process, together with mechanization of processes, are the means whereby we create surplus. Until surplus is created, people devote all their time and energy to survival. But with the creation of surplus it becomes possible to create reserves, to trade part of the surplus for goods that are available in other communities, to build capital and to provide services and leisure. None of these ends can be achieved while a community is striving just to survive.

For some people the term 'surplus' may have awkward overtones. It smacks of acquiring more than is needed and of having an excess, a surfeit. Undue addiction to that surplus may be the beginning of greed. But we should not allow these associations to obscure the basic premiss. Unless we can rise above the fundamental task of meeting the needs for subsistence, we are never able to speak of satisfying wants. There should be no moral objection to surplus as such: we speak readily of the bounty that nature offers. The surplus of fruit in a good year is part of the natural process and we rejoice in it. Likewise we should be thankful for the ability of humankind to create plenty. The state of plenteousness has traditionally been a cause for human rejoicing. In the context of economic activity, the creation of surplus is humankind's way to escape from the grip of poverty.

In an ideal world the surplus that is created would be wholly utilized in the formation of capital and the provision of services for the common good. However, as Adam Smith astutely observed in a famous passage in *The Wealth of Nations*, 'man has almost constant occasion for the help of his brethren, and it is in vain for him to expect to meet it from their benevolence only . . . It is not from the benevolence of the butcher, the brewer, or the baker, that we expect our dinner, but from their regard to their own interest. We address ourselves, not to their humanity but to their self-love, and never talk to them of our own necessities but of their advantages.'[2] Commerce and business are not disinterested activities and companies are not established for disinterested motives. The owners, the shareholders, engage in the enterprise for their private benefit. This benefit they derive as a share in the surplus that is created in the form of dividends, or in the form of the increased capital worth of the business. This is the profit element that motivates those who engage in business as shareholders and owners. Just as few people would be prepared to give their work without reward, so owners of businesses meet and serve the requirements of the customer in order to earn a reward. A utopian world might find its citizens willing to work solely at cost and for the general public good. But no such society has yet evolved. So realistically we settle for harnessing the self-interest of our fellows, in order to enjoy the benefits we derive from their efforts.

Goods and services

In the subsistence economy there is an inevitable concentration on the primacy of material goods. The means of survival in the subsistence economy are physical necessities first and foremost. This is why when we talk about wealth our first thoughts are usually about material things. On our television screens we see life in communities where the bare physical necessities for survival are lacking. The very first imperative of the economic process is to remedy that situation. The person who is starving is not interested in the way in which the food is presented on the plate. That degree of added value comes much later.

The initial task to get us out of the subsistence economy is the creation of wealth by producing material goods. It is worth noting that the word 'good' – in the sense of a commodity – is employed by economists to represent the missing singular of 'goods'. The singular 'good' usually is an abstract noun and means usefulness, benefit or blessing, whereas the plural 'goods' denotes the concrete embodiment of usefulness. Thus the material means of satisfying a human need are described as 'goods' – a term which carries a strong connotation of benefit and blessing.

Once a surplus of goods has been created, that surplus can be traded for other goods and also for services. Economists have traditionally differentiated between *goods* and *services*. Goods, as we have seen, are material commodities that have use; services are generally non-material ways of meeting human needs and wants. Services are based upon actions. Thus the *Oxford English Dictionary* defines 'service' as the action of helping or benefiting or as conduct tending to the welfare or advantage of another. It is clear that we are again concerned with well-being. Services are acts that contribute to the state of well-being and thus constitute wealth creation.

It is important to recognize that the provision of services is an integral part of the wealth-creation process. In popular thinking wealth is widely perceived as possession of material goods. But many of today's needs and wants do not require material goods to satisfy them. Many of what we now regard as the good things of this life, such as delight in the arts, are aspects of economic activity. It is interesting to observe how a sport like football, which began as a way for people to fill leisure time and to take exercise, has become an important part of the economic life of both the developed and the undeveloped worlds. People are prepared to pay handsomely for the entertainment provided by football teams and by individual players, though its material content is negligible. Awareness of the non-material nature of much wealth-creation activity has major significance in any present-day discussion of the subject.

It is evident in the economies of the developed world that the traditional distinction between manufactured goods and services is one of decreasing significance. We still refer generally to the richer and economically more developed countries, the members of the OECD, as industrialized economies. Yet in many of the so-called industrialized countries of the world, such as the USA, UK, Germany and Japan, far fewer people are employed in manufacturing today than in services. The percentage of those employed in the so-called service sector has been steadily rising since the early 1970s with corresponding falls in the numbers engaged in manufacturing. Similarly, the percentage of GDP represented by manufacturing in the OECD countries has declined, while the portion represented by services has increased. We have shifted to the weightless economy. Our wants and needs have become less dependent upon goods and upon things.

Some services are essential to the well-being of modern communities. We cannot conceive of a modern society in which substantial resources are not devoted to health care, to education or to leisure. These critical elements in our communal life are possible only when the necessities of life have been secured. In the subsistence economy, the daily grind of providing food and shelter leave nothing to spare for education or health care.

Selling and marketing

In our examination of some of the terminology that can lead to misunderstanding of economic processes, we should briefly consider the mechanisms by which we establish how needs and wants are to be identified.

We are all familiar with the collapse of the communist system in the early 1990s. Shortly after it happened, the company for which I was then working decided to expand its operations into former communist Central and Eastern Europe. We manufactured commodity chemicals, materials that were used in further processes to make a number of household goods. The company employed a small, highly specialized sales force to promote our products. When the manager responsible for the new markets in Poland, Russia, Romania and Bulgaria began to set up his new sales force, he naturally wanted to recruit native speakers of the languages in those countries. He discovered very quickly that there were no salesmen or saleswomen in those countries. Under communism, sales personnel were not needed. Customers were told what they could have: they were not asked what they wanted.

The job of the salesman is to find out what the customer wants and to try to provide it. There is a commonly held view that selling is a deceitful activity that involves persuading the customer to buy something that he or she does not really want. This may apply to the trickster who appears for one day at the street corner. He can take the risk of selling worthless goods or articles that people later regret having purchased. The salesman moves to another street corner and repeats the operation. But to sell people goods that they do not want is not a recipe for repeat business. When I first joined the marketing department of Esso, we trained the sales force in what we called 'needs analysis selling'. The basic premiss of this approach was that the sales force had to work with the customer to identify what the customer's needs really were. It was fundamental to our philosophy that the sales force should recognize that to sell goods that the customer did not want was a recipe for going out of business. It can be done once, perhaps, but not twice to the same customer. To revert to our earlier proposition that wealth is created by meeting needs and wants, it follows that to sell someone goods that they do not want is not part of the wealth-creation process.

The notion that selling and marketing are inherently deceitful activities dies hard. Much of the current discontent with the globalization of business is predicated on the idea that somehow people across the world are being coerced into buying goods that they do not want or goods that are defective. It is fundamental to the basis for the creation of wealth that this should not be so. No long-term wealth can be created by deception of the person who receives the goods or services.

The market

The key way of ensuring that this principle is satisfied is the operation of the much-abused and even more misunderstood institution known as the *market*. A great deal of ink has been expended on the concept of the market and the very term rouses strong feelings. This is not the place to rehearse all the arguments that have raged around 'market forces'. Given our perception of wealth as that which satisfies needs or wants, it follows that the consumer of goods and services should be free to choose what he or she wants. If the goods or services are not freely chosen then the consumer's wants cannot be satisfied. A corresponding freedom should exist for the supplier, of course. 'The market place' is the name we give to that process whereby freedom of choice is exercised.

Many argue that the term 'free market' is an oxymoron: that in the so-called free market of Western capitalism the consumer is coerced, deceived and corrupted into making choices that are not free. It is certainly hard to find conditions in which pure freedom of choice can be exercised, without any influencing factors such as the persuasive pressures of advertising or the use of a dominant position by particular suppliers. Nevertheless, consumers are not powerless in the market place and mostly regard themselves as able to exercise some considerable degree of personal control over their choices, despite such influences. It is unusual to find someone who considers that his or her choices in making purchases are completely dictated by external factors. Only where a monopoly exists is the consumer totally deprived of choice. It is fundamental to free-market capitalism that there should be competition between suppliers. If there is competition, the consumer has choice. That choice may not be without constraints but generally, in the developed world at least, it involves a great measure of freedom.

Alongside the view that the market place does not allow free choice and that both consumer and producer are subjected to manipulation and exploitation, there is another criticism that has to be recognized. On this view, the market is a free-for-all where no restraints upon corruption, deception and rapacity exist. This somewhat extreme characterization of the market is nevertheless widely held and colours much of the debate on globalization, not to mention discussion of the functioning of markets in the more developed economies of the world.

In its general economic sense, a market is a group of buyers and sellers who are in sufficiently close contact for a transaction between any pair of them to affect the terms on which others buy and sell. In a consumer goods market the quantities and prices of final goods are determined by the response of demand to prices and incomes and of supply to prices and costs. All these factors interact with each other to achieve the end goal of balancing supply and demand to the satisfaction of the parties involved. But participants are influenced by mixed motives and by conditions that vary from one individual to another. The decisions are human decisions, with all their inconsistencies and vagaries. The interplay and outcome of these confusing and conflicting factors is loosely called *market forces*, a term that often carries pejorative connotations. Given the unpredictable and inherently ungovernable nature of the human choices that are in play, it is unsurprising that 'market forces' has become a term of abuse. The functioning of such a system requires agreed conventions and rules. Without them the market would break down for lack of common understanding and trust. And so, in developed economies, market activities are the subject of regulation by trade organizations and by governmental agencies to try to prevent abuse and to provide the necessary assurances of consistency and fairness that participants seek. In no developed economy is there a legal market that is without any regulation or recognized disciplines.

Without rules, a market cannot offer the conditions that enable participants to act with confidence and security. Confidence affects the market place at many levels. First and foremost there has to be trust that transactions will be conducted according to commonly accepted practice. Furthermore there has to be trust that both parties to the transaction are able to see it through: the supplier has to convince the consumer that what is on offer meets requirements; the consumer has to convince the supplier that payment will be made. Also, both parties must have confidence in their own ability to meet the conditions for the transaction to be completed. So the consumer has to have confidence that he or she will be able to pay and the supplier has to have confidence that he or she can provide what is needed. Without that confidence, market activity ceases. Indeed, such is the degree of confidence that participants come to have that they trust in their future ability to complete their side of a transaction. The purchaser may borrow money, confident in his or her ability to earn sufficient to repay the loan. Likewise the supplier may borrow to purchase new equipment to make goods, confident that he or she will sell sufficient of them to earn the money to repay the loan.

The history of our present free-market, capitalist system, constrained within a democratically determined rule of law, is a short one: barely three centuries. Its history is well recorded but less well understood. What emerges is the picture of a system with many imperfections. The ideal market – where suppliers compete on equal terms, where consumers and customers exercise unrestricted freedom of choice, and where the consequential adjustments to the changes generated by technological innovation and by shifts in taste and fashion take place smoothly and without difficulty – is a long way from the reality. The trust and confidence that the market requires for successful delivery of goods and services are vulnerable to abrupt and sometimes irrational fluctuations in the moods of participants. Genuine full competition and unfettered freedom of choice are rare. The rules and regulations governing market processes are often inadequate in both concept and in application. The changes inherent in a market economy, due to such factors as technological change or volatile expressions of taste, may have devastating effects upon individuals and communities who are caught up in forces over which they seem to have little control.

When the serious social consequences of the instabilities and attendant side effects of volatile 'market forces' were first manifested, they usually occurred within relatively small geographical areas. Thus as weaving technology changed in the fifteenth and eighteenth centuries and offered competitive advantages to communities not previously strong in the textiles field, so workers in one place found their skills and livelihood threatened by another group in a neighbouring country or even in the same one. Industrialized countries have gradually established support and intervention mechanisms that are designed to moderate the worst social and economic consequences that may occur. These mechanisms, of course, are often of limited effectiveness. Within relatively homogeneous and traditional communities, such as a typical Western European country, these measures can command general assent, though never without some qualification.

As business has globalized and the Western model has been adopted across the world, these same problems have manifested themselves at the international level. New technologies or changes in fashion that render a commercial activity less viable may now take place, not in a neighbouring town in the same country but somewhere on the other side of the world. So the difficulties that call for major and painful adjustments occur across the global economy. As the consequences of changes in the wealth-creation process assume global proportions, so the imperative to look closely at its moral credentials becomes more insistent.

Notes

1. Richard J. Foster, *Money, Sex and Power: The Challenge of the Disciplined Life*, Harper and Row, 1985, p. 1.
2. Adam Smith, *An enquiry into the Nature and Causes of the Wealth of Nations*, bk 1, ch. 2 ('Of the Principle which Gives Occasion to the Division of Labour').

♦ 4 ♦

Towards a Christian
theology of wealth creation

As we have seen, two millennia of Christian thought and debate about humankind's economic activity shows disengagement and a disinclination to affirm it. Breaking with its roots in Judaism, in its early years Christianity was more concerned with the next world than with this one. Belatedly, the scholastics sought to come to terms with the business of wealth creation but in a theoretical way which was forced to retreat in the face of reality. The Enlightenment and its principles of reasoned methodology applied to the industrial process created further discomfort. Christianity found it easier to concern itself with the wretched social consequences of the industrial revolution than with the industrial activity itself. From this preoccupation followed an alignment of much Christian commentary with socialism and the state corporatist approach to economic matters. This, in turn, led to some agonizing reappraisals when Soviet communism collapsed, leaving free-market capitalism as it had evolved in Western democracies as the most successful and dominant form of wealth creation. Discomfort has become greater as economic forces dominate Western culture in the early twenty-first century. If Christianity is to relate meaningfully to the human condition as experienced within this economic phenomenon, some further reappraisal is called for. Christianity has to accommodate realistically to the forces that dominate contemporary Western – and many other – ways of life.

To call for this adjustment does not signify that there is, as has been argued, an 'end to history'. Free-market capitalism within a democratic framework may well have become dominant, but history teaches that economic systems are in a state of continuous change. The aspirations and creativity of humankind are great agents for change. The system contains within itself the seeds that will ensure transformation. There has never been a single economic model and within the capitalist free market itself there are many versions. But the importance of economic activity cannot be ignored and it calls for a balanced Christian view on the creation of wealth, irrespective of the political or economic variations through which it comes about. This requires a theology of wealth creation.

Theology is the study of God and, since it attempts to represent statements of belief consistently, it must place such statements within the context of nature and history, of which human economic activities form a part. Theology endeavours to formulate directives for life in the world, including ethical behaviour in relationships. This implies, as we have argued previously, that the activity itself should be inherently ethical if normative ethical behaviour is to be defined within it. A Christian theology of wealth creation would therefore seem to be a prerequisite for a Christian input to business ethics.

In this chapter we shall try to set out some bases for a true Christian theology on wealth creation. Such a theology must take account of the realities of the world as we know it. While Christianity may seek the perfectibility of humankind, it should be firmly grounded in recognition of these realities. Christian theology is not a handbook on good behaviour nor does it offer detailed prescriptions for application in the field of economics or any other human activity. But a theology of wealth creation should be practical as well as theoretical, addressing the subject as it is encountered in practice. For many ordinary people the language of theology has become opaque. Our terminology and our concepts should endeavour to avoid this trap.

In his book *Called to Account*,[1] Richard Higginson, Lecturer in Christian Ethics at Ridley Hall, Cambridge, sets out to bring Christian theology and business practice together. His approach is to examine case studies in the light of biblical and other Christian teaching, as a way of supporting the individual Christian in his daily work in business and helping him to address some of the dilemmas that he may meet. Higginson opens up many valuable insights into the relationship between business and Christian theology, particularly insights into biblical understanding. The following reflections upon fundamental Christian teaching are indebted to some of the insights that Higginson's book offers. His study is a rare example of serious thinking about what God and our work have to do with each other.

The Old Testament

A proper starting point for our examination lies in the Bible itself. I am aware of the dangers for the layman in venturing into this field. Biblical interpretation is for the specialist. For every biblical text that is quoted to substantiate a particular point of view, it seems possible usually to find another that contradicts it. This is very much the layman's predicament and I am the first to recognize that the use of biblical texts requires putting them into context. God's revelation in the Bible, as elsewhere, is rarely unambiguous. We should therefore be wary of drawing dogmatic or authoritarian conclusions. We shall not try to identify within the Bible specific guidance in the field of humankind's economic activities. Rather, I shall endeavour to argue that the Bible generally accepts the wealth-creation process as a necessary part of life, while at the same time drawing attention to its dangers, to the abuses of wealth and many of the difficulties associated with the activities that sustain it.

We have already noted that the Old Testament is generally positive about wealth, seeing it as a blessing, rejoicing in abundance, recognizing the responsibilities that wealth imposes upon those who possess it and accordingly offering quite detailed commentary on the morally proper conduct of business. There is little in the Old Testament to suggest that the creation of wealth, in the sense that we have defined it – as the provision of goods and services to meet human needs and wants – is anything but a morally laudable activity. Warning notes are sounded with regard to the accumulation of wealth and the dangers of addiction to it. In particular the Old Testament is concerned with the dangers associated with money and finance: lending at interest to fellow Jews was wrong; exploitation of the weak and unfortunate unacceptable. Typical of the admonitions in this regard are those from the prophet Amos:

> Hear this, you who trample upon the needy, and bring the poor of the land to an end, saying, 'When will the new moon be over, that we may sell grain? And the sabbath that we may offer wheat for sale, that we may make the ephah small and the shekel great, and deal deceitfully with false balances, that we may buy the poor for silver and the needy for a pair of sandals, and sell the refuse of the wheat? . . .
>
> 'And on that day,' says the Lord GOD, 'I will make the sun go down at noon, and darken the earth in broad daylight. I will turn your feasts into mourning, and all your songs into lamentation; I will bring sack-cloth upon all loins, and baldness on every head; I will make it like the

mourning for an only son, and the end of it like a bitter day. (Amos 8.4–6, 9–10)

But as we have already noted in Chapter 1, the act of serving one's fellows through business is affirmed in the Old Testament, welcoming the benefits that it creates and declaring that this is a manifestation of God's approval. Wealth is good as long as the responsibilities that it brings are accepted and provided that certain norms are observed in the process of its creation.

The New Testament

There is no body of evidence in the New Testament that Christ rejected these traditional teachings. Allowing for the fact that Christ lived in an agricultural society, the terminology of business and commerce is widely used, with no suggestion that it was inappropriate in the context of teaching about the Kingdom. Terms such as 'debts', 'payment', 'wage', 'price', 'buying' and 'selling' occur frequently in Christ's recorded usage. If wealth creation and its vocabulary are to be seen as doubtful, Christ was remarkably politically incorrect in his use of language. Likewise, as is frequently pointed out, a lot of the parables and stories that Christ tells are drawn from the world of contemporary economic activity. Many of these stories seem to embrace business and commerce without reservation (the parables of the pearl of great price; the workers in the vineyard; the talents; the lost coin[2]). Other parables refer to some of the more dubious aspects of human behaviour in the world of business (the hard-hearted servant; the rich fool; the dishonest manager; Dives and Lazarus; the rich ruler[3]). But even here the normality and acceptability of the activities involved are taken for granted. These parables were not intended as a commentary upon economic life: Christ is using the stories to explain what he wishes to say about his main teaching regarding the Kingdom. However, the point to be noted here is that Christ does not deny the world of business but accepts it as part of the normal everyday life around him.

The accounts of Christ's own life show that he was the beneficiary of created wealth. The magi brought him gifts of gold, frankincense and myrrh; ointment was applied to his feet; he enjoyed the best of wines at the wedding feast in Cana; in another miracle he provided bread and fish for a good meal. He worked in the carpenter's shop. So he was not outside the world of business activity and the processes of adding value.

There are nevertheless a large number of passages in the Gospels that indicate hostility to aspects of wealth and its creation. In his study *Hostility to Wealth in the Synoptic Gospels*,[4] Thomas Schmidt illustrates in detail a clear strain of what he calls hostility to wealth in the synoptic Gospels of Matthew, Mark and Luke. Christ does not refer to wealth as a gift from God nor to the benefits that wealth can bring. He speaks of the good that wealth can bring in the service of others. But wealth is seen more generally in terms of its spiritual dangers for the individual possessor. Christ, argues Schmidt, calls for dispossession as a requirement upon his disciples (for example in Mark 10.17–31). Christ's warnings about wealth are secondary to this question of discipleship. Above all Christ is saying that the possessions of the wealthy are an impediment to spiritual growth and impair relationship with God. The point is illustrated in a number of passages – such as Matthew 19, where Christ says that it is easier for a camel to pass through the eye of a needle than for a rich man to enter the Kingdom of God, or Matthew 6, where Christ exhorts his followers not to be anxious about such matters as food or shelter. St Francis followed Christ's admonition quite literally. For most interpreters of these passages, however, the message is to beware of the potentially damaging effects of excessive attention to the material goods of this world, not a requirement upon all Christians to assume a state of poverty.

Some have interpreted the incident of Christ cleansing the Temple as a protest against trade. However, examination of the context shows that Christ was protesting against the abusive practices of the money-changers, who were fleecing the faithful if they arrived without the currencies needed to purchase the sacrificial doves. His protest is against exploitation and dishonesty, not trade as such.

Perhaps the two places in the Gospels that express the most negative attitudes towards wealth are the passages where Christ tells the man to sell all his goods and to embrace a state of poverty (Mark 10), and where Christ specifically states that no man can serve two masters: God and mammon (Matthew 6.24). These two passages merit further comment.

The story of the young man who had great wealth and was told to give it away has great emotional impact. Christ's injunction comes at the end of the story, however, after the man has affirmed that he has led a virtuous life in all respects. Only the barrier of undue attachment to worldly goods stands between him and God. There is an implicit recognition that this is the last barrier, not the first. In other words we find here a strange omission that pervades the New Testament and which we would today find unacceptable: there is no mention of the damaging effects of poverty. The rich young man was able to present himself as a good person partly because he was free of the cares that beset the poor.

Christ's statement that we cannot serve God and mammon appears *prima facie* to present a major challenge. The statement seems to offer no option: we have to choose God. But there is another option that is not articulated, which is the use of mammon in the service of others. In rabbinic literature the term 'mammon' has no pejorative meaning, referring simply to possessions and gain. But in the New Testament mammon is several times associated with unrighteousness, suggesting that it is the abusive aspect of possessions that Christ is concerned with. To confuse matters further, in Luke 16.9 Christ says that we should make friends for ourselves by means of unrighteous mammon. So it does not seem from Matthew 6.24 that Christ intends us to abandon all endeavours to create wealth. The stark message about serving two masters is again placing emphasis upon the individual and the dangers for the individual of undue addiction to wealth. And the passage from Luke appears to endorse some accommodation to the realities of life.

Despite the thesis put forward by Schmidt and others that the New Testament is unarguably hostile to the creation of wealth, it would be incorrect to derive from these negative emphases a rejection of wealth creation. It would defy common sense for all followers of Christ to take literally the injunction to pay no heed to matters such as food, drink or clothing. Christ is not urging his followers to invite death through self-neglect. A sensible interpretation will see the words as a warning to the individual against an *undue* concern for material things which displaces spiritual concerns. Christ is arguing for a proper sense of priorities. Wealth is that which serves human needs and wants, and Christ's insistent message is a reminder that such needs and wants are not exclusively material, but rather that the greatest wealth creation lies in serving our need for God. Equally, alongside Christ's warnings about undue attachment to worldly goods, we should recognize the implications of the imperative to provide for the poor. This requires the wherewithal to do so. The Good Samaritan needed resources to alleviate the sufferings of the man who had been mugged on the road to Jericho. Relief of poverty demands wealth.

The negative tone about wealth in the New Testament is part of a wider phenomenon. The New Testament contains relatively little commentary on social issues. Wealth is seen almost entirely in terms of its spiritual dangers for the individual, with little consideration of its wider social benefits. At no point in the Gospels do we find recognition of the social ends that wealth serves or the improvements that it makes possible in people's lives. The damaging effects of poverty are disregarded while the dangers of addiction to wealth for individuals are stressed. There are parallels in other aspects of New Testament teachings. The teachings about the use of power and the gift of sex are similarly oriented to the behaviour of individuals and less towards their general societal implications. In short, we cannot expect to find in the New Testament a worked-through social gospel. Christ was teaching individuals how to bring about the Kingdom. He was not offering a handbook on social behaviour. As Schmidt himself states, 'the evil of wealth consists not primarily in lack of care for the poor but in independence from God.'[5]

It is clear from these comments that a theology of wealth creation requires more than reference to selected texts from the Bible. The generally positive views contained in the Old Testament are to some degree qualified by the emphasis in the New Testament upon the spiritual dangers that wealth entails for the individual. With the experience of two thousand years of Christianity we have a deeper perspective upon which to draw than was available to the early church. Richard Hooker, the sixteenth-century Anglican theologian, identified three main sources for Christian understanding: scripture, God-given reason and tradition. To this trinity other thinkers have added experience. A theology of wealth creation should draw from these additional wells of Christian wisdom.

Christian doctrine: creation

The first chapter of the book of Genesis describes in metaphorical terms God's act of *creation* in bringing the universe into being. According to Christian belief God created all things and his act of creation was an act of love. God was not obliged to create and Christians believe he did so because he willed to bring creatures into existence to share in the benefits of his love. It is of the essence of that sharing that the reciprocal love of human beings for God should be freely given.

Because God seeks freely given love, not the forced submission of slaves, it follows that human beings can exercise choice. And we observe freedom of choice in operation every day of our lives. Indeed, so unconstrained is our freedom that we are free to deny and reject

God. Despite the influences of heredity and of environment, our power of self-direction is sufficiently free for us to be held responsible by our fellow men and women. Social life is built upon our freedom of choice and our individual responsibility for the choices we make.

What I have said so far about creation and free will is oversimplified. Within the Christian understanding of creation are a number of paradoxes and tensions that demand analysis. We should not attempt here to develop an extended theology of God's creative acts and purposes.[6] But there are aspects of Christian thought about creation that are germane to our thesis and which we should explore further.

The very term that we have used – 'the act of creation' – implies a single event in time. However, we can see that creation was not a single event in time. There was no time before God created it, so logically there was no 'before'. But, within the context of time, creation is a continuing process, and human beings seem to play a part in it. We act out a small role by helping God develop the potentialities of creation itself. Our contribution may be small and may appear insignificant, but it helps to shape the world and possibly to bring into being things that add to the perfection of the universe (and also to its imperfections). We know that the universe in which we live is in a state of continuous change. God is the creator, but through the dynamism of change – which includes the outcomes of our acts of free will – humankind is allowed to participate in God's ongoing creative act.

Over the centuries Christians have had to face a major challenge regarding the nature of the created universe itself. God, we say, is omnipotent and omniscient. An all-powerful and all-knowing creator is thus 'responsible' for all aspects of creation, which includes pain and evil. If God is the creator of everything, knows everything and causes everything, does he then bring about the decisions that I believe to be my own free choices? The metaphor of the story of creation in the book of Genesis illustrates this dilemma. Adam and Eve freely choose to disobey God and eat the forbidden fruit. Yet it was God who created the tree and its fruit and caused it to be in the garden. Moreover, being omniscient he knew in advance that Adam and Eve would succumb to the temptation to pick and eat the fruit.

The problem of divine foreknowledge and human freedom has exercised Christian thinkers over the centuries and is fundamental to our understanding of creation and the role of human creativity within it. We are still learning about the nature of creation itself. But it does seem that we are now in a position to question the simplistic concept of God's omnipotence and his omniscience. In his essay 'God's Power: a Process View',[7] Ian Barbour identifies a number of reasons for such a questioning. He points first to God's respect for the integrity of nature, whereby he does not intervene frequently or coercively in the process, having set boundary conditions and constraints to it. God works 'subtly in co-operation with the structures of nature rather than by intervening unilaterally'.[8] Secondly, he points to the ubiquity of pain and suffering as integral and possibly essential elements in human life, partly as contributors to moral development and possibly the product of metaphysical necessity. Barbour's third argument for questioning the classical view of divine omnipotence lies in the reality of human freedom: 'The experience of choice', he states, 'seems to be an indelible feature of first hand personal knowledge . . . Moral choice is frequently called for in the biblical literature'.[9] God has foreknowledge of our decisions, but, Barbour argues, God's omniscience does not extend to choices that are unknowable until they are made. In short, 'if time is real in God's experience, human freedom implies limitations in God's knowledge of the future'.[10]

I have concentrated on this aspect of our understanding of creation because I would argue that free choice and free human creativity are essential elements in our search for a theology of wealth creation. It is implicit in Christian understanding that creation is itself good (Genesis 1 repeatedly says, 'And God saw that it was good'); as Keith Ward explains, 'The creative process, the exercise of free creative imagination and skill, and the finished product, are just good in themselves, for their own sake . . . Thus you explain why something exists by showing that it is of intrinsic value: it is good that it exists'.[11]

We should not set arbitrary constraints on our notions of human creativity. It is not confined just to the arts. That would be a very limited view. Human beings are creative in ideas, in the construction of societies, in the invention of machinery, in the formulation of scientific theories. We are capable of exercising our creativity in any field – and that includes the creation of wealth and the provision of new goods and services to meet the wants and needs of our fellow human beings. The painter demonstrates creativity through painting; the businessman does it through entrepreneurial activity. Humankind's ability to find ways of serving the needs and wants of fellow human beings is a prime manifestation of our creativity.

Before leaving the subject of creation, there are two further points to note. In the natural world we see both creation and destruction. Species evolve and become extinct; landscapes are formed and destroyed by natural forces such as flood or earthquakes. There is a continuous process of creation, transformation and destruction. Within creation itself are the seeds of destruction and change. And so it is with the human creative process. Sculpture may entail the cutting down of trees to be carved, the breaking up of stones to be sculpted. Ideas are superseded and in a sense destroyed by newly formulated concepts. It is like this with the act of creating wealth. Food is grown for consumption – the destruction of the fruits or the seeds that nourish us. Oil is burnt to meet our need for warmth or power. We change and also destroy part of the natural environment in which we live. The point that I wish to make is that wealth creation is not unique in this respect. Human beings, in their role as creative agents and executors of change, are creators, changers and destroyers and accordingly form part of the natural processes that govern the universe in which we find ourselves.

We have referred frequently to the exercise of free will as a fundamental aspect of creation. Indeed, it seems that the requirements for free choice and freely given love are critical determinants of the nature of our universe. The exercise of free choice is one of the aspects of wealth creation that we noted in Chapter 3 when we considered the function of the market. The market is one area where we exercise free will. It is the dynamism of those choices that drives the wealth-creation process. If I am not able to make my choices freely then the very act of wealth creation is denied because I cannot choose what I need or what I want. We shall look later at the implications of such choices.

I have endeavoured to establish wealth creation as a fundamental manifestation of humankind's participation in the continuing process of God's creative acts. We are co-creators with God and in exercising our freedom of choice in this field we are working out part of our role in the development of the created world. Choice and the consequences of choice seem to lie at the heart of God's purpose in seeking creatures who will love him as freely as he loves us. The exercise of our free will is integral to wealth creation itself and that activity is therefore part of our wider creative role. Viewed in this light, human wealth creation should be seen as fundamental to a full understanding of creation itself – a critical element in a balanced theology of wealth creation.

Christian doctrine: incarnation and redemption

The secularization of much modern life in the Western world has created a polarization: there are perceived to be two spheres of human experience, the spiritual and the material, with little common ground between them. Of all the world's major religions, Christianity is the one that should enable us to come to terms with this apparent separation. The mystery of the *incarnation* is the key to bridging the divide between the religious and the secular spheres of life, between the spiritual and the material. From the early creed of Nicaea, formulated in AD 325, and the expanded definition authorized by the Council of Chalcedon in AD 451, Christians have felt the necessity to set out in words the unique nature of Jesus Christ as being both human and divine, defining his special nature as an object of faith. That duality offers a unique Christian perspective on our experiences of everyday life.

The precise nature of the incarnation is a mystery that no formula can adequately explain. In 2 Corinthians 5.19 St Paul affirms that 'in Christ God was reconciling the world to himself'. In Philippians 2 he states that Christ had a divine nature but was born in the likeness of men. Repeatedly in the Gospels, those who meet Jesus are confronted with the question of the nature of his person: 'And they were all amazed, so that they questioned among themselves, saying, "What is this? A new teaching! With authority he commands even the unclean spirits and they obey him"' (Mark 1.27); 'Who then is this, that even the wind and the sea obey him?' (Mark 4.41)

What the incarnation says about God's relationship with the world in which we live is of considerable importance in a theology of wealth creation. Early Christianity was tempted towards the Manichaean view that the material world is evil. The incarnation, however, precludes any notion that God is concerned only with certain parts of human life. The participation of Jesus in the everyday events of life in contemporary Palestine has to be interpreted as God's assurance that the material world is good. As the Revd Jack Mahoney has pointed out, the incarnation is far removed from any concept of God as a kind of divine absentee landlord distanced from his creation. The understanding that God has participated in this world enables us to emphasize that God is actively present in the business activities of humankind as we bring new fruits into existence and celebrate the providence of God: 'If his delight is to be among his human children, he has invited us all to share his delight and his loving enterprise.'[12]

If the mystery of the incarnation affirms that God participates in the material world, the great Christian doctrine of *redemption* offers the further promise to humankind that we can be freed from dependence upon material things and from our propensity for making bad choices. The term 'sin' is one with which some Christians today are rather uncomfortable. It is more comfortable to believe that nature or nurture reduce our own individual responsibility for the choices we make. But, while upbringing and genetic inheritance may predispose a person to act in certain ways in certain circumstances, people cannot on that account shrug off personal responsibility for decisions they make. In large measure these are free acts and when one behaves contrary to the promptings of conscience (a matter to which we shall return in Chapter 6) one is often making a deliberate choice to do so. The propensity to act in ways which one believes to be wrong is what Christianity has traditionally referred to as humankind's sinful nature – a tendency that St Paul expressed clearly in his letter to the Romans: 'I do not understand my own actions. For I do not do what I want, but I do the very thing I hate' (7.15).

The truth of the incarnation safeguards the grace, mercy and forgiveness of God and this is the basis for a gospel of redemption for sinful humankind. Whenever our behaviour is misguided and perverse, our understanding of God's redemptive purpose can enable us to start again, to redress the wrong we have committed, to correct the faults we have acquired. No one is beyond God's forgiveness and the redemptive power of God's love as made real through the life of Christ. And so it is with humankind's activities in the field of wealth creation. When we make mistakes and misapply our creative gifts in that sphere, forgiveness and redemption are available. There is nothing that defines wealth creation as standing outside the power of redemption. Like all human activity it may be abused and misdirected. But it is never beyond the reach of God's love and forgiveness.

Michael Novak's theology for democratic capitalism

Michael Novak is one of the few theologians who have addressed the question of wealth creation. We noted in Chapter 2 that he had contributed to the debate following the collapse of the communist system in Central and Eastern Europe. In his book *The Spirit of Democratic Capitalism*[13] he identifies some important elements for a theology of democratic capitalism and we should note them as a helpful contribution.

In this book Novak is concerned to provide a theological validation for the democratic capitalist model. Although this model has proved remarkably effective and durable it is, I believe, unwise to see it – as Novak seems to – as the model that is suitable in its Western form for all other societies and all other cultures. When terrorists crashed aircraft into the World Trade Center in New York in the name of Islam, that was a protest against the very model of democratic capitalism that Novak so warmly commends. The terrorists were seriously misguided. But they fearfully demonstrated that the particular form of wealth creation which has proved so successful in the West is by no means universally regarded as acceptable. We shall address some of the considerations raised by 11 September, in particular the globalization of modern business, at a later stage. At this point I wish simply to draw attention to a criticism that can be made against Novak's outline theology – namely that it attempts to justify in theological terms the superiority of one particular system of wealth creation.

Novak defines the key features of democratic capitalism as acceptance of a market economy, accompanied by respect for human rights to life, liberty and the pursuit of happiness and supported by institutions moved by the ideals of liberty and justice for all. He believes that a political democracy is compatible in practice only with a market economy, both systems being nourished by a pluralistic liberal culture. The logic of capitalism, with economic liberties dependent upon political liberties, leads inescapably to democracy. Under the pressures of capitalism, repressive regimes are pushed towards political freedom. The outcomes of this process are not equal: capitalism does not result in equality. Nevertheless, argues Novak, the inequalities are not fixed because opportunities exist for every person to better his or her condition.

Novak is not indifferent to the deficiencies in capitalist prosperity and the criticisms that are made against it, such as its tendency to promote hedonism and profligacy, its dependence upon negative human characteristics such as greed and envy, and its promotion of an ambitious, adversarial class of entrepreneurs. He counters these deficiencies by pointing out that a democratic capitalist society is not committed to any one vision of a social order, but is flexible and responsive to change.

Novak puts forward Christian doctrines that he judges to have been powerful in leading humanity to establish institutional practices which have made economic development, political liberty and a moral-cultural commitment to progress emerge in history as a realistic force.

First he points out that the doctrine of the Trinity represents God more as a kind of community than as a solitary individual. So, to build a community within which individuality is not lost is to show forth God's life. How then can a human community be built without damage to human individuality? Novak contends that within a political economy, every component has a degree of autonomy, yet each system is dependent on the others. This differentiation permits other sorts of community – like families, neighbourhoods, trades unions – to flourish. These are mediating communities that make the life of individuals and of states possible. Within this formula he denies that the freedom of the individual ends, as some would contend, in alienation. The patterns of communal and individual life in democratic capitalism reveal a society's highest ideals – the concept of community that is enshrined in the doctrine of the Trinity.

Novak also considers the doctrine of the incarnation, which, he claims, teaches us to learn to be humble, think concretely, face facts and train ourselves to realism. It is a doctrine of hope but not of utopia. The point of the incarnation is to respect the world as it is and to recognize its weaknesses: 'The Incarnation obliges us to reduce our noble expectations, so to love the world as to fit a political economy to it, nourishing all that is best in it'.[14]

In addressing competition Novak argues that the will to power must be made creative, not destroyed. God is not committed to equality of results. Competition is the natural play of the free person, a measuring of oneself by some ideal and under some judgement. He argues that competition for money is beneficial to society: 'Few societies have invented an incentive so innocent in itself, so self-multiplying, so socially binding, and so utterly dependent upon the common social health'.[15]

The doctrine of original sin tells us that human liberty can express itself in evil as well as in good. The chief aim of democratic capitalism is to fragment and check power, not to suppress sin: 'A free society can tolerate the public display of vice because it has confidence in the basic decency of human beings', and 'the concept of original sin does not entail that each person is in all ways depraved, only that each person sometimes sins'.[16]

The separation of realms, according to Novak, is clearly expressed in the Gospel of Matthew: 'Render therefore to Caesar the things that are Caesar's, and to God the things that are God's' (22.21). Novak argues that the political and economic system cannot be infused, in an obligatory way, with Christian values and purposes. A market system must be open to all regardless of religion or faith. To try to run an economy by the highest Christian principles is certain to destroy both the economy and the reputation of Christianity. Nevertheless each Christian should follow conscience and cooperate in coalitions where consensus may be reached.

Finally Novak considers *caritas* (a word he prefers to the greatly over-used word 'love'). It is the ideal of willing the good of others. A system of political economy, claims Novak, meets the demands of *caritas* by reaching out, creating, inventing, producing and distributing, raising the material base of the common good: 'The highest goal of the political economy is to be suffused by caritas'.[17]

It is not necessary to accept in their entirety Novak's claims for the particular economic system of democratic capitalism in order to find some cogent elements for the development of the balanced Christian theology of wealth creation that we are seeking. His discussion is helpful because it takes a realistic approach to the world of economic life and does not shelter behind an unrealistic concept of what the Christian vision should be.

Democracy and wealth creation

Michael Novak presents the case for democratic capitalism as the most moral and most commendable system on offer in the world today. Francis Fukuyama's *The End of History*[18] supports that view and suggests that this system will prevail over all others globally. But this is a somewhat simplistic view of things. The broad description of free-market democratic capitalism embraces a wide diversity of forms of expression. *The Economist* has outlined some of these diverse forms:

- The American model features flexible labour and product markets, fierce competition and profit maximization, offset by widespread inequalities, low welfare benefits and poor public services.
- The Japanese model encourages loyalty and high skill levels, high-quality public services and a cooperative culture, offset by reduced capability to meet market competition and a poor use of resources.
- The East Asian model offers a wide range of characteristics, with a shared openness to trade and with high levels of saving.
- The German model provides good public services and welfare with social harmony but many restrictions on the labour and product markets, resulting in inflexibility.

- The Swedish model has open markets, comprehensive welfare provision, and narrow wage differentials, offset by sluggish growth and reduced incentives to work.
- The Dutch model is characterized by a high degree of common sharing and cooperation and flexibility on social benefits, accompanied by large amounts of part-time work and unduly large numbers of people on sickness and disability benefit.[19]

This wide diversity demonstrates the flexibility that is available within the capitalist wealth-creation process alone, as it has evolved so far. *The Economist* did not refer to the French or Singaporean models, which are different again and which illustrate even more that there is no single model that displaces all others.

The process by which a society may establish mechanisms for stable wealth creation is indeed complex. Market capitalism and liberal democracy are both features of the dominant system that has evolved successfully in Western Europe, the Antipodes and North America and – to some degree – in other parts of the world also, for example Japan, Taiwan, Singapore and Thailand. In *The End of History* Fukuyama adds a third ingredient for success – a secular, rational set of beliefs. These three elements may be necessary, but not sufficient conditions for the establishment of a stable basis for the generation of wealth accessible to most of the population of a community. David Landes, in *The Wealth and Poverty of Nations*,[20] draws similar conclusions from his in-depth historical survey of the processes by which different societies have created wealth over the centuries (in Western Europe he identifies, as an example, the ingredients for the success of the industrial revolution as the autonomy of intellectual enquiry, the creation of a common language of proof and the ratiocination of research).

In particular, the current success of market capitalism in liberal democratic societies suggests some kind of synergy between the two elements of democracy and prosperity. This link is examined in depth by Niall Ferguson in his book *The Cash Nexus*.[21] Unsurprisingly he reaches the conclusion that the relationship is considerably more complex than is implied by either Novak or Fukuyama and that there are many other factors that have important roles to play in the economic success of a society. Nevertheless, Ferguson does tentatively conclude that economic growth may promote the spread of democratic initiatives. Moreover, the key features of democracy – the rule of law, separation of powers, individual freedom, universal suffrage and the capacity for non-violent change of government – are generally favourable conditions for wealth creation, but not a guarantee of it.

Thus although substantial, widespread creation of wealth may not be the certain outcome of a democracy, it has very rarely been a stable feature of *non*-democratic societies. The most effective forms of wealth creation, when freedom for individual initiative is secured, do seem to be closely allied to democratic forms of government.

Winston Churchill famously described democracy as 'the worst form of government – except all those other forms that have been tried from time to time'. Democracy may not be a perfect form of human governance. It does, however, possess certain characteristics that commend it from a Christian perspective – notably its respect for the individual person, its concern for human rights and its unwillingness to wage unprovoked or aggressive war. (History offers only a few instances where a democracy has aggressively initiated war.) Such claims are, of course, qualified by our recognition that no human society can attain perfection. The fact remains that prosperity seems to contribute towards the establishment and preservation of democratic forms of government and this is significant in the theological implications of the creation of wealth.

The negative aspects of wealth creation

Unhealthy appetites

No serious examination of the bases for a true theology of wealth creation can afford to disregard some of the substantive criticisms that are offered against wealth and the processes by which it is created. From a theological perspective, perhaps the most damaging arguments are those that point to the dangerous emotions and desires that wealth arouses and stimulates. The Ten Commandments represent for most people a primary signpost for moral behaviour (albeit they contain some injunctions scarcely heeded today, such as forbidding the making of graven images and keeping the Sabbath day holy). They instruct us to avoid covetousness, the desire to take possession of our neighbour's wife, servant, ox, ass or any other thing he owns. Covetousness is closely allied to other undesirable emotions such as envy, acquisitiveness, attachment to material goods, and greed. Christian teaching has warned against these desires on the grounds that they are damaging to the spiritual health of the individual and constitute a hindrance to the development of our proper relationship with God. The thrust of much of

Christ's teaching, as we have observed, was to warn against undue attachment to possessions and the temptations of greed.

It cannot be disputed that the needs and wants which the creation of wealth sets out to meet can very easily turn into covetousness, acquisitiveness and greed. A true theology of wealth creation will understand this and take into consideration the necessary constraints on these feelings. The very definition of greed as inordinate desire for something poses the question 'What is moderate or acceptable desire?' There is no general answer: each case should be examined on its merits. But the issue that arises is whether the risk of stimulating excessive desire represents a sufficient reason for refraining totally from the activity of prompting wants in the first place. Reason suggests that this is not so. Money, sex, power and other objects of human desire all present the danger of turning the innocuous into the dangerous. Human life would come to an end without sexual activity, yet we know that inordinate sexual desire can have fearful consequences. Likewise, the exercise of power – for example by politicians or by a policeman – is a necessary element in the maintenance of civil society. Yet the improper use of power is dangerous and can imperil civil society if abused. In these cases immoderate behaviour presents a potential danger, but that is not sufficient reason for total abstention from sexual activity or the exercise of power. And so it is with wealth creation. The potential abusive stimulation of human wants is not reason enough to proscribe the activity. What our theology should seek is the basis for ensuring moderation of excessive and inordinate desire.

Inequality and unfairness

The creation and possession of wealth are widely perceived as the occasion for much inequality and unfairness. At the global level we are affronted by the contrast between affluent communities, like those in Europe and North America, and those that barely have the means to survive, as in sub-Saharan Africa. The rewards to individuals engaged in business are not equal: the huge emoluments paid to senior executives in some companies are vastly different from those paid to employees lower down the organization. These are but two examples of the inequality and unfairness that are apparent in the sphere of business and economic activity. They cannot be easily overlooked. Inequality of outcome is clearly inherent in the process of wealth creation. It can also be argued that equality of opportunity is likewise unattainable in this field of human endeavour. Does the inequality that characterizes the creation and distribution of wealth constitute a serious issue in a theological examination of the subject?

In *Inequality and Christian Ethics*[22] Douglas Hicks attempts an examination of Christian attitudes to inequality and unfairness. He points out that 'inequality among persons' is a theological claim about people's moral status in relation to one another and principally in relation to God. Beyond this point we become involved in answers to the question 'Equality of what?' Appropriately Hicks quotes Archbishop William Temple, who in *Christianity and Social Order* put the matter very succinctly: 'Apart from faith in God, there is nothing to be said for the notion of equality'.[23]

Our notions of fairness and justice lead us to object to certain gross forms of inequality. Yet obviously inequality is inherent in the whole of existence. A man who is 1.80 metres tall cannot be equal in height to one who is 1.85 metres tall. Some aspects of inequality are of little importance – for example my inability to compose music comparable to that of Schubert has minimal significance in any wider scheme of things. Many kinds of inequality, such as our ability to run or jump, or to write or do mathematical calculations, are just accepted as the way things are. Perhaps what offends us about the inequalities that are part and parcel of our relationship with wealth is the fact that wealth is itself something that we have created and distributed. For that reason it does not seem to be part of the natural order of things. Furthermore, at the basic level of providing food, clothing and shelter, the unequal distribution of wealth may well be a matter of life and death.

Christian tradition strongly emphasizes the principle of equality before God, while offering little impetus to address particular forms of inequality in society. Equality before God asserts that God loves all people equally. But only in very special conditions, such as those within a religious community, does equality form part of human societies. Indeed the philosopher Robert Nozick argued in *Anarchy, State and Utopia* that there are incompatibilities between our notions of freedom and of social justice:

> no end-state principle or distributional patterned principle of justice can be continuously realized without continuous interference with people's lives. Any favored pattern would be transformed into one unfavored by the principle, by people choosing to act in various ways; for example, by people exchanging goods and services with other people . . . To maintain a pattern one must either continually interfere

to stop people from transferring resources as they wish to, or continually (or periodically) interfere to take from some persons resources that others for some reason chose to transfer to them.[24]

Thus, if we postulate a hypothetically perfectly egalitarian distribution within a society, it would become less egalitarian as the consequence of people's decisions to transfer their shares as they see fit. Freedom and equality do not sit together in total harmony.

A theology of wealth creation has to come to terms with the reality of inequality. Free will and the attendant freedom of choice are both fundamental to the human condition. Humankind has found no just mechanism that enables society to restrict freedom of choice in such a manner that perfect equality can be obtained. Even if that were so, free choice would upset that perfect state. And choice is at the heart of economic prosperity. Humankind has to recognize and live with the uneasy balance between the inequalities that result from freedom of choice exercised within an economic system, and interventions to mitigate those inequalities. Interventions that impair freedom of choice may reduce economic prosperity. In practice this comes down to the community taking action to address gross and unacceptable inequality, while recognizing that full equality is neither attainable nor even desirable. Our experience shows us that the measures we adopt to mitigate economic inequalities are rarely fully effective and may well bring about other, unintended consequences. That is not a valid argument for not making the effort but it does warn us against unrealistic expectations for an outcome that is manifestly fairer and more equal. The persistence of inequality is not a sufficient justification for withdrawal from economic activity and thereby forgoing the benefits it provides. It is part of the Christian understanding of the human condition that we cannot find perfection in this existence, though we may continue to strive for it.

Competition

Competition is an aspect of the free market that attracts much adverse criticism. It is often seen to be wasteful, aggressive and destructive. When objections are raised to 'market forces' they are generally intended as a rejection of competition. In Chapter 3 we noted that free choice, and the avoidance of monopolies and of cartels, are important requirements for the creation of wealth. Without choice there is no reliable method for establishing what people want. Competition is the process by which people are offered choice. It has therefore become an integral part of wealth creation in the Western free-market system.

From a theological perspective, it is the motivations inherent in competition that give rise to concern. In competition there are winners and losers. St Paul sometimes refers to competitive racing (for example in 2 Timothy 4.7) and in 1 Corinthians 9.24–5 he points out that only one runner wins the prize. Winners imply losers. This situation, it is sometimes argued, excites dangerous emotions of aggression in the contestants. According to this point of view, the business of competition is akin to war. In the market place, however, it is somewhat different. The loser can try again elsewhere. Defeat is not usually the end of matters. The purpose of competition is to serve the requirements of others, not to eliminate the competitor. The use of the language of war that sometimes occurs in descriptions of commercial competition is misguided and misplaced. The different suppliers in a competitive market are vying with each other to meet the demands of the customer – and that is a very different motivation from seeking to eliminate one's competitor.

An argument frequently made against the competitive environment of the market place is that the same benefits could be secured through cooperation, which would be less wasteful. A Christian perspective may set out a vision of harmonious cooperation compared with the aggression of the market place. Such an ideal may be desirable but it does not follow that there is no place for regulated and fruitful competition in areas where it is beneficial. Cooperation and competition are not mutually exclusive. An economic system can utilize both. The critical concern about competition is that it should be shaped to serve human ends and not become an end in itself. Also, it should be noted that the absence of competition is not necessarily a recipe for cooperation. Indeed, in the absence of competition a society may be presented with a less attractive option, where there is no choice and no innovation. The competitive market place is perhaps the price to be paid for the fruitful deployment of human creativity.

Limitations to wealth

The last negative feature of wealth creation that I wish to consider is a common misunderstanding about the nature of wealth, namely that it is limited. We have seen that before the industrial revolution wealth was indeed limited. In agrarian economies there were very real constraints upon supply – the weather, the availability of cultivable land, restrictions on what crops could be grown, etc. Hence it was generally understood in pre-industrial societies that the supply of goods was limited and that some form of rationing was needed to prevent famines and extreme deprivation. In such economies, where supply is constrained, one person's meal might well be at the expense of someone else's hunger.

The changes that occurred at the time of the industrial revolution in Western Europe meant that the creation of wealth was no longer a zero-sum game. Humankind's capacity to produce goods was no longer restricted as before. The ability to provide more food from the same amount of land was enhanced at the same time. The harnessing of power and the application of technology have given humankind the means to supply the needs of huge increases in world population. Where shortages of raw materials or of land threaten our ability to continue to provide goods such as food, substitution occurs to make good the deficiency. The ability to produce has been transformed – although the ability to distribute the goods effectively for all humankind has not matched the growth in productivity. That, however, is another issue.

The Malthusian prediction that the Earth could not support its growing human population proved unfounded. That there are finite material resources on the planet remains true. But human creativity has demonstrated over more than two centuries an ability to provide for a much larger world population. It will form part of the argument of this book that it will be possible to meet insatiable human wants and needs if we recognize the necessary adaptations and changes in our concepts of wealth. Wealth creation is not a zero-sum game. It is not a valid criticism of our wealth-creation capability to suggest that one person's plenty is the cause of another person's deprivation.

Final reflections

Max Weber quotes a passage from John Wesley that expresses a strange paradox. At the end of the eighteenth century Wesley wrote:

> I fear wherever riches have increased, the essence of religion has decreased in the same proportion. Therefore I do not see how it is possible, in the nature of things, for any revival of true religion to continue long. For religion must necessarily produce both industry and frugality and these cannot but produce riches. But as riches increase, so will pride, anger and love of the world in all its branches. How then is it possible that Methodism, that is, a true religion of the

heart, should continue in this state? For the Methodists in every place grow diligent and frugal; consequently they increase in goods. Hence they proportionately increase in pride, in anger, in the desire of the flesh, the desire of the eyes, and in the pride of life. So although the form of religion remains, the spirit is swiftly vanishing away. Is there no way to prevent this – this continual decay of pure religion? We ought not to prevent people from being diligent and fruitful: we must exhort all Christians to gain all they can and to save all they can; that is, in effect, to grow rich.[25]

It is important to recognize that Wesley went on to argue that Christians, having gained and saved, should then give all that they could. But his words do present in a very clear form an essential dilemma that faces the Christian with regard to wealth. Our endeavours to improve the human condition contain the seeds of alienation from God.

Weber quoted John Wesley to illustrate his thesis that it was the Protestant ethic that stimulated the modern phase of economic history and the emergence of capitalism. Certainly the Protestant ethic commends work and frugality. Hundreds of sermons preached by Victorian clergymen in the nineteenth century testify to that. Work does seem, on a wider scale, to be fundamental to the human condition.

In an interesting article in *Faith and Business Quarterly*, entitled 'Work – A Missing Sacrament',[26] the Revd Carol Williams looks at the Christian understanding of sacraments and argues that restriction to the traditional seven is an unnecessary constraint. A sacrament is 'something sacred', 'the outward and visible sign of an inward and spiritual grace' sanctifying certain important aspects of junctures in the life of a Christian person. Work, argues Williams, is omitted from the sacramental canon, despite being a huge part of human life and part of its natural process. The notion of adding value is of the essence of a sacrament, perhaps most notably in the Eucharist, which commemorates Christ's act of taking bread and wine and adding to their value as a manifestation of his continuing presence with his followers. In a similar manner the creative aspects of our work add value to both material and non-material goods – as we saw in Chapter 3. It is from this perspective that a Christian theology can develop.

Christ said little about the spiritual and social dangers of poverty. He identified the allurements of wealth and possessions as potentially major impediments to a proper relationship with God. Equally, however, Christ pointed to a responsibility that we have towards the poor. His followers have examined the consequences of poverty and have accepted an obligation both to care for the poor and to work to eliminate poverty. This is the 'option for the poor'.

On the first Maundy Thursday, Christ issued a new commandment to his followers – to love one another. He demonstrated in a very practical way how that could be achieved – by service. We have argued that wealth is created only by serving the needs and wants of our fellow human beings. At the same time as we serve them we exercise the option for the poor because we create the only means by which poverty can be alleviated – wealth. As in so much of the human condition, there is a paradox here. We deploy dubious motives such as greed as the means to overcome poverty. For the Christian, the paradox can be resolved when the motive of greed is replaced by that of service. It is the consistency of ends – the alleviation of poverty – and of means – service to our fellows – that forms both the basis for a theology of wealth creation and also its moral purpose.

It is not possible in this book to develop a complete theology of wealth creation. I lack the competence to do so and it is not my principal purpose. What I have sought to do in this chapter is to point to some areas that seem to me to be fruitful resources for a fully developed theology.

Reflection upon the life of Christ and his teaching has identified the imperative which we refer to as the 'option for the poor'. The plight of the abjectly poor is an affront to the conscience of every Christian. In underdeveloped countries and in developing countries poverty generally signifies the absence of basic necessities to sustain life – food, water, shelter and clothing. No Christian can find that acceptable. As communities rise above subsistence, different needs arise and the definition of poverty changes. In Western economies people without access to means of transport or such goods as fridges or washing machines are sometimes deemed to fall into the category of the poor. Poverty has become a relative condition. We shall examine later, however, whether poverty has always to be seen in material terms. That has been the conventional way of looking at poverty but the clear implication of Christ's warnings is that there is an equal danger of spiritual poverty too. We shall argue that wealth creators should address that form of poverty also.

The alleviation of the condition of the poor can be achieved only by the creation of wealth. Like many other human activities, it is clumsy and dangerous and manifests many inadequacies and imperfections. But if we are concerned to alleviate poverty, it is the only way, as one must will the means in order to attain the end.

Notes

1. Richard Higginson, *Called to Account: Adding Value in God's World – Integrating Christianity and Business Effectively*, Eagle, 1993.
2. Respectively, Matthew 13.45; Matthew 20.1–15; Matthew 25.14–30 (cf. Luke 19.11–27); Luke 15.8–10.
3. Respectively, Matthew 18.23–35; Luke 12.13–21; Luke 16.1–13; Luke 16.19–31; Luke 18.18–27.
4. Thomas E. Schmidt, *Hostility to Wealth in the Synoptic Gospels*, JSOT Press, 1987.
5. Ibid., p. 136.
6. For those who wish to pursue a deeper understanding, Professor Keith Ward's *Religion and Creation* (Clarendon Press, 1996) or his more light-hearted *God: A Guide for the Perplexed* (Oneworld Publications, 2002) offer careful and detailed examination of the complexities of a modern Christian understanding of creation.
7. Ian Barbour, 'God's Power: A Process View', in John Polkinghorne (ed.), *The Work of Love: Creation as Kenosis*, SPCK, 2001.
8. Ibid., p. 3.
9. Ibid., pp. 6–7.
10. Ibid., p. 7.
11. Ward, *God: A Guide for the Perplexed*, p. 118.
12. Revd Jack Mahoney, 'Christian Approaches to Wealth Creation', paper delivered to a consultation on 'Attitudes to Industry in Britain', St George's House, Windsor, September 1990.
13. Michael Novak, *The Spirit of Democratic Capitalism*, Madison Books, 1991 edn.
14. Ibid., p. 344.
15. Ibid., p. 349.
16. Ibid., p. 351.
17. Ibid., p. 357.
18. Francis Fukuyama, *The End of History and the Last Man*, Hamish Hamilton, 1992.
19. *The Economist*, 10 April 1999, p. 90.
20. David Landes, *The Wealth and Poverty of Nations*, Little, Brown, 1998.
21. Niall Ferguson, *The Cash Nexus*, Allen Lane, 2001.
22. Douglas A. Hicks, *Inequality and Christian Ethics*, Cambridge University Press, 2000.

23. Quoted ibid., p. 114.
24. Robert Nozick, *Anarchy, State and Utopia*, Basil Blackwell, 1974, p. 163.
25. Quoted in Max Weber, *The Protestant Ethic and the Spirit of Capitalism*, trans. Talcott Parsons, George Allen & Unwin, 1930, p. 175.
26. Carol Williams, 'Work – A Missing Sacrament?', *Faith in Business Quarterly*, 6:2 (Summer 2002).

♦ 5 ♦

A moral soup

The postmodern climate

Finding a starting point today for a Christian input to business ethics appears unpromising. We live in a world of unprecedented moral uncertainty, the world of postmodernity.

The term 'postmodern' is very general. Postmodernity is easier to characterize than to expound. Following the example of Paul Lakeland[1] I shall generally use the term 'postmodernity' rather than 'postmodernism' because the latter implies that we are talking about a movement or an identifiable school of thought. That would be misleading. (We shall not here be considering the term 'modernism' as applied in the field of the arts, but as it relates to the world of ideas.) By its nature postmodernity is fragmentary, offering a multiplicity of ideas and ideologies, reflecting an atomization in our culture rather than something coherent.

It is well outside our purpose to review the history of ideas and so we shall not explain in any detail how the postmodern world of doubt and uncertainty evolved in the Western world. The medieval world held an Aristotelian view of natural ends and accepted governance through generally acknowledged authorities and institutions. This view was challenged by the rationalism of the Enlightenment. Reason was used to question authority and institutions and also previously held notions of values and of authority that were independent of humankind. On one hand the Enlightenment led to the empirical method of science, of knowledge based on repeatable scientific experiment. In the world of ideas, confidence in reason expressed itself in the spirit of progress – the optimism of modernity. But the seeds of doubt were sown at the same time. In his *Treatise of Human Nature* (1739) David Hume, the leading philosopher of the Scottish Enlightenment, explicitly claimed that values are not inherent in things, but are bestowed upon them by human attitudes and feelings.

As the word 'postmodern' indicates, postmodernity describes the climate that succeeded the assurance of the age of modernity, with its confidence in the notion of progress through reason and science. Modernity was conscious how much our ideas and beliefs are influenced by the changing knowledge of the day, but it nevertheless believed that reasoned reflection could save humankind from being simply at the mercy of either ancient tradition or modern fashion, and could help us to discover underlying universal truths. Against this, the postmodern mind regards the power of reason with scepticism and is inclined to ask 'What reason?' and 'Whose rationality?' Reason, the postmodernist would argue, is itself just part of the particular way we are and the beliefs we hold, a manifestation of a particular culture which does not guide us to any kind of universal truth.

It is often stated that the erosion of confidence in humankind's capability to make progress towards any kind of moral improvement was greatly assisted by the catastrophes of the 1914–18 Great War, followed by the barbarities of the Holocaust and the atrocities within communist Russia and communist China. At much the same time, postmodernity was building upon the Enlightenment's emphasis of the individual to argue the subjectivity of values. In postmodernity there are no certainties; no firm metaphysical foundations; no plausible grand theories. Certain trends in science appeared to support this bleak view. The postmodernist points to the chaos and randomness which is inherent in the material dimension of our universe and argues that the whole edifice of creation and existence is no more than a gigantic accident. The perplexity of Don Quixote, who was confused as to what constituted reality, has re-emerged as an archetype of our time.

The notion that there are no certainties available to us, but only subjective judgements, was given particular prominence by the logical positivists. They were heirs to the tradition of scepticism that originated in the first questioning of the effectiveness of reason as a tool for establishing certainty. They asserted that any utterances that are not empirically verifiable are nonsense, that is, they are inherently incapable of having any meaning. In his brilliant monograph *Values: Collapse and Cure*,[2] Lord Hailsham quotes a passage from one of the leading logical positivists, Professor A. J. Ayer:

'If I say to someone 'You acted wrongly in stealing that money' I am not saying anything more than if I had said 'You stole that money'. In adding that this action is wrong I am not making a further statement about it. I am simply evincing my moral disapproval of it. It is as if I had said 'you stole that money' in a particular tone of horror, or written with the addition of some special exclamation marks ... It merely serves to show that the expression of it is attended by certain feelings in the speaker.[3]

This passage makes clear the logical positivist position. Pronouncements on matters regarding morality or aesthetics are no more than expressions of feeling. In effect, that terminates any meaningful discussion on such subjects: *de gustibus non est disputandum*. There are no objective criteria by which we can evaluate such expressions. We are not even able to agree upon the precise meanings of the words that we use in debate on moral or aesthetic matters: they have no validity outside the thought of the individual who uses them. There is no shared or common understanding because there is no objective basis for such understanding. This nihilistic position demands that for any statement to have status other than that of a mere opinion it must be observable, measurable according to objective criteria of calculation and verification by experiment. Reason, being itself highly subjective, offers no assistance.

At this juncture it may be helpful to draw attention to certain aspects of postmodernity which will appear in our later discussion. First, it must be pointed out that the postmodern notions of individual autonomy, and the attendant views that there is no real possibility of shared understanding, do not hold in all societies at the present time. Postmodernity is principally a phenomenon to be found in Western European and North American culture. It is not much to be found in other cultures, notably Islamic societies. And within Western culture, postmodernity is by no means unchallenged. Indeed Western political philosophy is still animated by the hopes and aspirations of the Enlightenment for some kind of universal civilization grounded in a rational morality. Egalitarian communism may have failed but the vision of a homogeneous common understanding persists. As John Gray points out in *Enlightenment's Wake*,[4] however, this is inconsistent not only with the particularities of militant religious groups or active ethnic identities but also with the whole postmodern mindset of individual autonomy and the elevation of individual rights and choices. There is a tension here. We accept the Judaeo-Christian emphasis upon the individual and upon personal responsibility for one's actions. Our societies protect individual rights and freedoms and the basis of our well-being is founded upon the liberty of each individual to pursue his or her own interest. We still largely accept Adam Smith's assertion that cumulatively this works to the common good and we expect a degree of shared purpose and endeavour in society. However, the tension between atomization and the common good is to be found not only between cultures but also within postmodern Western culture itself.

Second, as we have already noted, it is fundamental to postmodernity to challenge institutions and concepts of authority. The Enlightenment greatly reduced respect for such institutions as the Church and government. The authority that they represent has been further eroded by postmodernity. Intellectual respect for authority as a concept and for the role of institutions in upholding the concept has been severely challenged. Few examples of respected authority that is beyond challenge persist in Western culture. If the opinions of individuals are supreme, then notions of universal unchallenged authority lose much of their validity. Who has the right to tell me what I should do, what I should think, what is acceptable? I am my own authority.

A third notable aspect of postmodernity lies in its origins within the sphere of academic and intellectual debate. It did not begin as a practical way of life. Linguistic analysis` – which constituted the basis for the logical positivist assault on the objectivity of values – is not the everyday concern of ordinary folk. Dr Johnson, when presented with the proposition that the existence of physical matter was questionable, responded by kicking a stone and saying, 'Sir, I refute it thus.' Most of us, if faced with the proposition that the meaning of words is questionable, respond, rather in the manner of Dr Johnson, by our continued use of them. Our common sense, we might point out, tells us that the claim that propositions which cannot be verified are nonsense is an utterance which is itself incapable of verification.

In the everyday world, while philosophers like Ayer voided words of meaning people continued to employ value terms like 'beauty', 'cruelty' and 'justice' and to make traditional assumptions about their commonly accepted meaning and significance. Likewise, with regard to authority, it remained normal behaviour for pupils not to argue that their ignorance was as valid as their teachers' knowledge; aircraft pilots and ship captains are generally deemed to be vested with legitimate authority. In short, postmodernity originated as a canon of abstract notions that did not at first greatly affect everyday life for ordinary people.

An overview of the societies of modern Western Europe and North America suggests that postmodernity is no longer just an abstraction. These societies are characterized by strong assertions of the rights and freedoms of individuals, by fierce questioning of all institutions and authorities, by the atomization of beliefs and the widespread rejection of traditional forms of religious observance. Previously accepted moral standards are now doubted and people seriously question any obligation to adhere to norms that are not prescribed in law. Indeed the law itself is repeatedly called into question. Such commitment as is generally artic-ulated to principles of justice and morality is largely based on a distilla-tion of the conventional wisdom of liberal democratic regimes. There is little coherent conception of the common good – the result, according to Alasdair MacIntyre, of our fragmented moral vocabulary.[5] The new liberalism demands a neutrality of viewpoints, based upon an ideal of equality which demands equal respect for a great many divergent conceptions of what is good. In such a world morality is a private habit, rather than a common way of life.

It is difficult to offer conclusive evidence that the atomization of society, the climate of moral relativity and the rejection of traditional notions of authority have led directly to a collapse in social behaviour and concern for the common good. Most societies have complained that contemporary behaviour is more depraved than that of previous gener-ations. The widely voiced view that modern Western society is collaps-ing because of a failure to accept common values is not just a present-day phenomenon. Moreover, even if we accept as valid the evidence that is usually cited – increases in crime and lawlessness, sexual licence, violence, manifestations of disorderly and anti-social behaviour, refusal to obey legitimate authority such as the police or the teacher – it is difficult to attribute these disturbing factors solely or even principally to the influence of postmodernity and, in particular, to a loss of shared values and of a common language and understanding on matters of morality. There are many other factors that could account for a decline in social coherence – for example, our cultural respect for the individual and his or her rights to his or her opinions, or our concern for liberty and the freedom of individuals to pursue their private interests to the point where they may conflict with the same liberty of others. Human beings have a propensity to wilfulness and selfish behaviour, a propen-sity encouraged by the complexities of modern existence, which make it more difficult to impose common standards on any minority that cannot countenance obedience to the rules that society formulates.

Even if the evidence for a real breakdown in the consensus required for an ordered society is as yet inconclusive and even if the causes of such breakdown (if it has really taken place) are complex, the fact remains that the basis for assembling a moral basis for our liberal demo-cratic societies has been eroded. In *After Virtue*, MacIntyre points out that there is now no rational way of securing moral agreement in our culture on issues such as whether or not to fight wars, whether or not to allow abortion, how to limit or allow choice in education. He argues that emotivism (the view that moral judgements merely express the emotions or attitudes of the speaker) rests upon the claim that all attempts to provide a rational justification for an objective morality have failed, and points out that society has not reckoned with what would happen if this were widely believed to be true. Since the collapse of the Aristotelian view of morality, all other attempts to create a common moral vocabulary have failed, but most modern moral debate utilizes fragments from that Aristotelian tradition. We shall later address MacIntyre's argument for a renewal of the tradition of the virtues and 'the construction of local forms of community within which the moral life could be sustained so that both morality and civility might survive the coming ages of barbarism and darkness',[6] and his claim that the dark ages are already upon us: 'This time however the barbarians are not waiting beyond the frontiers, they have already been governing us for quite some time'.[7]

MacIntyre was an early voice warning us of the perils facing societies that have lost the basis for moral dialogue. Many others have followed, such as John Gray and Rabbi Jonathan Sacks.[8] In 1996 Archbishop George Carey initiated a debate in the House of Lords on the importance of society's spiritual and moral well-being, decrying moral relativism, the 'widespread tendency to view what is good and right as a matter of private taste and individual opinion only'.[9] The debate provoked a flurry of further concern across British society – a concern which is regularly and forcefully articulated, often with a call for a return to 'traditional values'. The US historian Gertrude Himmelfarb, an expert on Victorian values, calls for these values to be revisited.[10] John Elford has recently called for a Christian morality to be creative, innovative and non-judgemental.[11] These are hardly inspiring remedies but they do reinforce the dilemma that the uncertainties of postmodernity present to a society that has lost its moral bearings.

An example may illustrate this condition in which we now seem to be inescapably caught. Some years ago I happened to be listening to a news broadcast on the radio. On that day one of the notorious Kray twins, gangsters who had for years exercised a rule of terror in the East End of London, was being given a traditional East End funeral, with black horses drawing the hearse, top-hatted professional mourners and so on. The radio journalist was interviewing a woman who had known the

Krays from their childhood. She reminisced about them and lauded their good qualities, how they had helped to carry her shopping bags and how kind they had been to their mother and to friends. As the eulogy continued, the journalist felt constrained to interrupt and to question this portrait of the Krays as benevolent, well-intentioned souls. He pointed out that they broke the law, engaged in the drugs and prostitution trade, beat people up and – if they felt so inclined – killed them. The woman responded by stating that the Krays murdered only other criminals, not ordinary innocent law-abiding people. She clearly regarded this as acceptable killing. Murder, the ultimate taboo, the universally forbidden act had been relativized: it was no longer the status of murder itself that was at issue but rather the perceived worthiness or unworthiness of the murder victim. And if the victim was an unworthy person then the murder was morally acceptable.

The moral domain

It is perhaps useful and prudent at this juncture to clarify some terms and concepts. There are many different understandings of the words 'moral' and 'ethical'. In this book they will be regarded as synonymous – which in origin they were. 'Moral' derives from a Latin root; 'ethical' from a Greek one. The root words meant custom or behaviour. But we shall use these words to refer to that field of thought which is concerned with issues of good and bad, right and wrong.

Morality is concerned with discussion of what should govern behaviour and the application of general principles to particular circumstances or classes of cases. This poses the question as to what we are talking about when we use moral language. Are we back in the world of postmodernity, referring simply to emotional preferences, to matters of custom or of whim? A helpful definition of 'moral' is to regard it as a consideration of behaviour which befits or does not befit human beings as human beings. This implies an end, a vision of what is befitting, what should govern human behaviour. The sense of duty or of obligation that is expressed in words such as 'ought', 'must' and 'should' forms part of the general vocabulary of moral debate.

The concept of a vision or an end-purpose implied in consideration of what constitutes fitting behaviour gives rise to the term 'teleology' or 'teleological'. These terms derive from the Greek word *telos*, meaning 'end'. Thus teleology is the doctrine of final ends – the view that our behaviour should be governed by the end-purpose or design that it is intended to serve. This is an important concept. We shall not make extensive use of the terms 'teleology' or 'teleological', however, but will endeavour to confine them to our consideration of Christian insights into morality.

There is a good deal of human behaviour that may fall outside the moral realm. There may be no moral significance in choosing to drink a cup of tea instead of a cup of coffee. The term 'amoral' is used to refer to such neutral acts. But again one must guard against careless common usage, which often employs 'amoral' to imply the infringement of a moral code. We should note that what is *prima facie* an amoral act, with no apparent moral implications, may well form a part of behaviour that *does* fall within the moral sphere. Thus a simple matter, like a mathematical calculation, assumes a moral dimension if it is part of a wider set of actions that result in a bomb being dropped upon a city. The effect of behaviour upon other people raises a moral dimension.

Right and wrong, good and bad

Up to this point we have restricted our use of the expressions 'right and wrong' and 'good and bad'. These sets of terms are frequently used without much discrimination. But although they share certain characteristics – they have an action-guiding or prescriptive function, and are applied to acts because of something about the nature of the act which provides a reason for applying the word – there are differences. 'Good/bad' have comparatives ('better/worse'), but 'right/wrong' do not. Not all acts need to be described as 'good' or 'bad', but all acts may be regarded as 'right' (in the sense of 'all right') or wrong. Right does not carry any allusion to the character of the agent performing the act; good, however, is used to describe an act because it is the sort of act that a good person would do in the circumstances. Finally, an act would generally be called 'right' because we have first asked if it was 'wrong' and, if it is not, we call it 'right'. This is not true of the use of 'good'.

Partially arising from the distinctions that we have noted, a morality of 'right and wrong' is likely to be black and white in nature: it will prohibit certain kinds of behaviour, and behaviour that is not prohibited will be allowed. A morality of 'good and bad' on the other hand allows for gradations between success and failure in attaining the ideals that are embodied in its concepts of 'good'. I believe that it follows that it is difficult to establish a morality which combines elements of both 'good and bad' and also 'right and wrong'. Christianity has endeavoured to do so at various times. It enjoins 'Be ye therefore perfect' (Matthew 5.48) with the implication that failure to do so is wrong. It follows that if we are to seek the perfection implicit in 'right/wrong' morality but fail we are 'wrong'. In Christian terminology this means we are all sinners. I do not believe that this counsel of perfection is particularly helpful in the context of business ethics. For reasons to be explored later, we may have difficulties in identifying perfection (or what is unequivocally 'right') in the sphere of economics. President Lyndon Johnson is reported to have said, in response to a journalist who asked the question 'Are you sure that America is doing the right thing, Mr President?', 'Hey, boy, doing the right things is easy. It's knowing what the right thing is that's the difficult part.' That response has special relevance in the field of economics and business ethics.

We shall see as our discussion of business ethics develops that the terms 'value' and 'values' are widely employed. 'Value' in modern terminology is frequently used to indicate what was traditionally called 'good' or 'the good'. 'Value' also has a general usage. According to traditional Western thought, it is the task of the observer to develop the sensitivity to perceive the values presented to him or her. When we speak of moral value we refer to a special form of value with its own distinctive characteristics. Moral value or values are concerned with enduring perceptions of those overriding principles that guide people in what they do. We make value judgements in the light of the values we hold and by the application of the principles they imply. Even if we limit the notion of judgement to some kind of statement of preferences, some sort of principle is involved in forming that preference. We should consider some of the sources from which we might derive moral principles. In the particular field of business ethics, we will find that it is common to set out moral principles. From what source can such principles be derived? This is, of course, a fundamental question of huge importance that has exercised minds for centuries. I cannot therefore presume to offer more than some general reflections.

Sources of moral principles

First, we should address the postmodern response to this question, since we have recognized that we are conducting our examination in the climate of postmodernity. As previously noted, postmodernity would dismiss moral values as based upon nothing more than subjective personal opinion. And as we have already noted, this proposition is itself a metaphysical claim which, on its own terms, is no more capable of justification than moral statements.

There is a significant consideration that militates against the view that there is no foundation at all for moral statements. If we take two values such as kindness and cruelty, or courage and cowardice, we are able to recognize that they are enormously different. The perception of the difference is not constrained by the niceties of language or by any barrier of subjectivity. The difference can be perceived and understood, even if it cannot be totally defined. It is therefore a real difference. The fact that we are all able to distinguish kindness from cruelty (or courage from cowardice, or truthfulness from untruthfulness, etc.) gives some point to our debate. Even if we cannot agree upon a definitive interpretation of 'kindness' or 'cruelty', there is ground for fruitful examination of the difference.

We should take this consideration one step further. It is sometimes suggested that moral debate requires an acceptance of absolute, universal concepts. As we have seen, this notion is implied in the use of 'right' and 'wrong' as moral categories. That which is not wrong is right. An absolute value or good is one that is valid in any circumstances without qualification. Such absolute values would form the basis of standards of conduct. Many Christians are drawn to the notion of absolute values: 'Be ye therefore perfect, even as your Father in heaven is perfect'.[12]

There are a variety of arguments against moral absolutes. First, there is the objection that we have no means of deciding which principles are objectively absolute (the postmodern position). Second, and more important, the relative nature of moral principles can be argued from cultural analyses that point to the great variety of custom and belief in different cultures. The third argument against moral absolutes is, in part, a religious one: that it fosters a legalistic morality. The injunction to 'be perfect' is therefore not to be taken literally in the world of our present existence – but rather as an ideal standard by which this world is judged.

Thus we shall disregard in our consideration of the bases for moral values both the notion that such values are purely subjective and also that they are absolute. Our search will take us elsewhere. All the same, moral principles and their associated values cannot be conjured out of thin air.

In *The Origins of Virtue*[13] Matt Ridley explores the question of the origins of values in the light of Darwinian evolutionary theory. In the world of the selfish gene, which ruthlessly pursues its own survival in a never-ending and pitiless struggle, humankind is utterly selfish and individualistic. Thinkers such as Malthus, Machiavelli and St Augustine would to some extent share this view and look to culture to modify our behaviour. This, in turn, raises the question of why culture should develop cooperative sentiments, suggesting that there may be pro-social predispositions in evolution that explain them. Looking at such factors as the tit-for-tat model, which demonstrates that the pursuit of self-interest to the exclusion of any other consideration is eventually self-defeating, Ridley argues that our minds have been built to be social, trustworthy and cooperative and that the human mind contains numerous instincts for building social cooperation and seeking a reputation for niceness. In this model the cooperative person looks to long-term self-interest rather than being purely altruistic. Ridley suggests that moral emotions – or the 'moral sentiments' identified by Adam Smith – are mental devices for guaranteeing our commitment to others: 'The virtuous are virtuous for no other reason than that it enables them to join forces with others who are virtuous, to mutual benefit. And once cooperators segregate themselves off from the rest of society, a wholly new force of evolution can come into play: one that pits groups against each other, rather than individuals'.[14] Ridley's thesis is valuable and interesting, not least because it seriously qualifies those interpretations of evolution which offer no place for behaviour other than that which is entirely self-seeking.

As I understand Ridley's thesis, it is not the same as utilitarianism, which accords to moral principles an end outside ourselves by which they are justified. That end is generally considered by utilitarians to be the pursuit of human happiness, expressed by Jeremy Bentham as the greatest happiness for the greatest number. But neither Ridley's proposal of selfish imperatives for 'virtuous' or altruistic behaviour, nor the utilitarian position based on external justifications, addresses the question of authority for moral principles.

As we have already noted, contemporary Western thought is unsympathetic to the notion that behaviour should be governed by reference to any generally accepted authority. An extreme example of authoritarianism is represented by totalitarian regimes. The leader decides and lays down the rules: 'Might is right'. Somewhat less arbitrary is the rule of law. As citizens in a democracy we obey the law. If we dislike the law, we seek to deploy the mechanisms that may change it. Only in extreme cases is civil disobedience considered morally acceptable, where a conflict with individual conscience arises. Mostly democracies have identified the more common instances where this may arise (for example when requiring citizens to take up arms). It is frequently argued in Western democracies that the law should not be concerned with matters of morality. I have some difficulty with this proposition: the law *is* concerned with our behaviour and may, therefore, sometimes enter the realm of moral principle. The conflicts between religious or traditional modes of dress or food preparation and laws on safety and health are instances where law and morality may overlap. Totalitarianism is very likely to establish laws that infringe moral principles (for example, communist laws on freedom of expression or fascist laws on race). In general, democratic societies avoid that kind of conflict. For most citizens in democracies, obedience to the law raises few issues of moral principle. Accordingly, obedience to the law is not a moral issue: it is right to obey and wrong to disobey the law. The agent derives no moral credit for doing what law requires: he or she is not morally free to do otherwise.

More generally, what is the authority upon which moral principles and values are based? The authority of the law is secured through procedures set down in an established, agreed manner, a general societal consent from which the authority of the law is derived. There is no such agreed procedure whereby moral principles are established, which is why morality can often be presented today as an entirely personal, subjective matter. Universal consent, as we have seen, is not sufficiently watertight to constitute an unquestioned authority. Widespread assent is a valid and helpful yardstick by which moral principles may be established, but is highly questionable as a totally authoritative basis. It is on occasion fallible.

As we examine Christian perspectives on moral issues we are obliged to consider the question of divine authority. One sometimes hears people refer to God's authority as an unequivocal basis for moral principles. I should state my position on this matter clearly. While I subscribe to the view that it is generally possible to identify principles that are consistent with our broad understanding of God's purposes (as interpreted at particular junctures in history), I do not believe that we are able to invoke the authority of God as the unarguable and unambivalent justification of particular moral principles.

Bishop Richard Holloway, in *Godless Morality*, argues that 'the attempt by humans to discover a morality apart from God might paradoxically be God's greatest triumph'.[15] He contends that religion should be kept out of ethics and that 'What many people have clearly departed from is any sense that the moral life, lived intentionally and consciously, is consistent with blind obedience to any authority, including what is alleged to be divine authority'.[16] One key reason for rejection of absolute divine authority, argues Holloway, lies in the fact that many claims on behalf of God have themselves been subsequently rejected for moral reasons. Many religious moral systems have operated on the basis of fear. Today, argues Holloway, authority has to earn respect by the intrinsic value of what it says, not by force: 'we must do what we can to construct moral agreements that will have the authority of our reason and the discipline of our consent. It is not yet obvious to anyone today what the basis for a new moral understanding might be'.[17] Holloway compiles impressive evidence that we should be very cautious before accepting a moral principle on the grounds that it is God's will. History is full of examples of serious misunderstandings of God's will. As I have stated previously, God is sparing with his revelation in order to protect our freedom: likewise it is not possible with any certainty to articulate moral principles on the basis of revealed divine authority.

Where I have more difficulty in following Holloway is when he asserts that religion and ethics are separate fields and should not be brought together. Holloway defends this position principally on the grounds that it is not necessary to believe in God in order to have moral principles. This is true. What is more debatable is Holloway's inference that religion is therefore better excluded from any consideration of the bases for moral discussion. Just because religious systems have operated on the basis of fear, have been unnecessarily and unjustly rigid, and have failed to recognize the need for qualifications in the application of their moral principles, it does not follow that there is no part for them to play in moral discussion. In Chapter 6 we shall consider this further and explore the contribution that Christian thought can make to moral debate.

Conclusion

It may be helpful to summarize some of the main points that we have emphasized in this chapter. The erosion of traditional certainties regarding the bases and validity of value judgements, in particular those concerned with morality, gathered momentum throughout the twentieth century, resulting in a widespread view in Western societies that all such judgements are matters of personal opinion. That proposition is itself, however, incapable of definitive proof by any objective means. Likewise the attempt to void the terminology of moral discourse is invalidated by the commonsense recognition that there is a meaningful difference between such notions as kindness and cruelty.

There is, however, no commonly accepted foundation upon which our moral principles can be unequivocally based. The enlightened self-interest of the selfish gene or the utilitarian goal of the greatest happiness for the greatest number are inadequate as bases for comprehensive moral guidance. Universal principles, absolute moral standards and comprehensive authority are not available to us: all fail to satisfy in some respect. Nevertheless, the desire for guidance persists, even though much of the moral vocabulary that we employ has been weakened and relativized. We need such guidance to sustain viable community.

A traditional source of moral inspiration and dialogue was religion, but as Holloway points out, it has been shown to be a fallible source and one which, moreover, will no longer command total assent in our secular, individualistic Western culture.

Wherein, then, lies the Christian contribution to the development of an approach to business ethics? That is the subject of the next chapter.

Notes

1 Paul Lakeland, *Postmodernity*, Fortress Press, 1997.
2. Lord Hailsham, *Values: Collapse and Cure*, HarperCollins, 1994.
3. A.J. Ayer, *Language, Truth and Logic*, quoted ibid., p. 24.
4. John Gray, *Enlightenment's Wake: Politics and Culture at the Close of the Modern Age*, Routledge, 1995.
5. Alasdair MacIntyre, *After Virtue*, Duckworth, 1981, ch. 2.
6. Ibid., p. 263.
7. Ibid.
8. Gray, *Enlightenment's Wake*; Rabbi Jonathan Sacks, *Faith in the Future*, Darton, Longman & Todd, 1995, *The Politics of Hope*, Jonathan Cape, 1997, 'The Good Society: Social Challenges of the Twenty-First Century', St George's House Lecture, delivered at Windsor Castle 5 June 2000.
9. Archbishop George Carey, speech in the House of Lords, 5 July 1996, *Lords Hansard*, vol. 573, col. 1692; see also his article 'Morality is More than a Matter of Opinion', in the *Daily Telegraph* of the same day.
10. Gertrude Himmelfarb, *The De-moralization of Society: From Victorian Virtues to Modern Values*, Institute of Economic Affairs, 1995.

11. John Elford, *The Ethics of Uncertainty*, Oneworld Publications, 2000.

12. The Golden Rule – 'So whatever you wish that men would do to you, do so to them' (Matthew 7.12; Luke 6.31) – is sometimes seen as a universal absolute. This, however, is not the case because what we desire for ourselves may or may not be commendable. The same consideration applies to the negative formulation of the Golden Rule – 'Do not do to others what you do not want them to do to you.'

13. Matt Ridley, *The Origins of Virtue*, Penguin, 1996.

14. Ibid., p. 147.

15. Richard Holloway, *Godless Morality*, Canongate, 1999, p. 5.

16. Ibid., p. 8.

17. Ibid., p. 31.

♦ 6 ♦

Christian insights
and the ethics of business

Writers on economics and economic history frequently point out that the undoubted effectiveness of the capitalist free-market system that evolved in Western democracies accelerated as the economic sphere became increasingly secular. It is often further argued that the success of the economic process is due to its separation from the constraints of a religious framework. We have noted (in Chapters 1 and 2) that this separation was accentuated in no small measure by the inability of Christian thinkers to sustain a meaningful engagement with economic processes. This was, in turn, partly the consequence of reservations about the moral value of the very activity itself.

It is one of the fundamental themes of this book that the distancing of the Christian ethos from that of the field of economics and business is both unnecessary and damaging. The separation is damaging to Christian belief because it tends to remove from its perspective one of the most basic and potent human activities – the creation of wealth. It is damaging for the sphere of wealth creation because it cuts off the input of Christian moral understanding into the conduct of business affairs. Because the powerful phenomenon of the Western wealth-creation model emerged within cultures shaped by centuries of Christian belief and tradition, the severing of Christian input to the conduct of business affairs must be addressed. Business ethics raises the question of what contribution can be offered from Christian traditions.

Godless morality

Bishop Richard Holloway's call for a godless morality, discussed in Chapter 5,[1] seems, on the face of it, to close the door on anything like a Christian perspective on business ethics. He suggests that a morality without God is not only possible but preferable, and argues instead for a human-centred basis for moral approaches. It is not my habit to argue with bishops – generally a pointless exercise. But Bishop Holloway's proposition is, in some respects, fundamental to some of the matters considered in this book and it is therefore necessary to address it.

First, from the standpoint of a Christian believer it is unacceptable to argue that religious belief has no guidance to offer in the domain of morality. One's belief about the nature of creation, one's belief about the nature of God and his relationship to humankind, and one's endeavours to comprehend, albeit inadequately, God's purposes – all these factors will lead inescapably to the formulation of some kind of moral frame-work. At some point belief must be translated into behaviour, as St James so cogently puts it in his epistle: 'So faith by itself, if it has no works, is dead' (2.17).

There is, of course, no guarantee that humankind's inadequate reflec-tions upon how religious belief should be acted out in our daily life will provide foolproof answers. As Holloway points out, history has plenty of examples to demonstrate that religion can give rise to very dubious moral concepts and lead to behaviour that follows no morally accept-able principle. Morality based upon religious belief may be as prone to error as secular utilitarianism, or pragmatism. But, on Holloway's own terms, religious belief forms part of human endeavour to construct a moral framework for behaviour and is worthy of consideration on those grounds, if no other.

Holloway's principal objection to the intrusion of God into the moral debate seems to centre upon the misuse of the notion of divine author-ity. This notion manifests itself in assertions that we should or should not behave in certain prescribed ways because 'God wills it so'. Holloway quite reasonably points out that such assertions are generally a cover for the exercise of power and have, on occasions, been deployed to excuse behaviour which seems far removed from what any caring or loving God might demand – such as the massacre of people who dispute a particular arcane theological point, for example. To invoke God's authority as the unqualified justification for a particular moral prin-ciple is indeed dubious. If we use the established tools that we generally deploy to validate statements, we have nothing that assures us incon-trovertibly that we know God's will. For reasons mentioned previously, God does not bestow absolutely certain knowledge of his will. The assertion that any particular moral principle is God's will does not, therefore, constitute an acceptable argument for its adoption. To argue from such a proposition represents a distorted Christian perspective.

Where Bishop Holloway seems to be seriously misguided is in his apparent rejection of the fruits of two thousand years of reflection by Christian believers on morality. The heritage of Christian moral thought cannot be so lightly disregarded. Even for the non-believer, who does not accept the bases for Christian moral exegesis, the canon of Christian writing in this field constitutes an impressive and important element in the traditions we inherit. Christian moral teaching is important not because it represents God's will but because so much philosophical thought and discussion has gone into it.

An additional consideration that merits our attention is one so obvious that it is frequently overlooked. Although I have noted that present-day wealth-creation models evolved within a Western culture shaped by two millennia of Christian thought, we also have to recognize that Christian culture has itself been shaped by many different inputs. The evolution and spread of Christianity, initially in the Hellenic and Mediterranean world, then across most of Europe and finally embracing the whole globe, brought it into contact with other religions, other meta-physical systems, other cultures. Christianity was permeable to these influences and absorbed elements from all of them. Much Christian philosophical thinking, as we know, drew upon the philosophers of ancient Greece. In its early centuries Christianity showed itself highly adaptable to the cultures with which it came into contact. As Canon W. M. Jacob put it in a thoughtful editorial in *Theology*, 'In its infancy and youth, the Church demonstrated a dynamic capacity to move across cultural boundaries, to infiltrate thought, and for its own ends, to adopt and adapt institutions and practices to forward its mission.'[2] This is an interesting observation and we shall pick it up again later. What this porosity signifies for our present discussion is that Christian moral thought is not totally isolated from non-Christian influences. This has at least two implications. First, Christian moral understanding has been eclectic and has absorbed and developed other strands. The Christian contribution is, therefore, very rich and wide-ranging. We are not considering the results of an inward-looking, self-contained philosophy, but rather one that contains elements from many sources. Second, the eclectic nature of Christian moral thought means that it shares its perceptions and concepts with other schools of thought. Thus we should not argue that there is a uniquely Christian perspective on most issues in moral philosophy.

In short, Bishop Holloway's exhortation to exclude Christian input from moral debate would exclude the great wealth of understanding that it brings to the discussion. It would result in curtailing the rich cross-fertilization that has animated much of Western moral discussion in modern times.

It is important to address the issues raised by Richard Holloway, not only on account of who he is – a distinguished if controversial Christian thinker – but also because he represents a view widely held in our present society, namely that religion is a purely personal matter and accordingly has no role to play in such matters of common concern as the debate on the moral principles that should be followed in wider society. The remainder of this chapter will be devoted to elaborating upon the value of Christian input to moral debate, with specific concern for that field which we call business ethics.

Good and bad, right and wrong

In the previous chapter we briefly considered the terms 'right and wrong' and 'good and bad'. Right and wrong, we noted, bear certain connotations of absolute concepts: what is not wrong is right. If an act is right it cannot be wrong. This concept is importantly embodied in much of the law. If we obey the law we are right; if we disobey it we are wrong. 'Right' and 'wrong' are legalistic terms. The term 'legalistic' carries an uncomfortable implication for the modern mind, suggesting an oversimplified and unduly rigid approach. The modern mind, deeply affected by the onslaught of postmodernity and comparable modes of thought, resists the sharp categorization of our behaviour into simple categories of right or wrong and rests more easily with notions of good or bad. Even if we cannot quite define to complete satisfaction what we mean by, for example, the concepts of kindness or cruelty, we recognize that they are different and that there are gradations of behaviour between the two. There is little dissent if we classify kindness as better than cruelty. But we are uncomfortable with absolutes (partly because it is difficult to find any) and we sit more comfortably with relatives. So we would be less happy to say that kindness is absolutely good and cruelty absolutely bad.

This is not to deny that certain principles command such universal assent that they have the status of absolutes. The revulsion against torture and the universal taboo against wanton murder represent principles which may have the effective status of absolutes. My contention is that it is very difficult to define many absolutes in precise incontrovertible terms.

I suggested in the previous chapter that in the field of business ethics we would be more comfortable with using the terms 'good and bad' than 'right and wrong'. In large measure this derives from our general societal discomfort with absolutes. It also derives from the fact that much behaviour in business is governed by laws and regulations, to which the terms 'right and wrong' are more comfortably assigned. As we have already argued, moral debate is not concerned with obedience to the law, but with those matters where the law does not or cannot prescribe our behaviour. Business ethics is concerned with good and bad behaviour in the conduct of business affairs, in the grey areas that are not covered by law or regulation.

The field of human economic activity is inseparable from change. In seeking to create wealth by meeting human needs and human wants we are in pursuit of an unattainable good. Part of our thesis is a recognition that human wants are insatiable (a subject to which we shall return). Certainly our wants are fickle. Much of the changeability of human wants derives from the restlessness of human desire. It is not by accident that the term 'longing' was so important in the vocabulary of the Romantic poets. It was at that time that the major shift from economic man as producer to consumer began, so that human desire for variety became a paramount consideration. The resulting continuous change in economic activity imposed a discipline of constant re-examination of the moral approach to the process. Exhortations to thrift, for example, take on a different complexion when the availability of a commodity changes from scarcity to abundance. The ever-changing nature of business calls for continuous examination of business behaviour and recognition of the implications of change. It tends inevitably to discourage definitive statements of what constitutes right or wrong behaviour, although over time certain constant principles emerge, as we shall see.

We noted that one helpful definition of 'moral' is to consider it as that behaviour which befits human beings *as human beings*. This definition raises the wider question of how we determine what is fitting and this is particularly important in the field of business activity. Discussion of what is fitting implies an end, a vision that is the ultimate goal of the activity. There is endless debate about the purpose of business. The diversity of answers to the question reflects the wide-ranging impact that economic activity has upon human society. Many commentators impose a very limited purpose on business – that of 'making a profit'. We have argued in Chapter 3 that it is necessary to view the matter more widely, by looking at the definition of wealth creation as something that serves human needs and wants. Business is therefore subordinate to that end and the profit (or loss) secured is just an indication of the efficiency and effectiveness with which it is carried out. Profit is merely a means to a greater end.

The Christian perspective on the purpose of business is of prime importance as a guideline in setting a framework for business ethics. Christian moral thinking is based on a vision, an end for human beings. That vision is one of freely given, unconditional love (*caritas* or *agape*). It is a love given by God in the creation of the world and exemplified in the life of Christ, who offers himself as a human model and a human expression of that love. For Christians the objects of freely given human love are, according to Christ's own teaching, first God himself and secondly our fellow human beings. It is this which provides the vision, the end-purpose, the *telos* for all that we do as human beings. This is an enormously inspiring vision that has appealed to and sustained millions of human beings over twenty centuries. The teleology of business ethics for the Christian is formed by a vision of love and it is expressed in the concept of service through meeting the needs and wants of our fellows. Other ends, such as profit or the optimization of shareholder value, are, in Christian morality, subordinate. We also have here a fully comprehensive vision that provides an embracing framework within which other considerations can be placed and where priorities and relative values can be determined. It serves as an inspiration to the believer because of the call to the dual end of loving both God and our neighbour. It is equally a vision to serve the non-believer by establishing love for our neighbour as the determining vision for human activity. This is an end-goal that commands very wide – if not universal – acceptance, and, as such, provides a bedrock for moral discussion both for believers and non-believers. If we apply our rough and ready test for 'good' and 'bad', love and service to our fellow human beings will fall into the category of good, not bad. So we do not necessarily need the prop of a universal absolute as the bedrock for our moral debate; love for our fellow human beings provides a sufficiently widely accepted good to serve as the defining end-vision. It is the starting point for a Christian perspective for business ethics.

We sought to give meaning to discussion of good and bad behaviour by pointing to the general acceptance of the differences that are perceived between such polarities as kindness and cruelty or courage and cowardice. The perception of this difference allows particular judgements to be made but it does not offer any explanation of the basis for such evaluations. Christianity has, over the centuries, offered a number of grounds to assist us in making value judgements. Some of these are particular to Christianity, most of them are not.

What then are the tools that Christianity has offered to assist in the exercise of moral discernment?

The Bible, tradition, reason and experience as bases for moral discernment

The Bible is an undisputed source for Christian moral thinking. However, because the Bible was written and copied by human beings who are fallible it is unwise to regard it as inerrant. Some Christians do, but are obliged to quote selectively and to make questionable interpretations. There are many insurmountable obstacles to granting unquestioned authority to the Bible in matters of morality. While the Bible is frequently referred to as 'the Word of God', this cannot reasonably be taken to mean that every word of it is straight from God's mouth. We should therefore reject a 'Christian' morality based upon biblical inerrantism.

A more balanced approach to the Bible as a source for moral understanding is to accord it a special status as the fruit of millennia of prayer and reflection about God, coupled with accounts of special occurrences which have been interpreted as especially revelatory about humankind's relationship with God. The New Testament is a prolonged account of and reflection upon the significance of the special event of the life of Christ, pointing to the truth of the incarnation and the particular example of that life. This is some considerable distance from the notion of biblical texts as laying down unarguable and rigid precepts for strict application in all circumstances. Richard Hooker, the sixteenth-century Anglican theologian, pointed to the obscurity of passages in the Bible and to passages clearly intended for particular times and places, not for ever. Christians are required to judge in what measure a passage of scripture applies to particular circumstances.

The Bible does, of course, contain passages that are highly prescriptive, notably the Ten Commandments – the Decalogue. The last six of the Ten Commandments are intended to determine mankind's social obligations and are framed mainly in negative terms. As such they present a significant strand in biblical moral teaching and they command wide assent well beyond Jewish and Christian believers. There are other sets of 'commandments' in the Old Testament, the largest part of which are concerned with forms of worship and the attainment of ritual purity, aspects which fall outside the scope of our discussion. However, as we saw in Chapter 1, the Old Testament contains a number of injunctions regarding the conduct of business. These injunctions provide general input to Christian and Judaic moral understanding. The New Testament is both less prescriptive in social matters and less legalistic. Christ's teachings are usually couched in illustrative terms and directed principally at the spiritual well-being of the individual. Some of it, we have already argued – like the injunction to take no thought for tomorrow – is not to be taken too literally. Christ's teaching is not expressed in commandment form. Even when his recorded words sound like commandments they describe attitudes to God rather than legislation.[3]

The Bible represents an important input to Christian ethics, even if it is one that is not readily open to simplistic application. The Bible is conditioned by the thinking and circumstances that existed when it was written. It follows that some of it will be of little direct relevance to modern business practice. The Bible has nothing to say about nuclear energy or the implications of the use of computers. It can, however, offer a distillation of general wisdom about moral issues, formulated within the context of belief in God.

Christianity has drawn extensively upon other resources in the development of its ethics. The process of meditation upon moral issues within the Christian tradition did not come to an end when the last book of the Bible was written. Christianity today can draw upon the work of all those who have explored moral issues within the framework of Christian belief. The passage of time has, over two thousand years, sifted out what is of value in these reflections to be incorporated into the general canon of Christian moral understanding. This constitutes the second great basis for Christian ethics: *tradition*.

We have observed the consequences of adopting *reason* as an aid to Christian thinking in the Enlightenment and noted the role that reason also played in undermining traditional concepts of authority and belief. At the same time reason offered the launching pad for the empirical methodologies that brought about, *inter alia*, the industrial revolution. Reason has perhaps been a mixed blessing for Christian understanding and today we live in the ruins of pre-Enlightenment culture. The Enlightenment emphasized the use of reason as a tool to assist human progress – a notion now suspect, as reason itself has been questioned and relativized. Nevertheless, reason retains value. Although it is perhaps easier to know what is unreasonable than what is reasonable, we continue to use reason to enable us to derive valid conclusions from plausible premises. Reason requires us to respect scientific knowledge and Christian ethics today will take due account of that.

Another critical source of input to Christian ethics is closely allied to the need to accept scientific and technological knowledge. It looks to *experience* as a further input. Experience is not the same as tradition, which is essentially drawing upon the wisdom of the past. Experience calls for continuing examination of moral understandings in the light of new developments. For example, the discovery of the birth control pill and the development of genetic engineering have posed major ethical challenges in the modern world. It would be folly for Christian morality – or any other morality – to rule out human experience in such fields as a contribution to the evolution of moral understanding.

Some important features of Christian moral understanding

I believe that it follows from the nature of Christian moral discourse as we have characterized it and of moral debate in general that it is unlikely ever to be static. The evolution of our knowledge of the physical world, the creativity of human thinking, the changing nature of human societies, the waxing and waning of ideas and ideologies, and many other factors militate against stagnation. What J. S. Mill referred to as 'the deep slumber of a decided opinion' is not a feature of humankind's debate on morality. Even such deep-seated taboos as murder or the deliberate telling of untruth are, from time to time, brought before the tribunal of moral assessment for renewed discussion. Such revisiting is not always the consequence of moral relativism (although that may sometimes be the case) but is usually occasioned by new circumstances and new knowledge. The dimensions of moral debate do not appear to be finite. Has Christian moral understanding been able to find any *terra firma* upon which to stand in the moral quagmire that we inhabit?

Virtue ethics

So-called virtue ethics has shown great resilience as an element in Christian moral thinking. The concept of virtue is not Christian in its origin. It originated in Greek antiquity and was further elaborated by thinkers in the Roman Empire. To these concepts Christianity brought the ideals of virtue derived from scripture and, subsequently, from reason, tradition and experience. The notion of virtue was a vital feature of Christian moral understanding until interest waned with the advent of the modern period in the sixteenth century. Some thinkers then rejected virtue ethics in favour of natural law as the source for our comprehension of what constitutes 'the good' – that end which moral discourse pursues. Nevertheless, the ideals embodied in the concept of virtue have never been entirely displaced from Christian moral thought.

A virtue is described by Jean Porter in her essay on 'Virtue Ethics' as 'a trait of character or intellect which is in some way praiseworthy, admirable or desirable'.[4] We need not concern ourselves at this juncture with concepts of virtue which treat them as objective realities, the perception of which will inspire a person to attempt to create their images in human society through sustaining right relations with others. A virtue does not have to be an objective reality to fulfil that role. Today, as Porter asserts, virtues are normally understood to be morally praiseworthy traits of character. It would be an oxymoron to refer to a bad virtue: the contrary characteristics of a virtue are referred to as vices. Thus, while virtues do not have to be considered as universal absolutes, they do embody much of our understanding of 'the good' – that goal toward which moral discussion should direct our behaviour. St Augustine claimed that virtues are fundamentally expressions of Christian love, thus conforming to Christian teleological understanding. Virtue therefore constitutes a 'core' concept in the ideals to which we can aspire. The virtues cumulatively represent the traits that befit us as human beings.

Aristotle identified twelve moral virtues[5] and nine intellectual virtues.[6] Traditionally, Christian teaching has identified four cardinal virtues: prudence, justice, temperance and fortitude. To these have been added three theological virtues: faith, hope and love (charity). The cardinal virtues are important as ideals that sustain personal relationships. But the Christian concept of virtue is not limited to the cardinal and theological virtues. Other virtues have been identified and emphasized. Thus, when the aristocracy dominated society in Western Europe and military accomplishments were important, the traits that were emphasized as virtues included courage, honour and fortitude. At a later period, following the emergence of the bourgeoisie as a dominant force in society, the emphasis passed to such virtues as thriftiness, honesty and diligence.

Such shifts in emphasis do not necessarily mean that virtues are entirely subjective in nature. From a Christian perspective a greater degree of objectivity is accorded to virtue as an aspect of goodness. When Christians call God good, they are not expressing approval of

God. God *is* goodness. Thus, when creatures are good they are mirroring the absolute goodness that is God. This is a crucial basis of Christian moral understanding.

Virtues are thus an important part of the Christian perspective on business ethics. They can be of great help in answering the deep questions that may arise within the sphere of business and economic activity. It is part of our argument that careful and considered use of the concept of virtue can make a valuable and essentially Christian contribution to the subject of business ethics. As Jean Porter points out, 'virtue ethics is valuable because it provides a framework for reflection on the place of knowledge, will and passions in the moral life'.[7] There are virtues that are particularly valuable in this respect and provide a coherent basis for the development of business ethics.

Natural law
The concept of natural law is another element in the evolution of Christian moral thought. Theologians have invoked natural law as a reason for Christian moral teachings. Acts such as theft or murder are forbidden because they violate the good of rational creatures made in the image of God. Natural law is thus identified in some Christian schools with right reason and this has transmuted into a desire for a theory of morality, law and political organization that would allow for peaceful coexistence in the international order. But by the nineteenth century natural law theory was largely moribund; nature and reason were separated. Appeal to the 'naturalness' of things came to be regarded as unhelpful and arbitrary. Moral values could not be derived from facts about human nature, because we are not sure what human nature really is.

Nevertheless the concept of natural law persists in such contexts as the UN Declaration of Human Rights of 1948. It is frequently invoked as an alternative to total relativism and a basis for finding a shared understanding of the common good. It does, however, rest upon arguable presuppositions about what constitutes 'natural'. Also, the notion of a natural 'law' introduces the legalistic approach, which we have already questioned. The impact of natural law thinking in the field of business ethics serves to reinforce a notion that Christianity can offer some kind of ethical handbook, reference to which provides an unequivocally 'right' answer to ethical questions. As we have already made clear, we are disinclined to adopt this approach in business ethics. Indeed, I go further and argue that a rule-book approach in business ethics discourages the discussion that is essential in the formulation of moral principles to guide the conduct of business affairs.

The moral community

In *The Theory of Moral Sentiments* Adam Smith argued that much of our behaviour is conditioned by our need for the esteem of our fellow human beings. We seek their approval. We behave according to what we believe are their expectations. This is a somewhat cynical view of morality. But Smith's proposition contains more than a modicum of acute observation. When I was a small boy I desperately sought the approval of my parents and such virtuous behaviour as I was able to muster was in some measure conditioned by that concern. I worked hard at school and tried to obtain good marks because I knew that it would please them. I refrained (mostly) from gross behaviour because I knew that they would not like it. While affection and love for my parents was a root incentive to do what would please them, I was also in search of their approval because I needed it. As I grew older I formulated my own guidelines. It so happened that most (but not all!) of my behaviour continued to meet the standards expected by my parents and when it did not I was anxious to ensure that they were unaware of this. And to this day, long after my parents' death, I still measure my conduct in that way. I still seek their esteem, albeit posthumously. As a coda to this admission, let me note that as a very small child I had no idea *why* my parents expected me to behave in certain ways. In adolescence and middle age I sought reasons for the values to which they adhered and, to some degree, I am still learning the reasoning that lay behind their requirements. (To take a trivial example: it is only since eating in public places has become a commonplace that I have understood why my parents forbade it: it is not very pleasant for the observer!)

The present-day notion that the principles that should govern our behaviour are entirely a private matter does not bear close scrutiny. A totally private morality seems to presuppose minimal contact with other human beings. It is based on an assumption that a person's behaviour does not affect others, nor is it affected by them. Humankind being a gregarious species, this viewpoint can be sustained only within a limited range of our behaviour – that which is truly private and has no impact upon anyone else. Only a very small portion of what we do is of that nature. People who disregard this fact and ignore the consequences of their conduct on others are generally considered to be anti-social. In modern, large communities like the great cities of the world, the anonymity of the crowd may mitigate the consequences of engaging in anti-social behaviour. As long as we behave acceptably in the presence of people with whom we spend a lot of time – friends, colleagues, family – it is possible to act with indifference to the feelings of others – those with whom we do not expect to have contact again. Nevertheless, even people who adopt such a schizophrenic approach to social behaviour will feel constrained to accept the norms and mores of the people with whom they regularly have social congress. All but a few people are members of a group, a community.

The communities of which we form part are held together for different reasons. Most of us belong to different, overlapping communities: the family and friends; the community of people where we live; the community of our workplace; the community of the profession to which we belong or the sports club that we join. These different communities have varying requirements and behavioural patterns to which as individuals we respond. Within each community there is usually a tension between what we want as individuals and what we feel constrained to accept as participants in the wider community – a tension that we recognized as inherent in the activities associated with wealth creation (see Chapter 1). This is part of the heritage of Christian moral reflection that can be brought to bear upon this tension.

Within a small community with very clear and limited shared goals, for example a football team, it is relatively straightforward to identify some common modes of behaviour that will contribute to success or failure, well-being or discomfort. A football team will usually perform better if its members obey the rules of the game, subordinate individual prowess to the objective of winning, accept the disciplines of team strategies, maintain personal fitness and so on. If individuals fail to adhere to these disciplines, they will incur the disapproval of their team-mates. A common purpose assists in the sharing of disciplines.

Larger and more disparate communities with less clearly defined shared objectives – such as the inhabitants of a small town – may find it less easy to identify the behavioural patterns that will contribute to a happy, united and well-integrated community. When external threats occur, such as fires, floods or wars, people find it easier to subordinate individual preferences and everyone contributes to a clearly defined and more urgent imperative.

If we consider the formulation of shared values for huge communities – the whole human race, for example, or the inhabitants of an entire continent – it is even more challenging to achieve consistency of behaviour. Cultural and ethnic diversity replicates at the macro-level the diversities that individuals manifest at the micro-level. The differences begin to grate, the seams to wear, the joins to come apart. In extreme cases war is the consequence. It remains part of the optimistic vision that all humankind will one day share a common vision and common understanding, but that day has not yet arrived. The challenge posed by humankind's failure to achieve a common understanding and shared set of goals is clearly recognized and initiatives have emerged to address it. Perhaps the most notable endeavour was the adoption in 1948 of the United Nations Declaration of Human Rights. Efforts are now being made to complement that Declaration by a comparable statement of human obligations, formulated by the Interaction Council in 1997. Additionally the world's religions have come together in an endeavour to articulate the principles of a global ethic.[8] That a set of generally agreed principles can be developed would seem to be attainable. But is adherence to these principles within our grasp at present? The current state of play suggests that we may be some way from achieving a recognized global ethic that will command common assent and observance.

The magnitude of the task of securing and following a global ethic is daunting. In the face of that challenge it would be a great temptation to give up. Sir Winston Churchill, in his final words to the House of Commons in 1955, articulated the vision of perseverance in moving words:

> The day may dawn when fair play, love for one's fellow men, respect of justice and freedom, will enable tormented generations to march forth serene and triumphant from the hideous epoch in which we have to dwell. Meanwhile, never flinch, never weary, never despair.[9]

That is the exhortation to humankind's quest for a global morality.

Our present purpose, although more modest, remains considerable: the synergy of the Christian moral vision and the shaping of moral principles to guide humankind in its restless creative urge exhibited in our economic activities. The basis for that synergy lies in the recognition of two mutually interacting communities – the Christian moral community and the creative, serving business community.

Despite the warnings of Bishop Holloway that religion and morality are distinct fields and that the distinction should be sustained, I have argued that religious thought should not be separated from moral guidance. A religious construct is largely meaningless unless, through a theology such as that outlined in Chapter 4, it takes account of the essentials of our present existence, offering guidance for conduct. Faith without works is an empty thing. We bring our Christian heritage to bear upon our moral examination of wealth creation.

At this point a word of caution is in order. In what we are discussing it may sometimes not be possible to avoid using the adjective 'Christian' in relation to morality. However, I am unhappy with the notion that it is possible to spell out a specifically Christian morality. We know that Christians may sincerely reflect upon moral issues – such as the necessity of using force for example – and reach different conclusions. There is no unanimous Christian conclusion on matters of morality. There is a Christian basis for considering moral issues but not necessarily a specifically Christian answer to all the questions that arise.

As we have endeavoured to explain, Christian moral exploration has, over the centuries, formulated concepts of virtues, representing fundamental guides for our fitting conduct within the context of the Christian faith. Since these virtues are based upon love of both God *and* humankind, they command assent wider than the Christian community alone. The particular worth of Christian moral thought lies in the validity of concepts honed and tested over centuries and which have the assent of a particular community – the Christian community. The test of time and reflection bestows an authority that is difficult to deny: an authority of experience and use. The assent of a substantial community bestows the additional authority of practical application.

Although the ideal of a world community may, for the present, be unattainable, experience tells us that moral communities do exist. Adam Smith's observation that we seek the esteem of our fellows describes one such community: the community of those whose esteem and approval we desire. Other communities are more tightly defined: the community of a small village, the community of the medical profession, the community of a regiment of soldiers. For such definable communities it is generally possible to identify moral codes and standards that are accepted and observed by all members. Depending upon the nature of the community and its shared purposes, particular values will be emphasized. The community of doctors shares a set of values related to the preservation of life and the care of the sick; the values that motivate a regiment of soldiers will relate to loyalty, courage and discipline. The particular values that a community stresses respond to the character and *raison d'être* of the community.

It is through the concept of community that we can begin to identify some critical issues. One of the principal features of postmodernity is to argue that morality is subjective and personal. Moral values and moral judgements, it is argued, have no significance except to the individual. But communities, such as a group of doctors or soldiers, cannot function effectively on that basis. A sharing of values and the identification of shared rules of behaviour are prerequisites for effective achievement of group goals. Further, as the shared values are more carefully articulated and defined, the group develops a more acute awareness of the import- ance of those values, an awareness that is sustained by the opinions of the group members. The esteem that Adam Smith identified becomes a reinforcing element that encourages the translation of a general value into a concrete and practical force.

The process whereby the Christian community has reinforced the strength of values is the formation of conscience. Conscience is the inter- nal recognition of the moral quality of one's motives and actions. It is derived from immersion in the values that constitute the ethical frame- work by which the person operates. Reflection upon the basic virtues (the cardinal and theological virtues) enables us to identify further attributes that we deem also to be virtues, as well as those qualities that inhibit or prevent the pursuit of virtue, namely vices. The tradition of Christian teaching has been a constant reminder to Christians of the importance of virtues, particularly by reference to the example of those who have attained virtue in their lives. Conscience is not, of course, a peculiar possession of Christians: any seeker after moral guidance may be led to identify areas of special sensitivity. What Christianity offers is the cumulative wisdom and experience of thousands of seekers over twenty centuries. Aquinas described conscience as 'the mind of man making moral judgements' – in other words it is the judgement of prac- tical reason at work on matters of good or bad conduct.

Conscience formation is no guarantee that the outcome of delibera- tion will always be good. Conscience can err for a variety of reasons, because human beings are fallible. But it does reinforce personal respon- sibility for our actions. The identification of virtues as guides is not suffi- cient: we need to develop the ability to do what is good in particular circumstances. Perhaps Bishop Butler, the eighteenth-century thinker, expressed it most appropriately when he wrote, 'There is a principle of reflection in Man by which they distinguish between approval and disap- proval of their own actions . . . this principle in man . . . is conscience.'

I have tried to clarify why I believe that the Christian community has a special role and responsibility in matters of morality. In summary, the Christian faith is not pietistic. It cannot be separated from moral reflection and translation of that reflection into action. The identification of virtues as concepts around which moral principles may be shaped has been a vital component of Christian thought. Through centuries of reflection, Christianity has contributed to the formation of conscience, whereby our sensitivities in moral matters are sharpened and educated. In Western societies, the Christian community has special claims as the moral community, not in the sense that its behaviour is better, but in the sense that it is the custodian of a moral tradition and its application.

Why business ethics?

The world of business and economic activity constitutes another important and readily identifiable community in our society. It contains within it many other communities – companies, professions, trades, specializations and so on. As we have explained, the business community is fundamental to the well-being not only of our developed Western societies but also of developing and under-developed countries. The activity of creating wealth has, at its very heart, a moral purpose – the service to humankind of meeting its needs and wants. Business, like all other human activities, should be conducted in a morally acceptable manner.

The last statement requires further substantiation. Quite apart from those who deny any validity to moral understanding (a position which, I hope, need no longer concern us) there are many who argue that business is an activity to which no moral principles are applicable. What is most effective is best. Many businessmen appear to take this view. For instance, the head of a major British public business is reported to have said in 1991, 'If we were to apply the Sermon on the Mount to our business, we would be cooked within six months. Don't misunderstand me, ethics are not irrelevant, but some are incompatible with what we have to do, because capitalism is based on greed.' (The businessman quoted, I should add, is a confessing Christian.) I hope that earlier chapters in this book have satisfactorily demonstrated that business and wealth creation should be properly embraced within a Christian affirmation of human activity. To regard its conduct as beyond the reach of Christian moral reflection would be inconsistent with that conclusion.

The principal arguments for the development of a moral framework for the conduct of business relate to the fundamental role that it plays in our modern societies. Modern societies cannot function without business. Within the business field, ethical decisions are unavoidable. Legal and regulatory requirements abound but many daily decisions are taken in business which are not governed by legal and regulatory systems. This poses the question, 'Within what framework are such decisions to be taken?' The wider community will repeatedly ask that question until an answer is given. The need to provide an answer is part of the justification for business ethics.

Business ethics is a relevant subject in our society for other reasons too. The development of a moral framework is essential in order to enable the resolution of conflicts to be made in a consistent and publicly explicable manner. Human beings may not be totally rational but most of them are sufficiently rational to ask for consistency in behaviour, if for no other reason than it removes a degree of uncertainty with which they are uncomfortable.

Business activities, like most others, are conducted only with the consent and support of society. If an activity meets with the total disapproval of society, then the activity may well be forbidden. This represents a great incentive to business to behave in a manner that society will accept. The broad consent of society is not a moral principle in itself but consent is more likely to be obtained if articulated moral principles are followed. Despite the postmodern climate, most people have a disposition to recognize the good and the difference between good and bad. That judgement will be exercised with regard to business.

Notes

1. Richard Holloway, *Godless Morality*, Canongate, 1999.
2. W. M. Jacob, 'Editorial', *Theology*, vol. 102, no. 807 (May/June 1999), pp. 159–60.
3. See Richard Jones, *Groundwork of Christian Ethics*, Epworth Press, 1984, p. 35.
4. Jean Porter, 'Virtue Ethics', in Robin Gill (ed.), *Christian Ethics*, Cambridge University Press, 2001, p. 96.
5. Courage; temperance; liberality; magnificence; magnanimity; proper ambition; patience; truthfulness; wittiness; friendliness; modesty; righteous indignation.
6. Technical skill; scientific knowledge; prudence; intelligence; wisdom; resourcefulness; understanding; judgement; cleverness.
7. Porter, 'Virtue Ethics', pp. 107–8.

8. See Hans Küng and Helmut Schmidt (eds), *A Global Ethic and Global Responsibilities: Two Declarations*, SCM Press, 1998.
9. Quoted in Roy Jenkins, *Churchill: A Biography*, Penguin, 2001, p. 893.

♦ 7 ♦

Business ethics

It is sometimes cynically suggested that the phrase 'business ethics' is an oxymoron: a contradiction in terms. In other words, it is implied, the world of business is incapable of conducting itself in a morally acceptable manner and its very purpose is morally unattractive.

A leader in the *Financial Times* of 30 November 2002 stated the dilemma very pointedly. It claimed that Aristotle was right to say that there are some jobs where virtue is impossible; none the less,

> even if there are corporate Mother Teresas waiting out there, capitalism does not flourish on virtue. Successful businesses are created by risk takers who survive by exploiting opportunities against cut-throat competition – usually motivated by hope of big rewards.
>
> Their behaviour may be morally questionable on occasions and, if allowed to run to extremes, would undermine the operation of capitalism. But it is the state's job to curb excesses through law and regulation (where a repentant poacher is often the most effective gamekeeper). Better the hard work of creating the right business environment than the endless search for the Holy Grail of a saintly tycoon.

This leader is deliberately depicting a contrast of two extremes of behaviour – sanctity or villainy – and suggesting that because business people do not follow one extreme, they must perforce follow the other! It is a dilemma that is perniciously simple. Few achieve sanctity and even fewer are perfect in the attainment of virtue. That is true in all walks of life, not just business. But just because we are not capable of perfect virtue we should not abandon the attempt to pursue it. And that is true of medicine, teaching or business. Business is not uniquely incapable of true virtue.

In Chapter 4 we argued for integration of wealth creation into Christian theology. In Chapter 6 we sought to establish that Christianity offers bases for moral guidance in business, the vehicle through which most wealth is created. The Christian community represents a world-wide moral community, custodians of two millennia of reflection upon moral principles derived from the concept of a loving God who looks for freely given love in the world that he creates. Business and the wealth-creation activity that it performs are part of the ongoing creation, to which human endeavour makes its own special contribution.

The perception that wealth creation constitutes a totally secular activity has severely impaired any continuity of Christian input to the process, including moral contributions. We shall try now to put forward some bases upon which that discontinuity might be repaired.

The term 'business ethics' has been seriously overused in recent times, usually escaping the degree of intellectual and, indeed, moral rigour that should be applied. It remains, however, a conveniently broad term which is helpful in locating the theme that this book pursues. Broadly speaking the term 'business ethics' will be taken to embrace the ethical considerations that arise in examination of the goods and services that business provides; the way in which business people and organizations conduct the activities in which they are engaged and, thirdly, the responsibilities that business has towards society generally – as the consequence of what it does, or as integral to the activity itself. It is occasionally opined that 'the business of business is business', a view that would severely limit our brief. The impact of business upon society seems so self-evident that this aphorism's restriction cannot be taken seriously. Business is everybody's business in the modern world.

It is possible to take a minimalist view of business ethics: a philosophy of doing what one can get away with, entailing little if any consideration of what moral issues might arise. For such an approach the term 'business ethics' is hardly relevant: it is scarcely indistinguishable from amorality. Even in a postmodern, fragmented world such as we considered in Chapter 5, in practice few people completely disregard the wider implications of what they do. It is unlikely that any business activity conducted on such a basis would long escape critical attention. By definition business affects people, precisely because it is designed to offer them goods and services. The minimalist moral approach is not sustainable either in theory or practice.

The rules-based approach

One approach to business ethics is based upon rules. Rules are, of course, usually enacted through legislation and regulation. That is the role of government, as the *Financial Times* editorial points out. A rules-based approach to business ethics seeks, as far as possible, to limit debate to consideration of what legal frameworks should be instituted. Where no laws have been laid down, it attempts to remedy the deficiency and set out all-embracing rules to be followed. Under such an approach, discretionary decisions are avoided as far as possible. Doing the right thing or the good thing comes down to doing what one is told. Not only is a totally rules-based approach dangerous – because in extreme cases it absolves agents from any responsibility since they are just obeying orders (as, say, in the case of Adolf Eichmann) – but it is also incomplete. If a rules-based philosophy were adequate there would be a very limited need for lawyers, whose only task would be to formulate the rules and laws. Interpretation and adherence would follow automatically. As we know, this is not the case and, however desirable it might sometimes appear to be able to dispense with lawyers, the interpretation and application of laws and regulation is rarely beyond debate. So a rules-based approach to ethics is insufficient. Not only are rules themselves inadequate – hence the injunction to obey not just the letter of the law but also its spirit – but there is no means of anticipating all possible eventualities and addressing them by laws. There is always a very wide spectrum of behaviour in business, as in everything that human beings do, where decisions have to be taken with minimal help from prescribed rules, or indeed where no rules apply.

Let me cite an example from around the midpoint of my business career, which illustrates how a rules-based ethic can be deficient. I was responsible for negotiating a multi-million-pound contract with a major customer in the airline business. The contract involved the supply of aviation fuel to dozens of airports across the world. At that time the market was very unsettled, with threats to supply from disturbances in the Middle East, fluctuations in exchange rates and huge movements in the price of the raw material, crude oil. The main uncertainties were covered by special clauses, for example a provision linking the delivered price to unusual currency movements. Nevertheless, both parties sought a means whereby exceptional, unforeseen circumstances might give grounds for renegotiation of an aspect of the deal. It was customary to include in the contract, therefore, a *force majeure* clause to cover the unforeseeable – the traditional 'act of God'.

Unfortunately, my legal advisers insisted on including in the clause specific examples of eventualities that might represent *force majeure*. My latent fears deepened when the customer's legal representative readily agreed to the clause in that form, offering only the wry comment that it was now so wordy that we might consider setting it to plainchant!

In due course, a supply disruption occurred that provoked an increase in prices. We sought to increase the price of jet fuel to our customer. The relevant clause relating to supply interruption did not cover precisely the situation that had arisen. We were therefore obliged to invoke the *force majeure* clause. The customer disagreed, arguing that the specific examples it now contained invalidated the broader concept of *force majeure* because we had, in effect, tried to define what *force majeure* was. There was a lengthy argument, which our lawyers lost. By overzealous application of the rule-based principle we had effectively compromised the spirit of the agreement. The rules were counter-productive. We were, in the end, obliged to develop a solution that was consistent with the spirit of our agreement. I was profoundly grateful that my customer was prepared to agree to this rather than adhere to a strict interpretation of the letter. The customer observed the spirit, rather than the letter, of the contract in being prepared to negotiate a price adjustment.

It is, I hope, clear from preceding chapters that another approach to business ethics is more appropriate. This approach is based upon values and upon their interpretation in particular circumstances. Such a *modus operandi* cannot be wholly prescriptive but depends upon understanding and interpretation of underlying values. This approach is, however, comprehensive because – as I shall endeavour to show – if the value base is developed with sufficient care, it makes available guidelines that may be applied in all situations. This is not the same as claiming that a set of values guarantees a 'right' answer, as a rules-based approach seeks to do. But what it does provide is a framework within which structured examination and debate may take place.

Business ethics

It may be helpful at this juncture to consider further why business ethics is necessary and what its particular features are. Up to this point the thrust of this book has been to refer to the history and development of the wealth-creation process. The use of the term 'business', as in 'business ethics', does not reflect any change of direction. Wealth creation is conducted in many ways. The evolution of the modern term 'business' began only the eighteenth century, in its related senses of trade and commerce generally, or a company or corporation engaged in those activities. 'Business' is, therefore, simply the generic term for the processes and organizations that enable wealth to be created. While trade and commerce have existed in virtually every society of which we have any record, the phenomenon of the company or corporation as a legal entity is essentially a post-industrial revolution development. The 'ethics of business' is concerned with the moral purpose of the activity; 'business ethics' embraces the goods or services provided, the manner of providing them and the consequences of doing so.

If this sense of the term 'business' is comparatively recent, the identification of 'business ethics' as a field of study emerged much later. Interest in the ethical dimensions of business developed seriously in the 1970s, principally in the United States. There were several reasons for this. At that time a number of high-profile corporate scandals occurred, involving bribery and improper interference in the politics of some countries. A notable example was when the Lockheed aircraft corporation was accused of bribery and corruption. These cases put the propriety of business conduct on the agenda of public concerns. Furthermore, exceptional economic growth and prosperity in North America and Western Europe greatly increased the impact of business upon contemporary society. Household brand names, ubiquitous advertising, the proliferation of consumer goods, the evolution of a consumer culture, the emergence of giant, wealthy and powerful companies – all these and other factors thrust business into people's lives in a way not previously experienced. Business could no longer be disregarded as a potent dynamic force that shapes society. With its growing importance came, inevitably, greater concern about business conduct and the moral standards that govern it.

Yet another dimension that undoubtedly stimulated interest in business ethics was the crystallization of several vital issues, some of which transcend national boundaries and which are wholly or largely associated with business. The impact of humankind upon the natural environment and a rapidly sharpened awareness of the fragility of life on planet Earth emerged as one of Western societies' primary concerns. Since the 1960s environmental conservation has figured prominently in most opinion surveys of public concerns (although it has rarely been perceived as one of the foremost two or three for political action). Initially, in the 1960s and 1970s, concern for the physical environment was directed overwhelmingly at business and its operations. Recognition of the corresponding responsibilities of individuals emerged somewhat later. Other aspects of business that emerged as important public issues included concerns about health and safety associated both with products and with the processes used to make them; the misconduct of individuals within the world of corporate business; the treatment of employees, particularly as the transition from industry and manufacturing to services and high technology gathered pace in the 1980s and 1990s with resulting large-scale redundancies and unemployment; the accountability of multinational or transnational companies and the impact of their business upon both developed and less developed communities. All these issues – and many others – raised awareness, posed questions of accountability and moral responsibility, and roused a societal demand that business behaviour be more closely scrutinized.

Understandably the initial response to this kind of challenge was to introduce greater regulation and legislation. In some areas it was possible to effect significant constraints upon abusive behaviour, particularly when a problem fell entirely within the competence of a single legislative body, usually a national government. Even in these instances, however, the inherent limitations of the rule-based approach applied: the laws could not anticipate every eventuality and the introduction of new controls itself prompted different behaviour patterns. Moreover, the phenomenon of the multinational company, operating across many geographical and national boundaries, posed a problem that required transnational agencies to formulate and enforce regulation. In many fields such instruments already existed or were developed. United Nations agencies, the International Labour Organization (ILO), the Organization for Economic Cooperation and Development (OECD), the World Bank and other organizations sought to address issues of major concern, with varying degrees of effectiveness. Perhaps the most dramatic example of trans-frontier cooperation has been the evolution of the powers of the European Union and its programme to harmonize and make effective a wide range of measures in such fields as social affairs, employment conditions and environmental conservation. The fact remains that the success of all such initiatives has been limited, both by the in-built inadequacy of legislation and regulation to anticipate and address all issues and also by the difficulties of enforcement across national boundaries. The essence of moral dilemmas remains: there are large areas of business activity where laws and regulation are of little assistance. These are the areas where free and discretionary decisions are demanded for which the law offers no solutions.

Self-regulation and the values-based approach to business ethics

And so it was against a background of rising societal concerns about the behaviour of the world of business and the inadequacy of governmental or transnational agency rules that the desirability of self-regulation emerged. Advocates of the minimalist or rules-based approach were naturally unsympathetic. Those who were deeply suspicious of the whole wealth-creation activity (which – as we have seen – included many Christians) or who rejected the fundamental principles of freedom of choice exercised through the operations of the free market were sceptical. Just as turkeys famously do not vote for Christmas so, they argued, people engaged in business do not willingly or readily constrain their behaviour. The market is portrayed as amoral and even worse: conducted inescapably along lines that defy any sort of moral system. For such people only two solutions appear feasible: proscribe wealth creation entirely and/or legislate it out of existence. In practice – as opposed to theory – no one could or would behave in this way.

It has to be said that many practitioners and supporters of wealth creation and of business are very unhelpful in public pronouncements about business ethics. We have already quoted the *Financial Times* and even an eminent and successful British businessman who is also a Christian, contending that effective operation is not possible if ethical principles are applied rigorously. In an address at the inauguration of Oxford University's Said Business School, which he developed as an essay titled 'Good Business',[1] Professor John Kay quotes some revealing remarks by business authorities. For example, in its submission to the Hampel Committee on corporate governance the CBI, no less, stated, 'While business has relations with customers and employees, its responsibilities are to its shareholders.' The clear implication here is that business is *not* responsible to customers or employees. Sir Stanley Kalms, chairman of Dixons, the electrical goods retailer, said, 'The provision of goods and services of good quality to the company's customers at fair prices. What a glorious utopian (socialist) concept. There is only one price, monopolies excepted – the good old market price. Fair is a word I have never heard voiced in a pricing meeting.' One of the most celebrated amoral statements about business was made by the distinguished economist Milton Friedman of the University of Chicago: 'The social responsibility of business is to maximize its profits.' As Kay points out, it is inconceivable that practitioners in other walks of life such as politics or sport or the family would ridicule the notion of fairness, or that a teacher would accept responsibility to wife and family but argue that he had only 'relations' with his students. It is a strange and unfortunate aberration that a few senior business people feel able to speak in this insensitive and unpleasant way. And of course, it reinforces the impression that 'business ethics' is a self-contradictory term.

There are many grounds upon which it is possible to refute the notion of business as an activity to which no moral considerations apply. In Chapter 5 we considered the phenomenon of postmodernity and advanced some reasons why a value-free society is not only undesirable but is itself a nonsense proposition. No matter how inadequately articulated they may be, common understandings persist that guide and govern human behaviour. The community is one vehicle that promotes the sharing of such understandings and their coherent development. In Western societies, of course, the Christian community has over the centuries been a creative and dominant voice that has shaped the moral framework.

It cannot be credibly argued that business activity is a value-free zone, where it is not even necessary or desirable to address ethical considerations. Some argue that the profit motive is sufficient as a guide to conduct. But profit-making provides only minimal guidance to business people. Decisions at all levels have to take account of a huge array of factors and most decisions do not address the matter of profit directly or, in many cases, at all. Likewise, another simplistic nostrum, that business is solely about creating 'shareholder value', in practice offers little guidance for most business decisions. If we return to the definition of wealth creation as serving human needs and wants it becomes clear that business, the vehicle by which that goal is served, cannot restrict its end-purpose to simple mantras like 'profit' or 'shareholder value'. These are measures of the efficiency and effectiveness with which business discharges its much more complex role of assisting in the creation of wealth.

In her logically argued exposition of a philosophy of business ethics, Elaine Sternberg seeks to establish the end-purpose of business as the maximization of shareholder value over the long term by selling goods and services.[2] She accepts that to define the end-purpose of business as financial gain for owners is controversial, but rejects the trend towards a proliferation of additional objectives through serving the interests of a wide range of 'stakeholders'. Sternberg's case rests on the claim that the goals of business must be tightly focused, otherwise they become so broad as to be unattainable. Adoption of a limited but specific objective such as the maximisation of shareholder value has the helpful quality of clarity and avoids confusing the desirable with the essential. Thus, for Sternberg, any definition of business that incorporates social goals into the purpose of business would risk making business meaningless.[3]

Sternberg argues, correctly in my view, that what differentiates business from everything else is its purpose. She seeks to establish that all objectives other than the one she prescribes are inappropriate for business as such. Accordingly she rejects purposes such as promoting public good or fostering the physical or psychological well-being of employees. These, she contends, arise out of business but do not constitute its defining aim.

Most significantly Sternberg argues that it is not the defining purpose of business to produce goods or services or to add value because, although they are indispensable elements of doing business, they are not exclusive to business and therefore cannot serve as business's defining goal: 'The army, the courts and housewives supply services . . . but they are not businesses. Similarly, though planting a garden, painting a picture, and telling a joke all add value, they do not normally constitute businesses'.[4] In other words, if the nature of the goods or services or the way they are produced take any priority over maximizing shareholder value, then the activity involved is not business. Sternberg then proceeds to examine how businesses differ from other organizations such as families or clubs, seeking to demonstrate that her definition of its purpose is the only truly distinctive one.

It is necessary to consider Sternberg's thesis not only because her admirable clarity of focus serves most cogently to concentrate our minds. To some extent I agree with her thesis, especially the necessity for rigour and logic. However, I have to part company in certain important respects. First, it has to be recognized that business activity makes sense only in a prescribed context – that of creating wealth. The role of business is the performance of those activities whereby humankind's wants and needs are met and satisfied. Unless those needs and wants are met, there is no business, no shareholders, no added value, no long term. Accordingly this dimension has to assume priority as the end-purpose of business. Second, the end-purpose of satisfying needs and wants is truly universal to all humankind. To do this only by maximizing shareholder value constrains it within the operations of a free-market, capitalist system like that which has evolved in North America and Western Europe. Sternberg would no doubt argue that the term 'business' makes sense only in that context. But in considering the wider, but nevertheless tightly delineated, scope of wealth creation, we are able to adjust our sights beyond the limitations of one particular culture. Third, all human activity needs assent and support. The specific objective of maximization of long-term shareholder value cannot command that assent and accordingly has to be modified as a defining purpose. Maximizing shareholder value commands little assent as a fitting end-vision for human moral endeavour.

Finally, even on its own terms, Sternberg's rigorous limitation of the objective of business proves insufficient as the end-purpose by which a moral framework can be established. As she develops her thesis and seeks universal principles that underlie business ethics, Sternberg establishes two further cornerstones: distributive justice and ordinary decency.[5] This is not the place to elaborate on the case that Sternberg makes for these two principles. Suffice it to say that it is difficult to ascertain how these flow from the end-purpose of business as she defines it. As we shall endeavour to show, the wider purpose of wealth creation in meeting needs and wants can embrace these broader concepts and principles which she has felt necessary to add to the maximization of shareholder value.

Sternberg's thesis is important because it is remorselessly well argued and because it represents a widely held position. In putting forward a different proposition I hope that it is possible to be as rigorous and as clear as Sternberg in developing a teleological basis for business ethics.

Why is business ethics needed?

The conduct of business is pervaded by ethical decisions. They are unavoidable. When high-profile events dominate media headlines – financial scandals, bribery, environmental or safety disasters – they are seen as failures in a moral context. We have not yet considered in detail the moral framework for business, but it clearly is unlikely to embrace swindling, pollution or killing as acceptable practices. Important transgressions such as these are by no means what most business ethics is about. Ethical issues arise regarding countless routine and lawful activities – some of which may, if not handled properly, end up as a headline disaster such as a major accident.

Business is no different from any other human activity in this respect. A host of issues relating to justice, fairness, honesty, and respect for others are part of the currency of everyday life. Human beings are constantly exercising their free will in making choices. In most of these choices there will be ethical considerations. Ethics, it will be recalled, relates to behaviour that is fitting to human beings. Every time we make a choice we are consciously or unconsciously involved in some evaluation against that criterion. Business, of course, has a special sphere of decision-making that relates to its own end-purpose. Particular industries or even companies, it may be noted, are obliged to address very particular moral issues relating, for example, to safety, or the employment of people, or to health concerns. Business ethics, like ordinary life, is not generally concerned with high-profile crises but with the everyday routines to be followed in providing goods and services. Indeed, most major headline crises – such as a calculated fraud – usually arise from law-breaking rather than from a less unambiguous moral failing.

We all know about daily moral dilemmas: how do I correct my child when he has been disobedient?; how do I explain away without deceit awkward and embarrassing things I may have done?; how do I decline the invitation I do not want to accept without giving offence? These small instances of decision-taking are seldom clear-cut. The decisions involved are rarely about right versus wrong, but invariably about better or worse – varying shades of grey. And so it is in business. Many decisions are far from clear-cut and genuine disagreement about what to do is the norm rather than the exception. The roots and resolution of many everyday business decisions contain ethical elements.

Despite the siren-calls of the postmodern climate, decisions that involve ethical choice cannot be taken in a value-free vacuum. At the personal level a simple decision, such as how to decline an invitation I am free to accept but do not wish to, can raise minor ethical dilemmas. Should I dissemble and say, untruthfully, that I am otherwise engaged? Should I risk giving offence by saying that I do not want to accept because I am not interested? Should I be rude and ignore the invitation? The answer to each of these questions will invoke some kind of value judgement regarding my willingness to be untruthful or to avoid lying, to upset the other person or take care to avoid doing so, to observe conventional courtesies or disregard them. All these elements reflect reference to values that have, over time, evolved to guide our conduct. Only in the rarest of cases would a person be able to say that no consideration of the values of honesty, concern for the feelings of others, or courtesy was involved in even such a simple matter as declining an unwelcome invitation. The pre-existence and recognition of these values *before* I am faced with a choice of behaviour means that I do not take even minor decisions in a value-free context. And, as with personal dilemmas, so with business decisions. Whether we do so consciously or unconsciously, willingly or unwillingly, we resolve moral dilemmas by reference to guidelines of some kind. This poses yet again the all-important question: on what basis are these values grounded?

Humankind has devoted prodigious effort to the search for the answer to this question. In the twentieth century, postmodernity seemed to deny the validity of the question but the logical positivist position is a self-contradictory one. Every civilization seems to have addressed the question, thus providing never-ending work for moral philosophers. But for the people engaged in business, unending debate is not a practical option. Business is especially about action and making things happen: it is impatient with delay. Hence it is obliged to embrace and work to a value system that is practical and substantive. But because of the ever-changing nature of wealth creation and of the business activity that carries it out, the underlying value system must be soundly based, comprehensive and coherent in its own terms.

So let us consider a couple of modern ways of identifying a value base that might serve to underpin business conduct. The Institute of Global Ethics argues that an ethical foundation for all conduct is essential and that ethical decisions should be reached by a process of testing issues against a series of moral propositions that might include the following:

- an ends-based ethic, which looks at the consequences of different courses of action;
- a rule-based ethic, which would endeavour to find a framework to which everyone in the world would subscribe in the particular circumstances under consideration (e.g. the Categorical Imperative);
- a theological ethic with reference to spiritual values derived from religion;
- an ethic based upon the Golden Rule, the principle of behaving to others as one would wish them to behave towards oneself;
- an ethic of dignity based on treating other people as ends rather than as mere means.[6]

These moral propositions are drawn from different philosophical sources and together provide a useful sieve through which a decision may be filtered. In the context of business ethics, this way of tackling moral issues lifts the debate above considerations of simple commercial justification or technical feasibility.

Underlying the approach adopted by the Institute of Global Ethics is the assertion that a set of shared global values exists and that the principles contained within them can command assent everywhere. These shared values, it can be argued, will guide the decision-taker as choices are evaluated against principles such as those outlined above. The case for a canon of shared universal values is attractive and plausible but can be sustained in practice only by considerable imprecision. The main difficulties that arise from this approach derive from the absence of an end-vision, or *telos*, in the system from which the values derive. It can too easily become a morality of lowest common denominators.

Similar to the method commended by the Institute of Global Ethics is that used by the Co-operative Bank in Britain when it embarked in the 1990s upon a programme to present itself as the ethical bank. The bank consulted widely with its customers in order to identify what they, the customers, regarded as critical ethical issues and how the bank should respond to them. The bank then actively promoted the ethical stance that it derived from these consultations. For example, it maintained the principle that it would not accept as a customer any business that was a polluter of the environment (from which, it implied, it did not do business with chemical companies, for example).

The basis for the Co-operative Bank approach is the adoption of the values of the wider public. Without examining in detail the methodology whereby the bank established the ethical viewpoints held by the wider public, it is evident that this kind of approach can be both ephemeral and inconsistent. Views expressed by the general public in the democracies of Western Europe and North America are notoriously volatile. Nor is there much evidence to show that they are based upon in-depth examination of issues. Public opinion may be seriously affected by the media, by current events or by short-term concerns, none of which is a satisfactory basis for a moral framework to guide long-term behaviour.

Both the Institute of Global Ethics and the Co-operative Bank establish sharing of values as a key parameter in determining a value base for moral guidance. Clearly, general acceptance of the value base is crucial for an effective moral code. But the approaches that were adopted take inadequate account of the need for testing over a prolonged period for a value system to command assent and authority. Nor do they identify the end-purpose: the *telos*.

The elements of a Christian basis for business ethics

There are many possible methods of establishing a set of values for the conduct of business or any other human activity. It is one of the arguments of this book that Christianity offers a relevant, coherent and well-founded basis.

As noted in Chapter 6, the end-purpose – or *telos* – of Christian moral guidance is love. This is a much-debased word, devalued by carelessness and overuse. The English word 'love' embraces casual, physical love (*eros*), desire and affection (*philia*), and unconditional love (*caritas* or *agape*). In Christian thought *caritas* or charity (another debased word) is at the heart of humankind's relationship with God. Christians believe that creation itself is an act of divine love. The ultimate goal for human beings is to attain the freely given love both of God and of our fellow human beings. This is universal love or *caritas* in the sense of bringing all humankind together in union with the divine.

Hundreds of books have been written about *caritas*. It is beyond my competence or intent to add to the canon of writings about love. But the concept of love in this all-embracing sense is fundamental to our thesis of a Christian dimension to ethics and to business ethics in particular. It is critical for several reasons.

First, the concept of love as a unifying and fundamental principle would seem to be unique to the human species. There is no evidence that other creatures have developed such a vision as a basis for understanding their condition or governing their conduct.

Second, love is a concept with an appeal that extends beyond the community of Christians. For example, André Comte-Sponville, a French philosopher, is not a Christian but he identifies love as the basis for all virtues in his treatise on virtue: 'It leaves us perhaps with a certain idea of humanity in which all men are bound together: the Greeks call it *philanthropia* which they defined as "natural tendency to love men, a way of being which incites to charity and benevolence towards them"';[7] 'Love introduces into the sphere of human relations that distant goal of universality which was already suggested by compassion and justice . . . and infuses it, to the extent possible with a positive and concrete content'.[8] There is no guarantee that such love is attainable and in that respect, argues Comte-Sponville, it is like other virtues. In its absence we need other virtues to help us. None the less, according to St Augustine, 'A short and true definition of virtue is a due ordering of love'.[9]

The foregoing passages illustrate a general point. The concept of love is not only the inspirational thrust for a Christian moral framework but it also represents a virtue that commends itself to human beings who stand outside the community of Christian belief. Love is, to be dangerously brief, a virtue that commands a near-universal human consent. It is that quality which is fitting to define us as human beings.

The third reason why love is critical to a Christian perspective on business ethics is that it has been interpreted practically according to Christ's teaching, through service to our fellow human beings. Thus Christ himself, at the Last Supper, offered himself as a servant to his followers by washing their feet and commanded them similarly to serve their fellow human beings. The role of business, at its root, is likewise an act of service, meeting the needs of other human beings. For the Christian and non-Christian alike, the true role of business is to give service to others. Herein lies the basis for a Christian dimension to business ethics and a definitive interpretation of its end-purpose.

The formulation of a value system to underpin any system of morality requires an end-purpose. The great Christian doctrine of universal love can be applied in the concept of service to others, through business, as the fundamental moral principle needed to provide a framework for business ethics. The implications of love and service can thus be developed to permeate and inspire the principles we formulate to structure that framework. Hence Christian and secular thought come together to give moral purpose to the undertaking.

Communities are an important factor in the formation of moral systems. A community is sometimes a body of people who have, for example, a religion or a profession in common and who are unified by common interests. Since the very earliest times Christians have possessed a sense of common identity, a shared feeling of joint membership of a community to the extent that in apostolic times they endeavoured to hold goods in common. It is within this community – the continuing Christian moral community – that a moral framework has been developed which is based upon the all-important end-purpose of love, the defining virtue that establishes what is fitting behaviour for human beings. This is indeed close to a value to which all human beings can freely assent.

The Christian moral framework of virtue

I am no trained philosopher, still less in any sense an educated moral philosopher. At various points so far I have selected elements from classical and contemporary ethics in a somewhat eclectic fashion. I have assumed that within the cultures that characterize Western Europe and North America, the influence of Christian understanding has been fundamental to the moral climate that evolved. Furthermore, because Christianity is a religion based in time, through the event of the incarnation, and because it makes a claim to the universality of love, Christianity has interacted dynamically with other cultures, at boundaries which are permeable and evolutionary. Thus Christianity drew deeply upon the philosophers of ancient Greece and both nourished and was nourished by other religions and moral systems encountered throughout the world. These interactions have also been greatly expanded as modern transport and communication systems have increased contact and exchange. It is against this background that the elements of Christian moral thought can offer potential underpinning for business ethics.

In Chapter 5 we noted the work of Alasdair MacIntyre in resurrecting Aristotelian thinking about the virtues and we have also looked at the historical Christian context in which virtue ethics developed. In returning to virtue ethics as an inspirational source for moral discussion, one must be careful to avoid the trap of using history to resolve moral concerns. A morally praiseworthy virtue is not an ideal simply on grounds of antiquity. The changing circumstances of human existence on the planet call for continuous re-evaluation of virtues in a modern context. But the concept of virtue has emerged as a tested and valuable one. A virtue should not be considered in isolation. Taken together the canon of virtues may constitute the moral life but one or several virtues taken in isolation would not necessarily do so. Thus the practice of one particular virtue within the sphere of business would provide no overall guarantee of a morally acceptable life or a comprehensive moral code. For that, other virtues should be called into play. Additionally, it does not follow that an accepted virtue should be regarded as representing a 'divine virtue' or 'God's will'. As I have made clear, I regard with great reserve any claims that particular moral systems have unqualified divine authority: God does not seem unequivocally to reveal his will in that way. (To that extent, we concede the point to Bishop Holloway.)

But virtues represent a distillation of thinking in the Christian context and – against the inspiration of God's end-purpose of love – of the human excellences needed for the moral life. This thought-process has helped to identify special values that are associated with particular virtues. (We shall return to this when we consider the particular moral concerns that arise for different kinds of business.) Certainly virtues are a means to achieve particular end-goals that are identified as good. Continued reflection upon virtues, demonstration of them by example, and examination of them over long periods of time provide a readily accessible set of values when ethical dilemmas occur.

As noted in the previous chapter, Christian thought has traditionally concentrated upon four cardinal virtues: courage, justice, temperance and wisdom; and three theological virtues: faith, hope and charity. The Aristotelian virtues and the Christian virtues taken together represent a substantive, long-standing and profoundly thoughtful canon of excellences on which Christian moral teachers have relied. This canon of virtues is flexible: each virtue is open to re-examination and re-interpretation. It is not a canon which relies on appeal to a universal set of absolutes, with the exception of love.

It is upon this foundation that a Christian input to business ethics may be formulated. With the authority of the continuing Christian moral community and the weight of two millennia of reflection, it is a cogent basis for business ethics: a moral framework for the activity which has become a powerful force in the modern world and which has emerged in a culture shaped by Christian thought. The question to be addressed next is: how should a Christian heritage of virtue ethics be practically translated into a workable framework for business ethics? That is the subject of our next chapter.

Notes

1. John Kay, 'Good Business', *Prospect*, March 1998.
2. Elaine Sternberg, *Just Business*, Warner Books, 1995.
3. Ibid., p. 33.
4. Ibid., p. 34.
5. Ibid., pp. 79ff.
6. Rush Kidder, 'Clone Me Up, Scotty: Dolly and the Moral Supernova', *Insights on Global Ethics*, 7:2 (Spring 1997), p. 3.
7. Quoted from Pseudo-Plato, in André Comte-Sponville, *A Short Treatise on the Great Virtues*, trans. C. Temerson, Heinemann, 2002, p. 284.
8. Ibid, p. 285.
9. Augustine, *City of God*, XV, xxii, trans. Philip Levine, Loeb Classical Library, Harvard University Press, vol. 4, p. 345.

♦ 8 ♦

Just business

At first sight, the three theological virtues of faith, hope and love, and the cardinal virtues of prudence, justice, temperance (now often referred to as 'moderation') and courage, may appear abstract and imprecise. Present-day minds, tuned to measurement in objective terms as the defining criterion, do not take readily to unmeasurable concepts, such as prudence. This is particularly true in the world of business, where quantification and measurement provide the criteria of success or failure. Moreover, perhaps, familiarity with the terms used for the virtues places them in a penumbra of collective memory where our critical faculties are partially suspended. These words are part of a vocabulary that may have lost some of its power to rouse us, precisely because of overexposure.

The concepts of certain virtues have contracted as a consequence of history and experience. Take, for example, the virtue of courage. For many people courage is largely an excellence to be found in military activities or in situations of serious physical danger and hardship. Common parlance is unlikely to describe as 'courageous' the behaviour of laboratory workers diligently pursuing a research goal in the face of strict financial restrictions. Justice has been similarly constricted in popular thought: it is generally seen to be limited to the application of the laws and regulations within a jurisdiction. As for love or charity, one can hardly begin to remove the accretions of sentimentality and banality that have seriously debased the concept.

It remains a fact, however, that the concept of virtue is, beneath the distortions of overfamiliarity and carelessness, remarkably resilient. As our brief overview has indicated, there is no definitive version of virtue ethics. It is an approach that has the potential for continuous renewal and reinvigoration. It is because of the enduring power and validity of the concept of virtue that it presents a serious foundation upon which a systematic approach to business ethics can be built. Typically virtue is related to success. No one does well without courage, industriousness or wisdom. These qualities are about character and leadership. As such virtue ethics can commend itself to business.

Just war

We have already considered at some length the tradition of Christian unease about wealth, its creation and its distribution. Despite the considerations that have been adduced here and elsewhere, many Christians will remain uncomfortable. They will continue to question the ethical purposes and methods of wealth creation. It may be helpful to look at another human activity that has caused similar unease for Christians over twenty centuries: war. From the earliest days of Christianity war was regarded as essentially unholy and participation in it as problematic. The doctrine of the just war was gradually developed to guide people in those situations where the evil of war might – or even must – be accepted in preference to greater evils, such as oppression or inhumanity, that can be prevented or stopped only by armed conflict. To address these situations Christian theologians, notably St Augustine and St Thomas Aquinas, endeavoured to formulate the conditions for a just war. War is a continuously changing aspect of human conduct. The conditions of modern warfare, with the availability of weapons of mass destruction and the potential to deploy them at great distance in a highly depersonalized way, are very different from the armed struggles known to Thomas and to Augustine. These changes, it is sometimes argued, render invalid some of the guidelines that form part of the just war concept. The arguments about the justifications for engaging in war and about the ways in which it may be conducted have become more complex and less capable of simple resolution. Notwithstanding these difficulties, the conditions for a just war remain important factors.

It may be helpful to recapitulate briefly the traditional criteria for a just war:

1. Just cause: force may be used only to correct a grave, public evil such as aggression or massive violation of the basic rights of whole populations.
2. Legitimate authority: only duly constituted public authorities may use deadly force or wage war.
3. Right intention: force may be used only in a truly just cause and only for that purpose.

4. Probability of success: arms are not to be used in a futile cause or in a case where disproportionate measures are required to achieve success.
5. Last resort: force may be used only after all peaceful alternatives have been seriously tried and exhausted.
6. Proportionality: the overall destruction expected from the use of force must be outweighed by the good to be achieved.
7. Non-combatant immunity: civilians may not be the object of direct attack and military personnel must take due care to avoid and minimize indirect harm to civilians.[1]

Although serious questions are immediately raised by these criteria in the context of modern military conflicts (for example, what is the legitimate authority to sanction the use of force against terrorists, or what is the distinction between military and civilian personnel, as war has become increasingly mechanized and automated?), they remain helpful principles against which decisions and actions may be evaluated.

To my knowledge, nothing as systematic and carefully considered as the criteria for a just war has been developed by the Christian community to address the dilemmas raised by humankind's wealth-creation activities. It is one of the objectives of this book to argue that Christian thinkers should, albeit belatedly, address wealth creation in this way.

Of course, several difficulties immediately present themselves. First, war is mercifully not an everyday activity for most of humankind. Wealth creation is an everyday pursuit for a large proportion of the human race. Second, the consequences of war are immediately more critical than those of wealth creation and, indeed, diametrically opposed to them (war inevitably entails loss of life; wealth creation does not entail loss of life as an intentional outcome – though it may occur by accident). Third, war is – for the most part – conducted by sovereign states; business is the activity of individuals or groups of individuals. Fourth, war as an activity is relatively easily delineated; wealth creation is more amorphous and therefore difficult to delineate precisely. All these considerations – and many others – mean that the formulation of criteria for just business does not bear too close a comparison with the formulation of the criteria for just war. The two human activities are different and demand different approaches to the preparation of a framework for ethical critique.

It is not coincidental that the two great Christian thinkers who developed seminal versions of the just war doctrine (Saints Augustine and Thomas Aquinas) were also moral theologians and philosophers who played fundamental roles in the development of virtue ethics in their day. The importance of the key virtues is readily apparent in the just war criteria. The very term 'just war' invokes the virtue of justice, as does the criterion of just cause. The virtue of prudence is manifest in the criteria of right intention and probability of success. Temperance and justice underpin the concept of proportionality. The doctrine of just war embraces guidelines and principles formulated from a basis of virtue ethics. The elements of just business can build on the same bedrock.

I shall offer criteria to help develop a Christian framework for just business on the foundations of virtue ethics. These suggestions spring from my life of work in business, engaging actively in the creation of wealth, and also from prolonged reflection upon and participation in the application of moral principles in the conduct of business. Business and wealth creation are, above all, practical and focused activities. These initial thoughts are, therefore, inspired above all by considerations of practicality.

The theological virtues of faith, hope and love/charity/*caritas* are foundation virtues in Christian thought, and love, as we have already noted, is the virtue towards the attainment of which all other virtues contribute. These theological virtues are highly desirable in any board-room. Love itself translates immediately into human behaviour such as friendship, respect and esteem.

Each of the cardinal virtues is a practical expression of wisdom and invites consideration of behaviour that is conducive not only to acquir-ing virtue for the individual, but also to establishing and maintaining relationships. Christianity is primarily a call to individuals. Accordingly the development of the Christian moral framework has had a strong emphasis upon the behaviour of individuals, rather than the conduct of groups. In Europe, until the eighteenth century it could be assumed that the individual lived in a community of people who shared the same faith. The application of Christian virtue ethics in modern business must recognize two radically different factors: businesses are not individuals, but groups of individuals working to a common purpose; the society in which modern businesses operate is no longer one whose members share the same faith. These differences must constantly be borne in mind in examining the contribution of virtue ethics in the sphere of business. A totally individualistic view of behaviour based on virtues is not sustain-able, of course. While some degree of individual behaviour is related to the development of private characteristics of excellence, there are practical limits to the isolation of individual behaviour from its social context. Certainly Christ's teaching recognized that the behaviour of the individual was inescapably linked to its effects upon others. Virtue ethics, derived from reflection upon Christ's life and teaching, accepts the interrelationship between individual and group moral principles. Most of the canon of virtues derives its meaning from the social context: justice, for example, is a concept of little significance for the individual abstracted from other people. Virtues relate to behaviour that is likely to make and maintain relationships.

The cardinal virtues

The cardinal virtues of prudence, justice, temperance and fortitude underpin the canon of other virtues. They are the dispositions of character from which many other virtues are derived. Much present-day debate on moral matters is couched in terms of human rights and (to a much lesser degree) duties or responsibilities. But it is not difficult to establish the transition to rights and responsibilities from the fundamental concepts of virtue upon which they are based. The virtues – and in particular the cardinal virtues – are the foundation stones upon which most moral discussion is largely based. This is not to exclude other sources: the Bible, natural law and experience are among a wide portfolio of inputs to moral debate. None the less, consideration of the cardinal virtues in the context of practical experience is a helpful starting point in formulating the criteria for just business.

The term *prudence* is not usually part of our everyday vocabulary today. To the extent that the word is used, it is often employed as a synonym for caution. In the lexicon of virtues, prudence is a more subtle concept than that. It represents the ability to discern the action that is both necessary and possible in a given situation, assessing what is appropriate as conditions vary. Prudence enables a person (or group of persons) to differentiate between considered action and impulse, assessing the consequences of an act as well as the intentions behind it. This quality of asking what is appropriate behaviour in the light of changing circumstances enables the prudent to handle uncertainty. A key characteristic of prudence is the ability to defer gratification from the immediate to the longer term. The capacity to think beyond the immediate consequences of an act, and to apply acquired knowledge prudently, entails the ability to discriminate between different options with clarity and with awareness of the obligations entailed.

The relevance of prudence in the conduct of business is not difficult to discern. The ability to assess in a considered manner the full implications of a particular course of action is a critically important quality in the successful conduct of business, since all business activity entails risk. Prudence is that quality which reinforces good sense in looking at the wider implications of a decision beyond the immediate effects. Prudence militates against seeking short-term gain at the expense of long-term survival. In the oil industry, in which I spent most of my working life, the decision to invest in drilling for oil was a decision with huge implications. Millions of pounds are spent in drilling a well. If oil is struck, the benefits may well take seven to ten years to accrue from the moment of decision to drill. Such a decision indeed calls for prudence and the acceptance of deferred reward.

Prudence is perhaps at the root of one of the most fundamental requirements in business: the need for trust, fidelity and probity. These qualities or virtues may be summed up in the concept of honesty, which is generally held to be a major virtue in its own right. Honesty entails accuracy, the avoidance of misrepresentation, and consistency. All these attributes are essential in the building of trust, without which business cannot operate effectively. Prudence demands the consistency and openness of behaviour that are the preconditions for trust. Honesty is a virtue closely related to that of prudence and also to justice.

Justice, by contrast with prudence, is something that we talk about every day. But here again, one must beware of distortions that creep into common parlance. Very often justice is perceived simply as the application of laws and regulations in a society. This is a very limited aspect of justice and ignores those criteria which are relevant to justice but which go well beyond what any law can prescribe. Justice is concerned with fairness, with balancing rights and claims and with the treatment of all individuals as human. This quality of fairness may, indeed, be unattainable in its fullest sense but it is, nevertheless, a concept that is a good in itself, since it calls upon people to put themselves in the place of others and then to act accordingly: 'Do to others, as you would have them do to you' (the Golden Rule).

In the context of business, the virtue of justice affirms the principle of conformity to the law, both in spirit and letter. But it goes well beyond requiring legitimacy in this formal sense. Justice demands that fairness be always a consideration (*pace* Sir Stanley Kalms – see Chapter 7) and that a proper balance of conflicting interests be sought. The most obvious application of justice relates to the treatment of human beings (employees, customers, suppliers) in ways that are appropriate and fair. But justice is also the response to the wider call from society that due respect be paid to social expectations regarding such matters as the distribution of rewards or the conduct of competition between organizations. This response to social expectation seeks a degree of legitimacy and consent that goes beyond simple adherence to the law.

The third cardinal virtue is *temperance*. It is today often referred to as 'moderation' but I shall retain the traditional terminology because of its historical resonance. The virtue of temperance has also had its impact dulled by modern usage, which in the nineteenth and twentieth centuries tended to restrict its meaning to moderation in consumption, notably with regard to alcohol. The broader significance of temperance entails the exercise of sufficient self-control so as not to dominate or be dominated by others or by events. Thus temperance accepts our enjoyment of our desires but demands an avoidance of self-indulgence and greed. Temperance invokes a sense of what is proportionate (with its resonance of the balance required by justice) through reasoned selectivity. The implications of temperance are of special relevance in times of plenitude.

Temperance ensures that our emotions do not harness reason to their caprices. The concepts of balance and moderation that are called for by temperance are again highly relevant in the field of wealth creation and business. Self-control and restraint are critical determinants in our respect for people. For the provider of goods and services, this entails careful and balanced assessment of what these goods and services should be and the manner and degree to which desire for them should be stimulated. Similarly, where a wealth-creation activity involves consumption of a finite natural resource, temperance calls for moderation in that exploitation and some degree of just balance between the good achieved and the resource consumed. As with prudence and justice, temperance requires both proportionality and respect for people.

Courage, or fortitude, the fourth of the cardinal virtues, has traditionally been associated with military activity or with physical bravery. Courage is not a self-contained virtue; it serves other virtues. In general it is a highly personal virtue and can be put to bad as well as good use: history has many examples of courageous wickedness! In a broader sense, courage means the ability to withstand temptation despite the pressures of abuse, ridicule or misunderstanding – in other words to adhere to principle.

In the business context, courage embraces a particular attribute. It enables anxieties over the inevitable uncertainties and risks to be kept in perspective. Everyone engaged in business is well aware of the host of unpredictable factors that can provoke anxiety (inflation, changes in the conditions of trade, the emergence of new or stronger competitors, shifts in customer taste, etc.). Courage enables such developments to be addressed in a measured and considered way, as prompted by prudence.

Consideration of the cardinal virtues and an indication of how they may be related to behaviour in business provide a proven basis for a moral framework of values/virtues. From a Christian perspective, the cardinal virtues are unified in the theological virtue of love. It is important also to recognize the need for coherence in the principles embodied in the cardinal virtues themselves. As we have already noted, striving to cultivate one or even several virtues in isolation is insufficient. Morality is all of one piece. One of the great strengths of virtue ethics is its capacity to identify different attributes of excellence that may be particularly appropriate for a special circumstance or condition. Courage is of particular relevance in military activity; justice has resonance where human relationships are concerned. But if morality is to be coherent, it is desirable to seek the consolidation of virtues, not just an unrelated selection of virtues.

The attainment of wholeness and consistency across the range of virtues is to be sought by pursuit of *integrity*. 'Integrity' is yet another term that has acquired a constricted meaning. It is often treated as a synonym for honesty, the avoidance of lying, cheating or stealing. In this limited sense, integrity is often identified as a quality to which business should aspire. In this discussion, however, I would prefer to use the term 'integrity' in its more comprehensive sense as defined in the *Oxford English Dictionary*: completeness; soundness and freedom from moral corruption. In this sense, integrity calls for consistent attention to the range of virtues, not just honesty. And so the integrity of a person or of a company would signify its commitment to the range of virtues and the recognition of their interrelationships.

Criteria for just business

From the foregoing outline of the cardinal virtues and how they may be related to business activity, it is now possible to formulate some conditions for the just business. No attempt to set out such criteria can make a claim at this stage to be comprehensive. The criteria for just war evolved over centuries; the criteria for just business cannot be identified in a few hours. But it may be helpful to set out some initial considerations as the starting point for further discussion.

1. *Service. Businesses shall have as their primary purpose service to humankind through meeting human needs and wants.* This principle, of course, employs the economist's definition of wealth and is a theme that has been repeatedly stressed in previous chapters. It is an important principle that requires continued emphasis, for several reasons. First, from the Christian perspective, it firmly roots business in service to others, rather than in pursuit of secondary aims such as making a profit or maximizing shareholder value. Second, it provides the end-purpose required for a considered ethical framework for business. Third, it unequivocally orientates business towards a human goal and entails respect for all human beings.

The principle as stated, however, is insufficient. It makes no reference to such critical considerations as working for the common good, seeking to enhance human dignity, or addressing the social and economic consequences of business activity.

We should also recognize that businesses not only pursue the satisfaction of human needs and wants, but also create and stimulate them. In so doing, business will bring into play other considerations, some of which are addressed elsewhere in this discussion. By no means all human desires are admirable!

2. *Legitimacy. Business shall obey the laws and obligations of legitimate authority in the jurisdictions where it operates.* While we have repeatedly stressed that moral debate is concerned with those issues that fall outside the law, no moral framework is complete if it disregards obedience to properly constituted authority. This is an obvious but essential part of the pursuit of justice.

In modern business practice, adherence to the law is a complex matter. Many companies operate across different national jurisdictions and these may set out different requirements. When I worked in the oil industry, this was by no means an uncommon situation. For example, health and environmental legislation varies widely from state to state. In the 1980s and 1990s, as Western countries legislated to reduce and then forbid the addition of lead to petrol, other countries in Africa and Asia had less demanding laws. Decisions about the lead content for fuels sold in these countries were more complicated than simple adherence to what the law said. Companies had to consider whether different standards could be applied on health issues in different countries. In health and safety matters, what action a company takes to go beyond what the law demands is a decision frequently entailing consideration of what is technically feasible as well as what is in the best economic interest of all parties.

International protocols and requirements further complicate the simple principle of adherence to the law. Citizens of the United Kingdom and of other member states of the European Union are increasingly made aware of differing legal requirements set by EU and national jurisdictions, even although the EU has a machinery for harmonization of legislation. The situation becomes even more complex for an international business which has to take account of legal requirements within state jurisdictions and the non-legal prescriptions of United Nations agencies or supra-national institutions such as the OECD or the International Monetary Fund.

3. *Proportionality. Business shall ensure that the benefits it provides are proportionate to the costs incurred.* The principle of proportionality is fundamental in many aspects of the wealth-creation process and derives from the virtues of justice, prudence and temperance. An immediately obvious example that arouses great public concern relates to protection and conservation of the natural environment and the resources that it provides. Humankind's technical ability to exploit natural resources has the potential to wreak lasting and irreparable damage to the planet. Against this can be set the benefits that accrue, for example, in meeting human needs for food, warmth and shelter. There is a moral requirement upon business to seek balance and proportionality in these areas, encapsulated in the notion of sustainability.

The principle of proportionality has much wider application, however. All business entails risk-taking. The commitment made in providing any good or service offers uncertainty for the business entrepreneur. Will the effort expended in drilling an oil-well result in the discovery and production of sufficient oil to repay the investment? For the village shoemaker, will the purchases of tools and materials be rewarded by an adequate demand for the shoes he makes? Just as the shoemaker seeks reward for the risk he takes – he wants to earn enough to live on and something more (his profit) that he can use as he pleases – so the oil company looks for income that at least matches expenditure but – if it is to continue in business – also for something that rewards the risks taken when the well was drilled.

The mechanic or technician or cobbler wants to be rewarded for the skills which he or she has deployed in providing goods and services. No one in a developed economy works simply to subsist. But distributive justice requires that the rewards secured should be in proportion to the benefits provided.

The principle of proportionality is called into play in many situations. As a general rule in free-market capitalist systems, the forces of competition may well be a limiting factor upon potentially excessive rewards to be derived from a business activity. But competition can also lead to monopolies or near-monopolies. The principle of proportionality can serve as a guideline in those situations where competition is a very blunt and inadequate instrument for moderating excess.

A particularly vexatious example of excess is the remuneration for senior executives in large business corporations. For most senior executives in large companies, the constraints of market competition do not apply. The levels of remuneration are determined primarily within the boardroom of the company. It is in situations such as this that the principle of proportionality becomes especially relevant. Are the benefits to the organization proportionate to the costs of the remuneration package? (Conversely, it may also be the case that better rewards for a key executive would bring greater benefits to the organization and those it serves, a consideration that is sometimes overlooked.)

4. *Trustworthiness. Business shall endeavour to establish trust among the parties with which it is engaged.* There are a number of synonyms for trust: fidelity; faith; confidence; reliance. It is self-evident that trust and confidence are essential in every aspect of business activity. The company employee trusts that he will be paid for his work. The customer trusts that the goods or services paid for will be fit for purpose and meet expectations and requirements. The supplier trusts that payment will be made for the goods or services provided. The wider community trusts that the business activity is not destroying the environment, ruining the health of those who live near a factory, or endangering safety. Without trust society cannot function properly and of no aspect of society is that more true than of business. At the very heart of what business aims to do is an assumption that it can be trusted to meet the needs and wants of the human beings it serves.

Trustworthiness is akin to one of the theological virtues: faith. If I say that I trust my neighbour it means that I believe in him. Christians build their faith and trust in God. Yet faith cannot be measured. Our faith and trust in business is related in that respect. Anyone who observes the operation of a capitalist stock market can see the effect of trust and faith – or of their absence. When trust in a company is strong, its health – as measured by its share price – is also strong. But if trust is weakened and confidence ebbs, the share price falls, customers look elsewhere, employees seek another job.

Trust is closely related to the cardinal virtue of prudence because prudence recognizes the obligation that is inherent in human relationships to pursue constancy and continuity. Prudence avoids foolhardiness, which is corrosive of trust. Prudence affirms loyalty, which is a foundation for trust.

From trust flow a number of virtues that are particularly important in business. Trust is recognition of, and confidence in, the veracity of someone or an organization. Veracity is allied to honesty and fairness, the avoidance of lying, cheating or stealing – no business operation can be perpetuated unless it is based upon honesty. And linked to honesty are two other important virtues essential for business: transparency and accountability. Transparency is that degree of openness that builds trust. While certain commercial aspects of a business are rightly kept confidential, the records of its operations and finances should be as open and clear as possible in order to build and sustain trust. Likewise, trust is built if the principle of accountability is followed, whereby due responsibility is assigned and accepted – and where this is seen to be so.

5. *Reciprocity. Business should be based upon recognition of reciprocal benefits between parties.* We noted that the virtue of temperance entails for business a careful and balanced assessment of the goods and services to be provided. In particular, temperance recognizes the benefits of moderation and the perils of self-indulgence. These considerations can perhaps be addressed through due recognition of the reciprocal nature of business activity.

At its simplest, reciprocity is recognition that business transactions in a free market are about mutual benefits to the parties involved. Customer and supplier each look for satisfaction. Employers and employees are linked in a relationship of mutual interdependence, of which reciprocity is a critical component. At a more general level, society and the wider community seek reciprocity of benefits between the creators of wealth and those directly or indirectly enjoying the wealth. At the very heart of reciprocity is an acceptance of responsibility for others. That sense of responsibility is an essential aspect of business activity. The virtue of justice is reflected in reciprocity, calling, for example, for fairness in trade, awareness of contractual obligation and for due balance between product value and profit.

Temperance implies moderation. Similarly reciprocity implies a degree of balance in an activity. This concept is particularly important when one considers the role played by business and wealth creation in stimulating our wants. Examples of excess are never difficult to find: innocent pleasure in drink and food can turn into drunkenness and gluttony. The allure of an attractive person portrayed to promote a product can become sexually demeaning by adoption of degrading techniques. The provision of material goods can become the stimulus to endless acquisition for its own sake. Abuses of this kind arise when the reciprocal nature of business activities is disregarded. A truly reciprocal perspective will endeavour to avoid excess and exploitation.

It may be argued that the criteria for just business that I have put forward are limited in several respects. A businessman or -woman may find them rather general in nature. They require further refinement before they are translatable into policies and standards in the business context. A moral philosopher or theologian may well regard these criteria as simplistic.

I am happy to accept these criticisms. The primary purposes in setting out some preliminary thinking on the criteria for just business are these. First, it is an attempt to indicate a route by which the richness of Christian moral thought can be more directly related to the conduct of the wealth-creation process. This route takes as its starting point an examination of the primary virtues and initiates the process of developing from them a consistent and coherent value base upon which to build the structure of business ethics. In doing so we seek to avoid the dangers of a moral structure which is devoid of coherence and is merely derived from current received opinion – a kind of politically correct morality.

Second, these suggested criteria are not presented as a final statement. As I have pointed out, the just war criteria were developed over several centuries. The suggestions that have been offered as criteria for just business should serve as the starting point, not the end point, for continuing analysis and debate.

Third, although a business practitioner might find these draft criteria lacking in practicalities for direct application, they begin the process of linking traditional virtues to the realities of modern business. As such they may provide the kernel of a value-base related to business from which more detailed and practical guidance can be drawn.

Fourth, these criteria may constitute a bridge between the language of Christian moral understanding and business activity. It has been a key theme of preceding chapters that the discontinuity between Christian thought and business practice has been both regrettable and unnecessary. The synergy between the Christian faith and the world of wealth creation is fundamental to the well-being of human societies on the planet.

Establishing a link that can help nourish the development of business ethics will give greater coherence and depth to the study and application of business ethics.

In conclusion, let us return to the matter of individual and group responsibility. Christian moral thought has traditionally concentrated upon the behaviour of the individual and has somewhat neglected the responsibilities and the moral responses of groups, such as companies and corporations. The distinction between individual behaviour and that of a group to which the individual belongs is not clear-cut. Collectively the group has a shared responsibility for what is done in its name, although in fact only one or a few individuals may have carried it out. In modern organizations – and especially in modern business corporations – there is a critical need to ensure consistent understanding between the members of the organization and awareness by all individuals of the common purpose of the company. The vigorous tradition of the responsibility of the individual for his or her behaviour is extended to wider responsibility for the conduct of the organization to which he or she belongs. There is an important interplay between these two considerations – individual and group responsibility – as we develop the implications of the ethical principles by which business should be conducted.

Virtues represent excellences that are equally valid for the individual and for the group. Indeed, some virtues such as justice have full meaning and application primarily in the context of human relationships. This general applicability of the concept of virtues offers the means whereby consistency of behaviour by the individuals in an organization can be achieved. Consistency is of critical importance for a business: the improper acts of one individual can destroy it. The development of business ethics and the role of virtue ethics as part of the process are thus of great significance for wealth-creation activity.

Note

1. In setting out these criteria, I am indebted to General Sir Hugh Beach, who has drawn upon a summary prepared by US Roman Catholic bishops in a document entitled 'The Harvest of Justice is Sown in Peace: A Reflection of the National Conference of Catholic Bishops on the Tenth Anniversary of *The Challenge of Peace*', approved by the bishops in 1993 and available on the Internet at <www.nccbuscc.org/sdwp/harvest.htm>. Sir Hugh offers his expert opinion that no better framework for an ethical critique of military actions has been proposed than these criteria for a just war.

The formation of
corporate moral behaviour

Dilemmas posed by the weakening
of shared values in society

The emergence of business ethics as a serious discipline in the decades since the 1970s is, at first glance, somewhat surprising. Superficially there is an inconsistency in the fact that disquiet over the propriety of the purposes and conduct of business has emerged in a period widely perceived as one of uncertainty about the validity of moral standards in much of Western society. If a climate of moral relativism exists, why should the practitioners of business become more – rather than less – concerned about the ethical considerations to be applied to what they do?

It is difficult to determine with any degree of precision whether the contemporary moral climate is more or less rigorous, more or less consensual than that of earlier times. All periods are characterized by nostalgia for an earlier golden age when, it is imagined, higher standards of conduct obtained. The Roman writer, Cicero, famously lamented, 'O tempora, O mores!' – 'What times, what customs!' Every age has had its Cicero.

There are, however, a number of factors that influence our times in such a way that moral debate is indeed rendered difficult. As we saw in Chapter 5, a climate of intellectual uncertainty about the validity of any kind of moral statement emerged in the twentieth century and that has undoubtedly coloured much modern discussion. Furthermore, the strong Western tradition of respect for the individual and the individual's rights was reaffirmed in the decades following World War II. This was a reaction against the abuses and intolerance of the totalitarian regimes of fascism and communism. Respect for the individual and his or her personal beliefs and judgements was an important legacy of the Enlightenment. It was given powerful new emphasis in the 1980s and 1990s when the freedom of choice of the individual was accorded even greater importance through the operation of market economies, as their durability and effectiveness were confirmed by the collapse of commnism.

Other factors have undoubtedly contributed to a modern climate of moral uncertainty and relativism. Throughout history it is possible to detect major changes in moral perceptions. For example, biblical and later periods acquiesced in slavery. Its formal abolition from all modern states is a very recent phenomenon. (The last part of the world formally to forbid slavery was the Arabian peninsula, which did so only in the 1960s.) Religious faith and the principles derived from faith, in particular from Christianity, undoubtedly provided much of the impetus for this particular shift. Changes in humankind's technical capabilities are another vital force in prompting changes in moral perception. That process has become more significant in our times. It would be difficult to deny for example that modern means of reliable contraception have brought about radical changes in general attitudes towards sexual activity. Sexual intercourse in the nineteenth century was primarily about begetting children; much sexual activity in twenty-first century Western societies is essentially a source of pleasure, with scant regard for procreation. The development of weapons of mass destruction and their devastating application in two world wars drastically changed humankind's views on war between nations.[1]

Furthermore, while shifts in moral perception have taken place in all previous ages, the rate of change in modern times is undoubtedly more rapid and the changes are more widespread. Modern communications technology transforms the pace at which new ideas are spread, not only within communities but across the entire world. Just as ephemeral human tastes, like fashion in clothes or in music, sweep rapidly across much of the globe, so ideologies, ideas and viewpoints are made available instantly to huge numbers of people, without filtering by validating authorities. Few unquestioned authorities remain to guide the perplexed seeker after understanding. Mass communication has been accompanied by mass travel and by mass movements of people on a global level, adding to the diversity of influences that play upon individuals in modern societies. A Christian living in Western Europe or in North America may find himself the next-door neighbour of a Muslim or Hindu. The phenomenon of mixing cultures undoubtedly promotes a greater sense of relativism in the minds of modern citizens who live in the modern world of rapid technological change, mass communication and mass population movements. There is a significant dilution of shared experience, shared history and shared understanding.

Even if our current situation is not without precedent, it is evident that powerful forces are causing us to question the shared values that underpin attempts to formulate a moral framework for society. It is because these forces are so powerful that we devoted so much space to considering the bases for Christian moral understanding. A value base for moral guidance cannot be dreamed up in a vacuum. Predicated upon a vision of love and articulated over two thousand years of reflection and application through tested concepts such as virtue ethics, Christian moral understanding resides in an ongoing moral community and provides a robust bedrock among the shifting patterns of modern Western culture. For those in need of some stable points of reference in the moral soup of the twenty-first century, we have identified an established and proven source from which guiding principles may be derived – both for individuals and for groups.

The pragmatic consideration

At this juncture it is legitimate to ask why a moral framework is desirable for business. When in Rome, it is said, do as the Romans do. In a society characterized by moral flux and moral uncertainty, why should business endeavour to be different? What is the imperative upon business to explore the ethical bases of what it does and how it does it? There are two answers to these questions: one pragmatic, the other derived from principle.

There are very sound practical reasons why business should address the moral bases on which it conducts itself. Despite the picture we have painted of societies in a state of confusion on matters of morality, it is nevertheless true that society still functions on the basis of a great deal of shared understanding and shared values. It is certainly the case that contemporary Western societies are fickle with regard to the values that we uphold and even inconsistent in their application. For example, it is not uncommon to find inconsistent attitudes towards theft. People who would not dream of taking money from someone else's purse are untroubled by pocketing incorrect change in a shop or by dishonest insurance claims. Nevertheless, there remains a substantial body of behavioural criteria that commands near-universal assent. The bases for these criteria are not often articulated and even less frequently examined in depth. Thus, despite the egregious example of the lady quoted in Chapter 5 who relativized murder, the taking of life remains a taboo, as does gratuitous ill-treatment of living creatures, especially human beings.

There are many areas of loosely defined concern where a general consensus obtains – as in respect for one's fellow human beings; observance of laws; concern for protection of the physical environment; acceptance of private ownership; compassion for the sick, the infirm, the very young, the very old and the poor; detestation of cruelty and torture; affirmation of the desirability of education; and so on. These areas of shared values can readily be related to the concepts of virtue (and vice) that we have already discussed, and also to a commonsense recognition that without some measure of agreement on accepted norms of behaviour, society itself becomes intolerable. The very tension between private imperfection (the gratification of selfish desire) and common shared understanding can eventually induce shared values, as Matthew Ridley suggests in *The Origins of Virtue*.[2]

Business is, of course, an integral part of society. It exists to offer goods and services to members of society. Business is both critically dependent upon shared values within a society and, by the very nature of what it does, serves to transmit, reinforce and in some circumstances to stimulate certain values. As noted in the previous chapter, business is particularly dependent upon and instrumental in the establishment of societal values of trust. The most straightforward business transactions entail a very large measure of trust.[3] An example from personal experience may serve to illustrate this.

As a senior marketing manager for Esso I was responsible for negotiating the renewal of a worldwide contract with a major customer. The contract involved delivery of our products at many different locations in different countries of the world. For each location, the contract entailed a number of arrangements that covered product specifications, quality, service, availability and, of course, price. For some locations, I had authority to agree a price down to a specified level. To renew the contract, we provided a written offer for each location to the customer, who then negotiated with us to try to improve upon our initial offer. When it came to discussion of price, the customer always allowed the existing supplier the opportunity to make a revised bid to retain the business if a competitor had made a better offer. This was done without revealing the competitor's price, but merely by indicating to the existing supplier that his offer was not the best received, so that he could make one further revised bid.

On this occasion, the customer made it clear that for one very important location, our price was not the best offer he had received. Because I trusted the customer, I accepted that an improved offer was needed. I made a revised offer, the best price for which I had authority, and after some hesitation the customer indicated his acceptance (I deduced, but never knew, that I had presumably matched the competitor's offer). Shortly afterwards, the negotiating session was concluded and my colleague and I retired to reconsider and review the outstanding matters that had arisen. While I was working with my colleague there was a knock on the office door: it was the customer's purchasing director. He said that he had now received a new offer for the location which was better than mine. There was silence for a minute or two. I had nothing to say. I had offered my best and final price. Then the customer laughed and said that he had been too hasty: he had agreed to my offer too readily. But he stuck to his word. He had agreed with me to renew the business and would not go back on that. We had retained the business for that location.

I never forgot the honourable behaviour of that customer. He cemented a relationship of trust which, for the duration of the time that I was responsible, I tried to reciprocate. When a year or so later war in the Middle East disrupted supplies, I was able to ensure the best possible arrangements for that customer, a reciprocal manifestation of trust in response to his honesty. Of course, instances of mutual trust and honesty are regular features of business life. Without such confidence in the honesty of one's business counterpart, it would be nearly impossible to conduct business effectively. The example that I have given shows how business relies upon a societal shared value and also, by necessity and by its own example, how it can reinforce and strengthen values.

Business draws upon a heritage of shared values. In instances such as that just described, the application of the shared value of honesty reinforced trust and was in the commercial interests of both the companies concerned, since it enabled them to trade without the onerous added transaction costs incurred when legal instruments are used to compensate for lack of trust.

There is a further dimension to the importance of shared societal values for business. Despite the many uncertainties that litter the moral landscape of the twenty-first century, business does not operate in a value-free environment. There remain very considerable areas of shared societal consensus on behaviour. A company must be aware of and sensitive to these societal values. Business operates only with the consent and the support of society. If that consent and support is limited or withdrawn, the consequences for a company can be extremely serious. It may, in some circumstances, result in the withdrawal of society's permission for the company to operate. Some well-known examples illustrate the point.

In the 1990s, the director of Ratner's, a well-known UK High Street retail chain of shops selling cheap jewellery, made an ill-judged flippant remark in which he likened the quality and durability of the goods in his shops to that of a prawn sandwich. The public reaction was prompt and extreme. Upset both by the implication that customers were too stupid to notice that they were buying rubbish and also by the admission that the goods were indeed inferior, the public deserted the shops and the chain went out of business. Ratner's had disregarded one of society's values with regard to business, namely that goods sold should be of acceptable quality – not rubbish. Trust was lost by an apparent admission that the goods offered were not fit for purpose.

More serious and higher-profile examples show how dangerous it can be for a company to lose touch with the shared values of society and to give the appearance of disregarding them. The case of Shell International's misunderstandings with regard to the disposal in 1996 of its North Sea Brent Spar oil production platform by dumping it in the Atlantic is well known. The company had followed what it believed to be sound environmental and economic practice in seeking to drop the platform in deep water. What it failed to perceive was an orchestrated attempt by environmental groups to respond to public fears for the physical environment – fears that the proposed method of disposal would cause serious environmental damage. The cost to Shell of abandoning their preferred method of disposal and instead towing the platform to harbour and dismantling it was extremely high, of doubtful environmental benefit and damaging to the company's reputation for concern for the environment. Shortly afterwards Shell again incurred considerable adverse publicity and damage to its commercial interests because of the behaviour of its subsidiary company in Nigeria. Public opinion was outraged by accounts of alleged massive pollution of the Ogoniland area, where the company operated, and its signature of a joint-venture natural gas agreement with the Nigerian government, which was seen as collusion with an undemocratic regime that had just executed Ken Saro-Wiwa, an activist for restoration of democracy. The company was widely criticized for lack of concern for the physical environment and for human rights.

I can offer a personal footnote to the story of Shell's activities in Nigeria. In the early 1960s I worked for Shell in Africa and it was one of my duties to conduct an internal audit on the exploration units of

Shell's search for oil in the region of Port Harcourt, which was subsequently developed as a major oil province. General awareness of the dangers of human activity upon the physical environment was less acute than it has now become. Nevertheless, I recall that by the operational standards of that time we employees of Shell were justifiably proud of the care that was taken to minimize the adverse effects of what we did upon the pristine natural surroundings where we worked. We were also proud that the company was investing huge sums of money to find natural resources that would provide wealth for a newly independent country desperate for such investment. A great burden of expectation was placed on the company to maximize investment and help bring prosperity to the burgeoning population of a backward country.

How different it was some thirty years later. Shell's approach to environmental protection had degraded (in large measure because of the laxness of state participation and oversight of operations) and the massive investments were no longer seen as support for a newly emerging democracy, but rather as props to a brutal regime that had overthrown democracy. Shell had failed to keep its finger on the pulse of societal expectations and the revisions to values that had occurred during those thirty years. As a result, damage was done to Shell's reputation and to its business interests across the world. Its licence to operate was put at risk in some instances.

One can, of course, cite many examples where companies have in some way fallen short of societal expectations and where public outrage at perceived ill-behaviour has brought about severe restrictions upon a corporation or even its demise. Thus the notorious *Exxon Valdez* oil spill in Alaska in 1989 continues to inflict financial and operating penalties on the company. The Bhopal disaster in India was ultimately the cause of the disappearance of Union Carbide as an independent company.

The origin of interest in business ethics in the 1970s was, in large measure, a response to pragmatic considerations of the kind I have described. In the case of the company that I worked for at that time – Esso, the UK subsidiary of the company that would become known as Exxon – I have little doubt that attention to business ethics was initially heavily prompted by the adverse publicity given to dubious or illegal payments made to political parties in Italy. At the same time, the company management became aware that the usual comfortable assumptions made about employee behaviour were no longer valid. Residual shared values were strong but it was recognized that they could no longer be taken for granted. I clearly remember the offence that I personally felt when, early in the 1970s, I was for the first time asked to sign a statement that required me to declare any conflict of interest – that is a conflict between my own personal interests and those of the company. My sense of outrage was on account of the implied assumption that I would act improperly in such a situation. In fact, employees were asked to sign conflict of interest statements principally because it had become apparent that some employees no longer recognized the impropriety of such behaviour. A few senior managers had used their influence with contractors to the company to have private work carried out on preferential terms. In at least one instance, to my personal knowledge, the manager had protested that he was unable to see what was unacceptable in what he had done (getting a cheap swimming pool installed in the garden of his house). He was unable to recognize that the financial benefits he had obtained effectively prejudiced his ability to conduct business impartially on behalf of the company with the contractor concerned.

Factors such as these – the business benefits of shared values which reduce risk and transaction costs, the damaging effects of offending against societal shared values and the necessity of making clear to employees and other concerned parties what standards are to be applied – are all very cogent practical reasons why a business should be attentive to moral concerns and should endeavour to establish ethical standards of behaviour. Although there is a climate of moral relativism in society at large, although those moral sentiments of which Adam Smith wrote are weakened, although societal values are not fully or unequivocally articulated, these considerations nevertheless constitute very powerful factors in prompting a company to look at the moral framework within which it should operate.

Considerations of principle

In 1986, as one of a group of businessmen I was involved in the formal launch of the Institute of Business Ethics (IBE). At the question and answer session with a crowd of journalists, we were asked for our response to the accusation that business ethics was no more than humbug. In other words, the questioner implied, an open declaration by a company of its commitment to, say, honesty or environmental conservation or product quality is probably no more than a cynical smokescreen designed to conceal the company's true motives, namely expediency and profitability.

It is impossible wholly to counter an accusation that business ethics is no more than cynical and hypocritical public relations. In the next chapter we shall see that such deception may occur. One cannot prove a negative. One can never say with certainty that a statement of moral principle made by anyone – businessman, desert hermit or brain surgeon – is sincere. A statement about business ethics is, therefore, no different from such a statement made by someone in any other field of human activity. The hearer of the statement can never be certain and only subsequent behaviour will either confirm or disprove the sincerity of what is said. Human pronouncements on matters of morality will be subject to a degree of scepticism until a pattern of behaviour is established which can be related to the moral principles offered. It may be that the track record of many businessmen is poor. In a previous chapter we quoted some gratuitous and unfortunate examples of statements by businessmen that seem to encourage a degree of scepticism. It has been a general theme of this book that the secularization of business has encouraged this kind of amoral approach. But we have argued that business should not be regarded in this way: it is too fundamental to the human condition to be conducted without regard to any moral considerations whatsoever.

An amoral approach to business, as for any other human activity, is not sustainable in practice. All human behaviour is governed by some set of moral understandings, even if they are not necessarily articulated in any coherent manner. And although today we may be reluctant to affirm universal moral absolutes, we do not require a sophisticated moral philosophy to demonstrate that humankind does indeed differentiate behaviour in fairly consistent ways. It would be difficult to find individuals, let alone large numbers of people, who would sincerely and positively reject the traditional virtues of, say, justice, courage, temperance, honesty and kindness, and affirm the corresponding vices. 'Evil, be thou my good' is a position that mercifully few people adopt as a guiding principle in life.

Even the accusation of humbug is, in a sense, an affirmation of the validity of moral statements. I have long felt that there is a great deal to be said for hypocrisy in some respects. A sincere affirmation of intent to conduct oneself according to certain norms of behaviour, such as the pursuit of virtue, is highly desirable. But even if such a statement is made hypocritically it betokens an acceptance of the desirability of aspiring to those virtues. Hypocrisy is at least recognition of standards of higher conduct; it indicates preference for one mode of behaviour over another.

For the Christian, the aspiration to virtuous behaviour is qualified by awareness that perfection is not attainable in this world. We noted earlier the vocabulary of perfection that has featured in Christian thought. This has never, however, represented an expectation of perfectibility in human behaviour. Alongside our desire for the good, we have an in-built propensity to fall short. It is for that reason that we are more comfortable with the vocabulary of worse, bad, good and better than that of right and wrong. Just as in high-quality programmes we seek continuous improvement in performance, so in virtue ethics we seek continuous improvement towards virtue, but in full recognition that pure, unqualified virtue is not attainable. The journey of aspiration towards the good is valid for all human endeavour – and that includes business endeavour. And so businesses, like individual human beings, will undoubtedly fall short of the highest standards that are set. But failure to attain perfection or the highest form of virtue has never been regarded as sufficient reason to abandon the endeavour.

In the first part of this chapter we looked at the pragmatic case for business ethics. There is, however, a moral pursuit of excellence in business which is derived from principle. For the reasons that we have discussed and which derive from the sharing of values within the community, the end-purpose of an ethic based on principle is unlikely to be very different from one based on pragmatic considerations. A principles-based ethic has the considerable benefit of stating clearly at the outset the standards to be set. A pragmatically derived ethic will attempt to identify guiding principles to be pursued in order to achieve the practical end that is sought, rather than as ends in themselves.

The formation of ethical frameworks within business

Whatever the motivation for business to establish an ethical framework for the conduct of its operations – pragmatism, principle or a combination of both – the endeavour must start with an examination of what the organization exists to do, from which it is possible to proceed to consideration of the principles that it will seek to apply in its conduct. The purpose and principles of any organization are, of course, the responsibility of those who lead it. In the case of business that is the directors and senior management. Everyone working for a company has some responsibility for the way in which it behaves. But there is a special obligation to define its objects and guiding principles on those who are appointed to direct it. In part they may be acting in response to external imperatives, meeting the standards and expectations of society. In part they will articulate internal imperatives.

The process by which a corporation addresses this issue has much to learn from the practices and disciplines that have sustained Christians over the centuries. For individual Christians a way of life is based upon belief: a recognition of purpose and sustaining principles derived from that purpose. From that faith-based purpose and the guidance derived from it, each individual progressively develops a framework within which behaviour is formed. Different individuals place emphasis upon different things. The emphases that an individual pursues will generally either consciously or unconsciously relate to the conceptual framework of virtues (and vices) that establish the moral climate within which the Christian community lives. Depending upon a number of factors, individuals will concentrate upon certain virtues rather than others. The person who chooses a military career will doubtless place much emphasis on the virtues of courage, loyalty and self-discipline, for example; the person who feels drawn to teach may draw sustenance from consideration of justice and respect for individuals. Each person will formulate criteria that relate to his or her personal circumstances. Traditionally, this process has been known as a rule of life, a set of disciplines and self-generated guidelines that constitute a personal interpretation of how one should conduct oneself as a member of the professing Christian community. The exercise for the individual Christian is not conducted in isolation, but by drawing upon structures and insights provided within the Christian tradition. Part of that structure consists of the example given by others, by the teaching and counsel of others, by prayer and reflection upon the canon of Christian wisdom, by reason, by scripture and the countless other practices that have been developed to support and sustain Christians. The virtues and – negatively – the vices represent for the Christian signposts that serve to alert him or her in particular situations, guiding conduct in what gradually will become only a partially conscious process: the promptings of conscience. Conscience for the individual is the accumulation of internalized values, which gradually become hard-wired into his or her behaviour.

For the corporation or company a comparable process occurs. Even if the directors and senior management of the organization do not actively assume responsibility for the moral climate, a culture will none the less emerge, either consciously or unconsciously. As we have seen, there are very real dangers if the culture of behaviour is unguided and unresponsive to external considerations. The leaders have a very real interest in influencing the moral climate that shapes behaviour in a company. If the leaders do not lead, practices and customs gradually emerge and company philosophy is created by default.

Figure 1. The conceptual hierarchy within a corporation

Figure 1 represents the normal process by which a company sets out its purpose and principles and then systematically seeks to bring them into the very bloodstream of its daily conduct.

The pyramid diagram represents a conceptual hierarchy within a corporation. At the top stand the mission and supporting principles as set out by senior management. At the base is a sustaining level of monitoring, audit and control. In between lie other layers that represent different stages in the process of integrating mission and principle into the company bloodstream, the corporate equivalent of developing its conscience. Anyone who has worked in any well-organized company will be familiar with the intermediate layers of the pyramid: policies, standards, procedures. Even in very small organizations it is necessary to set out the way things are to be done. A one-man operation that provides plumbing or bookkeeping services will work to some kind of methodology embodied in procedures and systems, even if these are not written down. And consciously or unconsciously the one man will carry out those tasks to standards that he has set himself as the outcome of a policy decision to offer a higher or lower level of service.

Although much of what is represented in the pyramid is common sense and obvious to anyone who has some familiarity with business, it is useful to elaborate upon this structure in order to flesh out our thesis that insights from Christian understanding are relevant to business and the wealth-creation process.

Mission statements

The term 'mission statement', like so many others that we have discussed, has become sadly debased through inappropriate use. It is not always possible to encapsulate a statement of purpose or mission for an organization in one simple sentence, desirable though that may be. This is not much different for many Christians who might find it difficult to set out their beliefs in one simple sentence. Early Christians devoted much effort to the formulation of credal statements, many of which do not help ordinary Christians today (try the Athanasian Creed, for example). But Christ's summary of the law – love God and love your neighbour – provides a searing, challenging statement by which people may conduct their lives.

For business, there is great merit in senior management's preparing a considered and carefully worded statement that sets out the philosophy of the organization. A crafted mission statement gives clear and helpful focus not only to those who work for the company but also for all those with whom it deals. The use of mission statements is now widespread.[4] An example from personal experience may illustrate the point.

In the 1990s I was a director of the European operations of ARCO Chemical, a major US-owned company engaged in the manufacture of intermediate chemicals. It was a partially owned subsidiary of the Atlantic Richfield (ARCO) oil company, which had a strong tradition of observing good ethical practice. The ethical standards of ARCO did not occur by magic. They were the inspirational work of Robert Anderson, who led the company for many years and established its ethical climate. I never knew the man but undoubtedly he drew his moral inspiration from a philosophy formed by Christian virtues. The ARCO Chemical mission statement, which drew on the parent-company traditions, was as follows:

ARCO Chemical Company will produce chemicals, related products, and services in a manner that enhances value for our stockholders, customers, employees, and the public. To achieve this mission we will:

- Manage our assets to produce a superior return on our stockholders' investment;
- Sell high-quality, competitive products and provide superior service to customers;
- Create an environment for employees that fosters personal growth and allows individuals to achieve their full potential; and
- Operate our facilities in an environmentally responsible manner, provide a safe work place for our employees, and produce only those products we believe to be safe for customer use.

As someone who had personal responsibility for carrying out this mission and also for ensuring that it was understood and put into practice by employees of the company, I am able to say with total sincerity that all the colleagues with whom I worked accepted the imperatives that it contained. In the European region for which I shared responsibility we rigorously endeavoured to discharge our responsibilities to shareholders, customers, employees and the public. The aspirations to excellence or virtue contained within our mission statement were taken very seriously indeed – in every respect. The company was financially very successful and so in the fortunate position of generating the resources to discharge its self-imposed disciplines. In the six years that I worked for ARCO Chemical, the criteria for a just business that I suggested in Chapter 8 (satisfying the requirements of shareholders, customers, employees and the public; obeying the law; observing due proportion between benefits and costs; building trust; recognizing reciprocal obligations) were not only met, but met in full. I shall refer later to instances which demonstrate that the company mission statement was integrated into the way in which we operated.

The ARCO Chemical mission statement is both general, in that it sets out an intent to pursue general virtuous goals, and also specific, in that it addresses issues of particular relevance for a chemical company, such as concern for health, safety and the environment. This is important because it illustrates the necessity for the leaders of a company to examine most carefully those issues that relate directly to the business in which it is engaged. Broad generalities must also be translated into specifics if they are to have any effect.

Principles

Even the best mission statements are, by themselves, of limited practical value. A claim that one intends to make the best widgets in the world gives little guidance on how it is to be done, or on the implications of that aspiration. Aspirations have to be translated into practical action to be achievable. So it is with the Christian seeking to express his faith in his daily life: how does one love God; how is one to love one's fellow human beings? In business, as in the life of faith, one does not proceed directly from statement of intent to a statement of what one is going to do at the factory bench, at the computer terminal, at the shop counter. The very process that we have considered at some length is a prerequisite, both in the life of faith and in the life of work. On our pyramid it is represented by the level of principles. The principles for a company flow, as for an individual, from the end-purpose of the activity. In the case of a company that purpose will be to offer service in a particular way, such as cooking hamburgers, manufacturing scalpels for brain surgery, or designing bicycles.

Our putative criteria for just business in the last chapter identified some general principles, based on reflection upon the relevance of fundamental virtues, to serve as broad criteria for business activity. The second tier of Figure 1 (principles) will generally relate even more precisely to the sector of business activity in which a company is engaged. I worked almost entirely in the oil and chemical industries. It requires little reflection to understand that companies operating in those fields have obligations with regard to health, safety and environmental considerations. As a consequence, we worked to carefully thought-through principles that reflected our very special responsibilities in these fields.

Let me again illustrate the point by quoting the principles that were derived from ARCO Chemical's mission statement with its broad aspirations regarding health, safety and environmental performance. The company principles were as follows:

- We will operate with the highest ethical standard and integrity, as individuals and as a company.
- We will operate in a safe and environmentally sound manner.
- We will work to achieve superior profit performance.
- We will operate our manufacturing plants as cost-effectively and efficiently as possible.
- We will strive for complete customer satisfaction.
- We will encourage innovation and creativity in all work.
- We will encourage and reward personal initiative and team effort.
- We will encourage career development and individual growth.
- We will comply with all laws and regulations governing our business.
- We will treat all vendors fairly and equally.

I do not cite these principles because I regard them as exceptional. But they do illustrate some very relevant points. First, it is not coincidental that ethical standards and concern for safety and the environment preceded the principle relating to profit performance. It was a matter of cardinal importance in ARCO Chemical that safety and the environment were priorities. On several occasions a letter to all employees from the company president made this quite explicit: 'In all cases, profit performance is secondary to operating safely, in an ethical and environmentally responsible fashion and observing all laws and regulations.'

Second, it is worth noting that compliance with the law is spelled out in the principles, but that it comes *after* the self-imposed principles. Third, the endeavour to achieve complete customer satisfaction is at the root of what the business organization endeavours to achieve. Fourth, no fewer than three of the ten principles relate to respect for people, notably treatment of employees. But perhaps the most significant feature, again, is the careful examination of the issues that related most directly to the business we were in. And the principles themselves may be readily likened to the traditional virtues.

For those engaged in banking or financial services a different set of priorities and challenges demand the formulation of principles relating to such matters as accuracy of records, probity in the handling of money and avoiding the exposure of clients to undisclosed financial risk. If we take food companies, it is clear that they have special concerns for hygiene, purity and health. Each business has its special concerns.

The identification and formulation of principles with emphasis upon particular concerns for a company mirrors the framework that an individual Christian develops. Some people may be subject to particular temptations; the food junkie, the highly sexed, the acquisitive, the domineering will all – under the promptings of Christian reflection and prayer – identify areas in life that call for special concern. Often an individual Christian may adhere to a particular principle in pursuit of a particular virtue – a more positive approach than simply addressing weaknesses. The process to which we are referring has traditionally been called 'the formation of conscience' in Christian moral vocabulary. The formation of a corporate conscience is a recognizable development for many companies, at the point where those who work together are able to exchange opinions on the principles to which they operate, thereby sharing in common purpose and values.

The formulation of company mission and the establishment of guiding principles by senior management are necessary steps before the preparation of a company code of ethics. In some spheres of business activity, notably the professions, the existence of codes of practice is of long standing. This has been a distinguishing strength of professional bodies. Professional codes of practice for lawyers, architects, engineers, etc. serve the dual purpose of setting out norms of conduct to which practitioners adhere and which clients can expect. Although they were not encapsulated in written codes, the standards adopted by Quaker businessmen were similarly codes of conduct that conformed to clear ethical principles. Earlier still, medieval guilds placed professional requirements upon their members, often with a content that reflected that age by including specifically religious as well as business elements.

Codes

As noted earlier, in 1986 I was one of a number of senior executives who established in the United Kingdom the Institute of Business Ethics (IBE). The Institute is now an independent charity, sustained by subscriptions from companies and individual members. It originated from the aspirations of a group of practising Christian business executives – the Christian Association of Business Executives (CABE). CABE's vision is to encourage the application of Christian principles in business. To promote the application of ethical standards in business generally, the early goal of the IBE was to encourage companies to formulate and apply codes of business ethics. As part of its programme to promote the adoption of codes of ethics, the Institute published a series of guides and commentaries.[5] This programme undoubtedly contributed in the United Kingdom to growth in the number of companies adopting codes of ethics. Surveys conducted by the Institute since 1986 show a steady increase in their use among larger companies, over half of whom now have statements or codes of some kind.

Figure 1 locates codes of practice immediately below principles. This reflects the fact that codes of practice are derived from principles. A code of business ethics will be based upon senior management's commitment in principle to the application of moral guidelines within the company – just as a code of environmental practice would be based upon a principle that sets out aspirations on performance in that field. A code of business ethics cannot be drawn up on its own – it is to be derived from the mission and principles articulated for the organization. Again, the analogy to a rule of life for Christians is appropriate. For the individual Christian, a rule of life is derived from beliefs and reflection upon these beliefs and it is unique to the individual. While rules of life will share many features, each individual formulates his or her own rule. So it is with companies. The code should be purpose-built and be derived from the principles that have been formulated as guidance for the organization.

The guides and commentaries published by the IBE set out in practical detail the processes whereby a company code can be prepared, adopted and applied within the organization. *Codes of Business Ethics: Why Companies Should Develop Them – And How* contains a valuable list of no fewer than 62 subjects that may involve ethical decisions. This list serves as a useful check to help those responsible for drawing up a code. It assists in ensuring that a code is comprehensive. Not all 62 subjects may apply for any particular company, of course. The extent of the list, however, strongly reinforces the view that business is not an amoral activity or a value-free zone. Ethical questions may arise in almost every sphere of business. This is not the place to repeat the checklists and illustrative codes offered by the IBE. Our present purpose is to establish the bases upon which ethical dilemmas may be tackled, no matter in which area of business activity they may occur.

It is at the next level down the pyramid that a company starts to translate the good intentions expressed in its mission, its principles and its codes into good practice – by the formulation of policies. Within a company a policy is more detailed and more prescriptive than a code of practice. For all employees adherence to company policies will be a condition of the contract of employment. The policies must therefore be sufficiently precise to enable any departure from them to be identifiable and, if appropriate, dealt with by disciplinary measures. For example, in the field of personnel or human resources, one would expect a company policy on, say, equal opportunity or remuneration to prescribe in detail requirements on how employees should be treated. Policies spell out a company's *modus operandi* in relevant fields and in nearly every instance will relate back to the principle(s) from which the policy is derived and upon which it is based.

The application of the code of ethics must, of course, be general across all company policy. One of its purposes is to ensure consistency of behaviour throughout the organization. It would be perverse to forbid racial or sexual discrimination in the marketing function but to allow it in the finance department. A requirement for honesty cannot be imposed in the human resources field but ignored by computer staff. The code of ethics binds all employees whatever their job, whereas other policies may be more specific to particular functions and apply in practice to limited numbers of employees.

Because of the nature of the code of ethics – its general applicability and the fact that its requirements, such as honesty or accurate record-keeping, may not relate directly to particular business goals – there is a risk that its provisions may not be as carefully implemented or observed by employees as the requirements set out in respect of specific functions, such as safety or recruitment. The preparation and adoption of a code of business ethics is just the first step in discharging a company's commitment to moral standards. Implementation must follow the same route as the application of any other company code, illustrated in Figure 1 by the bottom three levels: standards, procedures and monitoring.

Implementing the code

The IBE has also developed useful guidance for the implementation of a code. *Applying Codes of Business Ethics*, published in 1995, identifies the following twelve steps for implementing a code of business ethics:

- integration of the code into the running of the business;
- endorsement by the chairman and chief executive;
- distribution to all employees;
- breaches of the code – what to do when faced with a potential breach;
- personal response to the code by employees;
- affirmation of the code as a regular procedure;
- regular review;
- contractual adherence;
- training of employees in issues raised by the code;
- translation of the code into relevant languages;
- distribution to business partners;
- inclusion of the code in the Annual Report.

This checklist is a programme of best practice that the IBE commends to all companies. If applied systematically and conscientiously it will go a long way towards ensuring that the code is effectively integrated into company behaviour. The way in which each organization tackles the task of integration will, of course, vary from company to company and the IBE publication also contained five case studies in which different companies set out this experience and the features that were specific to their organization.

It is relevant to extend our analogy with the formation of Christian moral standards and their integration by the individual into his or her personal conduct. At both the institutional level of churches and chapels and also at the personal level of self-examination and the pursuit of a rule of life, Christian practice has enabled and assisted people to translate the aspirations to higher standards of conduct (what we have identified as virtues) into normal daily practice. Some of the steps identified by the IBE will resonate in this context. The personal response by employees is analogous to the private commitment by individual Christians; regular review is something conducted by many ways of self-examination and the adoption of disciplines – for example during Lent. For the individual Christian, the integration of the code – the pursuit of virtue – becomes part of his or her unconscious behaviour pattern. It is the formation of Christian conscience, the integration into our way of behaviour of the concept of virtue. This, in due course, can become a kind of conditioned reflex: an automatic trigger of sensitivity when one of the signposts – virtues or vices – enters the frame. The process can be likened to the pickling of an onion in vinegar! If the process is properly done it is impossible when eating to distinguish what is onion from what is vinegar.

Adoption of the steps outlined for companies by the IBE is a process whereby corporate conscience is formed and the code of ethics is integrated into the bloodstream of the company and all that it does. I offer some considerations on this process that are drawn from my own personal experience in my business career.

The first steps – director endorsement of the code and its distribution to all employees, together with notification that adherence to the code is a contractual requirement – are invariably carried through quickly and effectively. More difficult and often less well prepared are the other steps without which the code will simply not be integrated into the running of the business.

Some of the additional steps are not difficult to implement. For example, at Esso it was customary at the time of annual reviews of employee performance to raise the subject of the code and to seek the personal response of employees. This was further formalized by asking employees to confirm on a regular basis that they possessed, had read, and understood the code, and to sign a document to that effect. In ARCO Chemical it was additionally the practice for the chief executive regularly to write personally to each employee, elaborating upon aspects of the code or drawing attention to areas where adherence had become weak or needed fresh emphasis. At ARCO Chemical, the directors of the European regional operations regularly reviewed the code and discussed its relevance and whether it needed updating. At board discussions of operational matters, it was not uncommon for the president or a director to refer to provisions within the code.

As an example of board awareness and integration of the code into the running of the business, I recall an occasion when a new plant was under development for one of the factories. An environmental and safety issue arose: if an unusual surge of flammable gases occurred should they be vented to air or flared? The technical considerations were complex and the appropriate solution was not immediately evident. Time was short, however, and there was a lot of pressure to reach an early decision. The director concerned referred to the hierarchy of priorities within the ethics policy, which established that environmental and safety considerations had priority over profit considerations and the related requirement for a quick resolution. He needed time to reach a balanced decision. The incident clearly demonstrated the integration of our principles and code into the bloodstream of our business decision-taking. Furthermore, the relevant minutes of the board discussion explained the decision reached and gave an auditable record to explain the delay. Application of the code of ethics was a normal part of conducting business. But it is important to note that the example was set at senior management level.

The task of training within the company in order to ensure awareness and understanding of the code is, in my experience, something that is often omitted or done inadequately. There is evidence of a growing recognition of the need for awareness training and some companies look to external resources for assistance. What is indisputably true is that unless senior management regularly take soundings and put in place a clear action programme, the training will not happen and there will be a risk that employees are not aware of the provisions of the code or will not fully understand them. This risk is much greater if the company has international operations which entail cultural and linguistic barriers. The IBE publication *Codes of Ethics and International Business* examines approaches to these problems and sets out guidelines given by some international business organizations.

Again, it may be helpful to draw upon personal experience at the international level in ARCO Chemical. As a director of the European operation I was concerned with ensuring awareness and understanding across some twenty countries in Eastern, Central and Western Europe. Employees from these varying backgrounds shared the penumbra of a common Christian heritage which had been fractured and fragmented by many pressures: interdenominational disputes; linguistic and cultural diversity; frequent changes in national and judicial boundaries; the imposition of ideologies like fascism and communism as well as the onslaught of different philosophies, such as modernity and postmodernity.

It was the practice in the company to conduct regular surveys of employee opinions. One survey revealed that employees had less than adequate awareness and comprehension of the company ethics policy. It was therefore decided at board level that a number of steps were called for. The first and most obvious need was to ensure that the code was translated into the principal languages of the workforce. The company had not operated widely across Europe before the late 1980s and the text had been made available only in English. This was clearly unacceptable and translations were produced. As a footnote it is important to understand that simplistic translations can be misleading. For example 'ethics' is not directly translated by *l'éthique* in French without qualification. Translation must be sensitively and expertly done.

To raise employees' awareness of the code, we conducted a series of seminars across the company, aiming for a degree of cultural and linguistic homogeneity for each group. The company president initiated and attended the first seminar. This was important for emphasizing his personal commitment. I personally led the other seminars. Each seminar threw up new issues and revealed matters to be addressed. Sometimes these were straightforward, such as ensuring that all new employees were given a copy of the code on joining. This simple procedure had not always been followed. More seriously, it was clear that some kind of explanation of the code's implications was necessary for most employees after about six months in the company, when a better appreciation of specific issues enabled an informed discussion to take place.

Part of the seminar consisted of exploring the ethical dimensions of case studies based upon real events within the company. This session was linked to an invitation to employees to raise questions or matters of concern (to help in this part of the seminar, an external consultant was engaged). From these informal discussions we learned many useful things – for example, some employees had clearly not taken literally our policy that forbade deliberate falsehood: they felt it to be acceptable in some circumstances. From the findings of the seminars, a detailed action programme, approved by the board, was adopted for implementation across the regional operation.[6]

My purpose in describing the steps taken at ARCO Chemical is not to claim that our approach was in any way superior or a model to be

followed. It could perhaps be claimed that to carry out such a programme in the early 1990s was somewhat exceptional. Many of the
lessons that we learned and the actions that we took have been adopted
elsewhere and doubtless in more sophisticated and effective ways. The
general point which the example of ARCO Chemical illustrates is that in
order for a code of ethics to become effective it must be handled like any
other company policy: it must be managed. And the management
commitment must both start and end with senior management.

The ARCO Chemical illustration covers the three bottom levels of the
pyramid in Figure 1. Normal management practice can be applied to the
integration of a code of ethics into a company's operations. Sound
management of any activity calls for the specification of company standards. Standards are achieved by spelling out the correct procedures to
be followed. And of course, all management entails follow-up and
checking, the essential elements of the bottom level of the pyramid –
monitoring, audit, control. What ARCO Chemical was doing was
setting out its standards, following procedures to ensure that the standards were met, and then verifying that performance matched up. The
procedure was no different from that of running a shop or managing a
production process. The more qualitative nature of the requirements to
implement a code of ethics should not be allowed to cloud the validity
of good management practice.

Monitoring

Let me give examples for each of the bottom three levels of our hierarchy. A typical standard to give substance to a code of business ethics
would set out the accuracy and completeness required in financial
records. A procedure to sustain the ethics policy might be regular
systematic workplace discussions of ethical issues. The monitoring and
audit of business ethics policy must, of course, be located in the usual
internal and external audit functions. This is the normal way of ensuring that all policies are being observed. A further method for ensuring
proper adherence to the ethics policy is to build in the ethical dimension
as part of managerial reviews of all company operations. And of course
the employee survey conducted at ARCO Chemical was a further
example of monitoring and audit.

The commitment to an annual company report, which sets out the
company performance on its social and ethical commitments, has now
become normal practice for some companies. Shell is a notable example.
The requirement to make a public statement does, of necessity, impose

managerial discipline upon a company's application of its code of business ethics. It is a costly exercise and one that is beyond either the resources or the needs of smaller organizations. But it does demonstrate conclusively that the integration of a company's code of ethics into all aspects of its operations is no longer a pious hope, expressed imprecisely in a mission statement. Attention to every layer in Figure 1 treats the management of business ethics as a routine management task.

Over twenty centuries, there has been a tradition for individual Christians and Christians in communities such as monasteries or schools to adopt a disciplined behavioural pattern in order to pursue the virtues commended by tradition and practice. Typical standards might be observance of scrupulous honesty or acts of kindness towards neighbours. Procedures to assist in attaining standards are reflected in practices such as regular prayer, Bible reading or attendance at worship. In some Christian communities the monitoring and audit functions are conducted by confession while others call for examination of conscience or the sharing of witness.

Gradually for the individual, the integration of conscience into daily life becomes partially unconscious. A Christian with a formed conscience is alerted and aware when behaviour engages an area where temptation may arise. The individual only rarely at that point consciously calls to mind the precise virtue to be pursued or the vice to be avoided. It is largely done on auto-pilot.

The absorption of principles and guidelines into the bloodstream of a business is not, of course, a guarantee of perfection. The process of decision-making through a filter of internal values may still result in behaviour that is open to criticism. What the formation of conscience and the disciplined life offer is a greatly reduced risk of unthinking lapses from moral standards and also improved likelihood of greater consistency. The process of examination as a conditioned reflex has merit for those reasons, whatever the outcome may be.

A properly developed and managed culture of ethical awareness in a company offers similar benefits: an immediately available set of criteria and guidelines, reduction in the risk of delinquent behaviour, and attainment of consistency. In a modern world of perceived moral relativism and acute public sensitivity to corporate behaviour, these are strengths that will serve a company well.

Let me illustrate my point with another example drawn from personal experience in ARCO Chemical, which enabled the company to handle a potentially disastrous crisis by the application of integrated and built-in standards established through a well-developed code of business ethics.

The company manufactured intermediate chemicals, that is to say products which were sold to other companies who used them to produce goods for final sale to the consumer. Our company did not sell to the general public. Although most of our products were commodities, manufactured in large quantities to fairly broad specifications, we also produced a limited range of speciality products. One of these speciality products was used extensively as a carrying agent in a variety of applications – medicines, ingredients in foods and in cosmetics, etc. Obviously, for such sensitive uses the product had to be quite harmless for human beings, and it was manufactured to the very exacting safety and health standards demanded by the US pharmaceutical specifications, which allowed less than 0.5 per cent impurity.

As manufacturers of the product we sold through distributors and agents who in turn sold it to pharmaceutical, cosmetics and food companies who incorporated it into their products for sale to the public. A problem arose when one of the distributors returned a batch of our product having detected an unusual smell. The product was analysed and found still to be within specification. Within the demanding limits imposed, however, quantities were found of a chemical impurity, the properties of which had not been tested for ingestion by human beings. It was imperative immediately to analyse the nature of the impurity and to establish whether any risk to human health was involved.

The situation we faced posed dilemmas of a legal, commercial, operational and ethical nature. The essence of the ethical dilemma was this: should the general public be alerted that some of them might have used a product containing the impurity, the properties of which were unknown? Against this we had to set the possibility of unnecessarily alarming people, most of whom would be unaffected since the degree to which the impurity had occurred was not known. The ethical dilemmas were immediately recognized and the company code of ethics and the principles from which it was derived were scrupulously observed.

The crisis management team of senior managers immediately initiated an urgent action programme. All batches of the product were withdrawn, all distributors and end-use customers were notified, and a crash programme to analyse and test the impurity was put in place, together with a comprehensive risk assessment to examine every relevant factor in order to identify any further hazard and to evaluate the risks to those who might have been exposed to the impurity. Competitors and other manufacturers and users of the product were notified and kept informed as the nature of the impurity, and the causes of it became known.

One of the critical dimensions to the crisis was that of cost. Our code made this a straightforward matter: health and safety had priority over considerations of cost. At no stage was the possible cost of action allowed to constrain what we did. The general principles of transparency and reciprocity were observed throughout the crisis. Nothing was concealed and full disclosure of all relevant facts was made to all parties who needed to know. Respect for people demanded that every possible step was taken to protect health and well-being. The virtue of prudence was invoked, as at every stage we asked ourselves, 'Has the necessary action been taken as quickly and as comprehensively as possible to establish the facts and to act upon them?'

The decision-taking and implementation of the programme was carried out with great speed as the situation demanded. This was facilitated in large measure because we in the crisis management team were working to well-considered and clearly articulated principles, because everyone – from the company president down – was fully versed in those principles and committed to them, and because our priorities were absolutely clear. The company code of ethics and its principles were part of the company bloodstream. The bases on which our decisions were to be taken were already understood: we did not waste time or effort starting from a blank sheet. We drew immense strength from a well-formed company conscience.

The outcome of the crisis was mercifully benign. The impurity turned out to be harmless. It was established that storage conditions at the depot of one distributor had produced the unusual concentration. Major changes in procedures were adopted to prevent any reoccurrence. Competitors and other users of the product were notified and general standards and revised procedures adopted by the relevant trade association.

This incident was a very dramatic ethical dilemma. The very survival of the company was put in question. The answers to several key questions that arose were far from obvious. For example, there was no 'right' answer to the question, 'How many people should be told about the impurity?' Our decisions had to be rapid and very clear; loss of time or misunderstandings could have had catastrophic consequences. The five members of the senior crisis management team had to trust each other's judgement and competence. I am convinced that our task was made immeasurably easier because the company had addressed its moral responsibilities beforehand and had established a clear and effective framework for dealing with the situation.

Just as many a Christian who faces a dilemma acts partly by instinct or conscience, so our management team operated to well-understood and well-integrated concepts of the moral imperatives to be followed. A utilitarian, pragmatic imperative would, in my judgement, have been insufficient. In a moment of extreme crisis, it was principles based on the traditional virtues established over two millennia of Christian experience that was needed. Ethical principles in the company bloodstream were not a guarantee of a morally acceptable outcome but they made it considerably more likely.

Notes

1. For a perceptive analysis of this phenomenon by the historian Michael Howard, see his *The Invention of Peace: Reflections on War and International Order*, Profile Books, 2000.
2. Matt Ridley, *The Origins of Virtue*, Penguin, 1996.
3. See Francis Fukuyama, *Trust: The Social Virtues and the Creation of Prosperity*, Hamish Hamilton, 1995.
4. For examples of company mission statements see Jeffrey Abraham, *The Mission Statement Book*, Speed Press, 1995.
5. Publications by the Institute of Business Ethics on the preparation, adoption and application of codes are as follows: Simon Webley, *Company Philosophies and Codes of Business Ethics*, 1988; Simon Webley, *Business Ethics and Company Codes*, 1992; Simon Webley, *Codes of Business Ethics: Why Companies Should Develop Them – And How*, 1993; Simon Webley, *Applying Codes of Business Ethics*, 1995; Simon Webley, *Codes of Ethics and International Business*, 1997; Martin Le Jeune and Simon Webley, *Company Use of Codes of Business Conduct*, 1998; Julian Cummins, *The Teaching of Business Ethics*, 1999; Martin Le Jeune and Simon Webley, *Ethical Business – Corporate Use of Codes of Conduct*, 2002.
6. For a more extended description of the company's method of tackling the question of promoting our code across different countries, the reader may wish to consult the following: 'Prepare to Make a Moral Judgement', *People Management*, 4 May 1995; *Managing Best Practice no. 26: Managing Business Ethics*, Industrial Society, 1996.

♦ 10 ♦

Beyond codes of ethics

Chapter 9 looked at the process by which the mission and code of ethics of a business organization can be integrated into the bloodstream of its operations in ways not dissimilar to those whereby an individual Christian may form his or her conscience. For both organizations and individuals, sensitivity to areas where ethical issues are likely to occur can be heightened. These sensitive areas are more readily identified for organizations if its mission and code of ethics are established, as has been suggested, by drawing upon bases for moral reflection and guidance established within the Christian community over many centuries. We have thus gone a considerable way to narrowing the gap between the wellspring of Christianity and the secular activity of wealth creation. For the Christian engaged in serving fellow human beings through working in business, the narrowing of that gap is of great importance, placing the activity within the understanding and nurture of faith.

But Western Christendom is not a theocracy. As we have seen, the economic activities of wealth creation have long been secularized. Christian moral teaching is grounded in a set of principles that offer general guidance, but rarely precise instructions. In this respect the activity of wealth creation is no different from, say, the practice of medicine. Conduct is guided by Christian principle, not Christian regulation. Inevitably tensions occur, simple answers to moral questions are not always obtainable, and, as with our behaviour as individuals, differences in interpretation arise. Indeed as we noted at the outset, some instances of, say, the stimulation of new wants or the appeal to acquisitiveness and greed may challenge traditional teaching. Preceding chapters have attempted to put forward a framework whereby such issues can be tackled within the Christian ethos, not outside it. It would nevertheless be simplistic to consider business ethics just as a subset of Christian ethics and to assume that a code of ethics formulated in the way we have outlined will provide the means of resolving all moral issues.

Adoption and implementation of a statement of principles and of a code of business ethics for self-regulation is no guarantee that a company and those who work for it will thereafter conduct themselves in a manner that is beyond reproach. For a start, it is improbable that universal agreement can be reached on what our best aspirations might be in any given situation. But more fundamentally, it has to be recognized that, as human beings, we are destined to fall short of our own ideals. At the heart of moral debate lies a paradox. Although we appear to be uniquely endowed as a species with the capacity for abstract conceptualization of standards such as the virtues and to translate those concepts into meaningful guidance for action, we are unable to match them.

For the Christian, this is no reason for discouragement. In the person of Christ, the Christian sees a perfection towards which he or she will aspire. But the aspiration is qualified by recognition that we are unable to attain the highest virtue by our own unaided efforts. In traditional Christian theology this imperfection in our nature is encompassed in the doctrine of the Fall: a recognition that things are bound to go wrong because our highest ideals are accompanied by an in-built selfishness that will always frustrate our best endeavours. For the Christian the pursuit of virtue is indeed its own reward: in our present existence we do not achieve perfection. The endeavour to attain virtue enables the individual to share in Christ's own participation in our present condition. To strive for excellence is our response to the command to love God and our neighbour. It is one of the most valuable and enduring aspects of Christian understanding to recognize that our striving for virtue is worthwhile in its own right, regardless of the inadequacies that we bring to the task.

For a business organization it is not necessary to subscribe to a doctrine of fallen humanity. As we have seen, for a company the pursuit of the moral good has the merit both of being commonsensical and of concentrating company attention upon its true mission. At the most banal level, an organization will corporately recognize that its efforts to achieve the best standards will never attain perfection. There will always be a shop assistant who fails to help the customer adequately; the finest design for the goods a company makes can always be improved. But by concentrating upon excellence in such routine matters an organization is pursuing ideals. There is a tightly woven web of aspiration towards the good, irrespective of whether it is based on pragmatism, on principle or on both. In this respect there is some congruence between Christian aspiration and pragmatic business purpose.

When an organization abandons the challenge of continuous improvement, it may well consign itself to extinction. Just as in nature, there are inescapable pressures for continuous adaptation to ensure survival, so in the world of business, the effects of competition demand a never-ending search for improvement. That imperative applies not only to goods and services offered but also to corporate behaviour.

Of course, if the senior management of an organization is not committed to its longer-term survival, then the imperatives of continuous improvement and aspiration to higher performance have no significance, and a statement of principles and a code of ethics are without validity. For the Christian engaged in business the pursuit of excellence – or virtue – represents an inescapable challenge that does not have to be set down in a code of ethics. Sadly, for the senior management of a company the moral imperative is sometimes set aside even where a code of ethics exists.

The Enron case

At the beginning of the millennium, public confidence in company behaviour was badly damaged by serious failures at several large corporations such as WorldCom and Enron. The collapse of the US-based Enron Corporation in 2000 is a notable example of a company that did not match up to the rhetoric of its company code of ethics. Enron had produced a comprehensive code of business ethics. After the collapse it became clear that senior executives in the organization had paid little regard to its provisions.

Indeed, the Enron Corporation went so far as to suspend a clause in its code. The clause read as follows:

> No full-time officer or employee should own an interest or participate, directly or indirectly, in the profits of any other entity which does business with or is a competitor of the Company, unless such ownership or participation has been previously disclosed in writing to the Chairman of the Board and Chief Executive Officer of Enron Corporation and such officer has determined that such interest or participation does not adversely affect the best interests of the Company.

At a board meeting in the autumn of 2000 it was agreed to suspend this clause and to allow the Chief Financial Officer (CFO) of Enron to run certain partnerships with other entities. The CFO, without reference to the board, further delegated the job to a subordinate. This act of suspending a clause in a company code of business ethics is probably without precedent. By any yardstick, it is difficult to see how it can be acceptable to suspend a moral principle that has been established and made public. It would be difficult to reconcile this with the criteria for just business that were put forward in Chapter 8. It is an extreme example of a case in which an individual Christian would find conflict between his faith and his job.

The circumstances surrounding the collapse of Enron have been extensively examined and reveal a culture in which behaviour such as bullying, misrepresentation and dishonesty was endemic. Law-breaking and accounting irregularities occurred at Enron to an extent that indicates that its senior executives treated the code of ethics as no more than a camouflage of corruption. It is difficult to avoid the conclusion that the code was little more than cynical insincerity. Little effort appears to have been made to bring the standards of the code into the bloodstream of the company's operations. As Groucho Marx quipped, 'If you can fake sincerity you've got it made.' The top executives at Enron certainly drew great material and social benefits for themselves under the cloak of sincerity and a code of business ethics. It was a particularly flagrant and immensely damaging instance of saying one thing and doing another. The senior management at Enron had no concern for the survival of the organization, nor serious regard for the principles they had publicly stated.

We all know from personal experience that failure to live up to our higher principles is not uncommon. We all do it. But it is unusual to find it done systematically. We fall short most often because of one-off lapses, because of inattention or carelessness. And so it is with businesses which, after all, are made up of communities of human beings. For the individual to lower his or her standards on occasion will generally be a private matter – something to be resolved within that individual's own conscience. When the inconsistency between behaviour and principle becomes public, so that friends or neighbours or colleagues notice it, the individual will then behave more consistently and be less tempted to cut corners deliberately. Adam Smith's observation that we all seek the approval of our fellows becomes a strong motivating factor.

Companies have very good business reasons to be seen to behave consistently – particularly in those areas where moral issues may arise. The public – shareholders, customers, legislators, employees, suppliers and many other groups that deal with the organization – react unfavourably to inconsistency in behaviour. It eats away at trust, the cement for all business dealings. It is for this reason, if for no other, that a company will rarely make a public statement of principle and then proceed deliberately to flout it. Enron is an unusual case. And as we know, Enron collapsed spectacularly, publicly and with humiliation and disgrace for those responsible. There is no long-term future for a business that behaves inconsistently and disregards the need for trust in its dealing with others. To that extent our criterion of promoting trust, with its underlying virtues of probity, transparency and accuracy, is not just an ideal: it serves sound business purposes.

Enron offers an interesting case study with regard to the effectiveness of external regulation or self-regulation. Enron appears to have abused its code of ethics as a cover for unacceptable behaviour. Senior management fell seriously short of self-regulation. The particular nature of much of the abuse that occurred at Enron related to its accounting practices. The company engaged in practices which meant that its financial statements were false or misleading. As far as I am aware Enron's accounts nevertheless complied with the applicable US accounting standards. The accounting rules of the United States at that time comprised some 4,530 pages of text. So although Enron executives were grossly deficient in self-regulation they nevertheless were able to comply with extremely demanding formal external regulation. Yet the sheer volume of regulation, in the absence of self-regulation, proved ineffectual in preventing fraud. The point is, I hope, abundantly clear: regulation and self-regulation go hand in hand. There is a clear resonance with the injunctions of Christ to go beyond formal adherence to the law.

No codes or statements of principle provide a safeguard against deliberate abuse and determination to deceive. This is true both of individuals and of groups of people such as business corporations. Private personal lowering of standards is less easily detectable, however. If I lie or cheat, I am the only person who is immediately aware as I do it. When a company sets out to deceive, it requires collusion. The Enron example showed that collusion happens – but experience tells us that it is more difficult to deceive when more than one person is involved. Trust among thieves is notoriously fragile. Moreover, when a company sets out its aspirations and its standards clearly and publicly, a much greater degree of collusion is needed to circumvent them. If standards are loosely stated and carelessly applied, it is easier for misbehaviour to pass unremarked.

A clear statement of business ethics within a corporation not only establishes a standard but also sharpens awareness if the standard is breached. Even at Enron, where a climate of disregard for its own publicly stated principles seems to have become endemic, the misbehaviour sounded alarm bells for some individuals within the organization. Their sensitivities were aroused by the perception that principle and practice were not consistent. It was for this reason that a senior executive at Enron voiced concern at what was going on. Enron had a whistle-blower.

Whistle-blowing

The act of raising concern about malpractice within an organization is commonly known as whistle-blowing. If an employee has concerns about wrongdoing there is a choice of three options in dealing with the situation: silence; raising the matter internally; bringing the matter to the attention of outsiders such as the media or the police. It is gradually becoming the practice in most developed countries to put in place legislation to protect whistle-blowers (for example in the United Kingdom the Public Interest Disclosure Act of 1999 is widely seen as establishing a benchmark for public interest whistle-blowing). The question of protection is a two-way street. Just as the whistle-blower should be safeguarded against penalization for raising uncomfortable matters, so too an organisation needs protection against malicious or false allegations. These are not easy issues to resolve.

Whistle-blowing does not have an encouraging history. There are several well-known examples of individuals who have drawn attention to corporate misdoing and who have suffered personally for having done so. For example Christine Casey, an employee with the toy-maker Mattel, became concerned that the company appeared to make exaggerated forecasts of sales which in turn might lead to misrepresentation of company earnings projections. Ms Casey drew her problem to the attention of senior management and suggested ways to fix the problem, but the response was not encouraging: her duties were changed and she received negative performance reviews. She left the company's employment and in 2000 filed suit against Mattel for constructive discharge (unfair dismissal). The judge ruled against her. Essentially she was not protected by whistle-blower laws on the grounds that she had made proposals to senior management rather than explicit complaints. US laws prescribe stiff penalties for retaliation against whistle-blowers, but they do not always offer full protection, as this example seems to demonstrate.

This experience is not confined to business corporations, of course. Whistle-blowers in, for example, the European Union have found their careers damaged and in some cases terminated because they drew attention to abuse. There is, sadly, an all-too-common instinct within organizations to reject the agent who raises uncomfortable matters because that is seen as a threat to the established pattern.

The prospective whistle-blower may not wish to seek a martyr's crown. It is therefore important in the context of business ethics that ways are found to address this issue. For the employee who feels discomfort with company behaviour and who wishes to raise the issue for consideration, mechanisms should be in place to enable this to be done without fear of reprisal. The virtue of justice, enshrined in the criterion of the acceptance of legitimate authority, demands nothing less.

Drawing upon experience in my own business career, I believe that a code of ethics can be made integral to company operations in a variety of ways. Some of the simplest and most obvious aspects of such good practice can provide the opportunity for employees to raise concerns. For example, the regular discussion and recognition of the code, as practised in Esso, gives the opportunity for an employee to raise matters of concern routinely and regularly with his or her superior or manager. This is particularly important at the time of employee performance appraisal, as a discipline both for the employee and the supervisor. If the problem that the employee wishes to raise involves the supervisor directly (who may be perceived by the employee as the key element in the breach of the code) then obviously an alternative way to raise the matter should be available. A variety of solutions exist. In providing channels for employees, it is important to take account of sensitivities that are wider than the company culture. For example, I found that in Germany employees were uncomfortable with the idea that they might take such a problem to the supervisor's own manager, that is, to go over his or her head. To do so perhaps offended against the German employees' sense of trust and loyalty. Again, in the Netherlands, employees favoured group or communal forums in which some issues might be addressed, rather than resorting to more formal procedures.

In the previous chapter, we noted that audit, controls and monitoring are basic disciplines that good management will integrate into a company's operations. The audit and control function should go far beyond the traditional concepts of merely checking the company records to ensure that proper records are maintained and that correct accounting procedures are followed. Both internal and external audits are now seen to have a wide remit to examine adherence to all company policies – and that includes the application of its ethics policy. The external audit, although it notably failed in the Enron case, is none the less a valuable vehicle for addressing delicate matters that are not necessarily covered by a rule-book. I recall that when I worked for Shell in Africa, as an internal auditor, I was concerned that some senior managers were treating company property in the company accommodation for expatriates as though it belonged to them personally. It was a very delicate matter to raise with one's superiors and I got round doing so by involving the external auditors; their more independent role enabled them to deal more easily with the issue. In some organizations today, external agencies are invited to conduct social audits that may extend to evaluation of how adequately its ethical standards are being met. There are even external standards against which performance may be formally measured, such as the Ethical Compliance Standards ECS2000.

For many companies it has become standard practice to offer a 'hot line' that a concerned employee may use to raise ethical concerns. At the time I worked in Esso, the hot line was handled by the company secretary/senior legal adviser. At ARCO Chemical, the company offered two options. The first was a confidential interview with the senior legal adviser. But for those who felt that an internal colleague or employee was an inappropriate person to handle delicate matters, an external consultant was available whose brief was to guard the anonymity of the employee unless authorized to disclose his or her identity. The consultant was then charged with bringing the matter to the attention of the company president in conditions of strict confidentiality. It has to be recognized, however, that the existence of 'hot lines' or other channels for voicing concerns is not an entirely satisfactory solution to the problem. Anecdotal evidence suggests that employees do not have great trust that their anonymity will be preserved or that complaints will always be treated in confidence.

The no-blame culture

What is particularly important is to establish a 'no-blame culture' where freedom to raise sensitive issues is normal. At ARCO Chemical, where I worked for seven years, we tried to create an open no-blame environment. This is perhaps illustrated by an example in the field of safety.

As a company engaged in the manufacture and distribution of chemical products, ARCO Chemical was acutely sensitive to issues of employee and public safety. The processes by which we manufactured our products were delicate and, if not conducted with due care, potentially extremely dangerous. Although it experienced one very serious explosion, entailing loss of life, at a factory in the United States (when critical but unrelated system failures within the plant occurred at the same time) the company otherwise had a very good safety record across its operations. Our objective was to anticipate and prevent accidents in an environment which was already almost accident-free. The company adopted a detailed programme to persuade employees to report any near misses that might have become or have led to accidents. This necessitated honesty on the part of employees in admitting mistakes, or even failures to observe safety procedures. For employees to do this, a climate of no blame is essential. On the basis of near-miss reports, it was possible gradually to build up a profile of the situations that were potentially the most hazardous and risk-prone so that these could be addressed by corrective measures *before* the accident occurred.

A similar culture of no blame is necessary before employees can be encouraged to support the code of ethics and its implementation. The climate of openness and discussion is essential if company standards and principles are to become its conscience and effectively to influence the conduct of employees and of the company itself.

In Chapter 8 we noted the importance of openness and transparency in the creation of trust, one of the criteria for just business. It is regrettably a characteristic of much business practice to disregard the virtue of openness. Only too often dubious excuses of confidentiality and the protection of proprietary information are used as the pretext for secretiveness and even deception. A degree of openness is essential if honesty is to be observed in many situations. For the Christian in business this is an area for concern.

The importance of process

No system of regulation, whether internal or external, can safeguard against calculated wrongdoing or mistreatment of those whistle-blowers who draw attention to it. Even the full force of law in a modern state is unable to deter systematic and collaborative misbehaviour. Internal codes and procedures for self-regulation are not a foolproof defence against the determined wrongdoer. The most that one can claim is that consistent self-regulation establishes a climate in which wrongdoing will be more readily identified and dealt with.

A more fundamental issue than that of calculated misbehaviour must be addressed as part of our examination of the case for self-regulation within business. In the grey areas in which moral dilemmas arise, it is often far from obvious what the morally acceptable course of action should be. Choosing between right and wrong is not difficult. Dilemmas arise when one is required to choose between conflicting goods. A simple example may illustrate that 'right' answers are not always obvious. Returning from a prolonged business trip I was faced with a serious delay in my flight. The airline in question was most apologetic and as recompense offered an *ex gratia* payment to all delayed passengers. In due course a cheque for £25 arrived at my home. A minor ethical dilemma arose. Should I pocket the money on the grounds that it was I who had suffered the inconvenience, or should I hand over the money to my company since my air fare had been paid by them? I leave it to the reader to decide what was the appropriate action to take. I think that an ethically acceptable case can be made for either option.

At a more serious level, let me refer back to the dilemma that faced the senior management of ARCO Chemical in the situation described in the previous chapter, when impurity was detected in a product used in sensitive health and food applications. It was by no means obvious at the time the crisis occurred which course of action was the most ethically acceptable. Take, for example, the question of how many people should be informed about the possible health risk that had arisen, and at what stage they should be told. At one extreme it was possible to argue that – given our lack of knowledge about the impurity that had been found in our product – we should have disclosed the problem only when we were in a position to recommend action to put matters right. This course of action commended itself on grounds of reduced cost, because it greatly increased our ability to retain control of the situation (particularly with respect to the popular media) and also because – as turned out to be the case – there was possibly no serious cause for alarm. The other extreme would have been to make a full-scale public announcement at once and to hand the problem over to the public authorities (and the media!). This would have avoided any accusation of cover-up and would have shared responsibility for future action very widely.

Needless to say there were many other factors which weighed heavily in our deliberations and which militated against either of the two extremes. Because we were working to a set of integrated values that were incorporated into management decision-taking, we were able to test our deliberations against clear and well-tried criteria. At the simplest level we were able to examine our thinking against a utilitarian consideration (how we could achieve the greatest good for the greatest number); against the Golden Rule (to do to others what we would have them do to us in comparable circumstances); against the legal requirements to be met in the different jurisdictions under which we operated. But these criteria demanded further analysis and qualification – which is where the company's own principles and code were applied. We gave due weight to factors such as respect for people; the priority of health and safety over financial considerations; the requirement for transparency and openness at all times; honesty and truthfulness. The close relationship of these considerations to the key virtues emphasized in Christian moral teaching discussed in previous chapters is clear. We are employing the same concepts and vocabulary. The ARCO Chemical management team dealing with the crisis reached conclusions that were consistent with these virtues and also met the demands of our corporate conscience. Information was freely and immediately given to any party – supplier, customer, agent or competitor – whose use of the product required them to take immediate precautionary steps.

Although it is possible that other managers, working to a code of ethics formulated in a different company, might have reached somewhat different conclusions, I firmly believe that the decisions we took would have commanded very wide assent. Though the classic virtues may not be absolutes, they embody sufficient wisdom, experience and general consent to enable those who follow them to reach conclusions that meet most moral criteria. The example I have used is an extreme one that carried enormous implications of health and safety and raised a multitude of moral questions to be answered. The ability of ARCO Chemical's senior management to handle the crisis was based upon immersion in a well-tried value system.

It follows from the argument I have put forward that the *process* by which a business tackles ethical concerns is of fundamental importance. The formation of corporate conscience is more complex than the formation of individual conscience. In the previous chapter we looked at the institutional procedures by which it may be done. The fact remains that a company is legally a separate entity from those who own it or work for it. So wherein lies the responsibility? In the UK officers responsible for the company can be held to be its 'controlling mind': if they act criminally, the company is criminally liable. But in many instances it is too complex to determine which managers constitute the controlling mind and whether they acted criminally as individuals. The establishment of a corporate culture of ethical principles helps to address this difficulty.

The potential ambiguities in the field of corporate responsibility, with the attendant legal difficulties that may arise, are sometimes used by individuals to avoid responsibility. If the legal situation is vague, it is difficult to determine where responsibility lies. Christian understanding is that we are all accountable to God and this presents a tension that is difficult to resolve satisfactorily.

Despite the examples of corporate misbehaviour that command media attention, such as Enron or WorldCom, observation tells us that most companies behave according to broadly acceptable ethical standards over long periods. Companies, large or small, that establish a good reputation will do so through the consistent application of principles and standards that are shared among employees and those who have dealings with the company. The formal articulation of these principles and a conscious endeavour to integrate them into everyday operations will serve a company well, especially in the postmodern climate of relativism and uncertainty. Only when important virtues have been embedded in the corporate culture can senior management begin to have confidence that due process will be followed when inevitable moral issues arise in the course of business.

It is the responsibility of management to maintain the value of a business in *all* respects, not just the value reflected in share price or in profit. It has long been accepted that goodwill is a true value of a business, and that the reputation that derives from adherence to a clear moral framework is an essential component of goodwill.

For the Christian, the concept of goodwill and the value of a reputation for adherence to virtue resonates strongly with traditional teachings. In the Old Testament we read of the esteem in which the virtuous person is held and how that virtue is derived from reflection upon the understandings offered by faith. In the New Testament, the Beatitudes and the Sermon on the Mount offer substantive encouragement for the pursuit of virtue. It is a matter of sadness and regret that the flow of Christian moral reflection that has served to guide individuals over the centuries has been so brutally ruptured with regard to their participation in the world of wealth creation. Countless individuals have followed the call to a better life anchored in pursuit of the virtues. The same process is available for the conduct of business.

Social responsibility

Much of our discussion up to this point has been concerned with the ethical implications of the purpose of wealth creation and the manner in which it is conducted. The formalization of business morality along the lines we have put forward, with its model in the formation of the individual Christian conscience, has the power to build a coherent basis for addressing ethical dilemmas as they occur. Although the process does not offer the certainty of perfect outcomes, it greatly reduces the risk of worse ones.

We all know from our daily experience that our behaviour invariably has consequences that go beyond our immediate intentions. The unintended consequences may range from the trivial (I reach for more peas to put on my dinner plate and upset a glass of drink over the table) to the serious (I park my car and a child emerges from behind it to cross the road and is knocked down by a motorist whose view was obscured).

It is the same with business. The most diligent consideration of the aims of wealth creation and the way it is carried out cannot take full account of the consequences. Serious attention to the principles embodied in virtue ethics will greatly clarify intentions and purposes within a sound moral framework by vividly focusing minds upon proper behaviour. But all human activity involves change: it is an inescapable outcome of our creative urge. And of no human activity is this more true than our engagement in wealth creation through the conduct of business. Every act of creation that we undertake entails some degree of change and sometimes destruction. Much of this change falls into the category of unintended consequences. There is, in fact, a spectrum of outcomes of our business activity which ranges from the deliberate (metal is mined, processed, converted into a utilitarian object) to the partially deliberate (a chemical process manufactures a specified product but also produces waste) to the totally unintended (the use of asbestos to insulate a building is found, years later, to have created a health hazard). Unintended outcomes may be beneficial or damaging.

There is, of course, nothing exceptional about this. We know that despite the apparent order in our universe, at one level it is based upon chance. Quantum theory tells us that if we know where a particle is located we cannot know the speed and direction of its movement. The behaviour of our world at certain levels is unpredictable. And so it is with wealth creation.

As the impact of businesses has grown, so it has become apparent that those engaged in business cannot disregard the social and other consequences of what they do. Among the first instances of this were the damaging social and environmental consequences of the industrial revolution. We have looked at the political response to the problems that arose and how contemporary Christian conscience sometimes espoused a socialist solution. We have now learned that public ownership and intervention may ameliorate these problems but do not solve them. The free-market system has shown great resilience in its varying forms and at the present time remains the primary and most successful vehicle for the creation of serious, widely distributed wealth. It is with the consequences of that system that much of our moral discussion is concerned.

Stakeholding

The so-called stakeholder debate was prompted by those who argued that business has responsibilities towards many groups in society – notably to employees, to customers, to suppliers and indeed to the general community. In its extreme form, stakeholder theory argued that such responsibilities should be formally determined. Others argued that businesses had responsibilities solely to shareholders. The debate stimulated much study and a number of interesting initiatives.[1]

This is not the place to debate the merits or demerits of stakeholder theory. As a practising businessman it never occurred to me that any company for which I worked could disregard the various sections of society which its activities brought it into contact with. But it is obvious that a company that disregards, for example, the concerns and interests of its customers will not long stay in business. It is no different if a company does not establish good relationships with other groups. Certainly the three major organizations for which I worked (Shell, Esso, ARCO Chemical) took those relationships very seriously and ensured that they were conducted according to the principles of reciprocity, one of the suggested criteria for just business. It is important to understand that in addition to providing goods and services to the community, a company may also make demands upon it. Recognition of those demands and some kind of appropriate recompense is called for under the principle of reciprocity.

Stakeholder theory is relevant to our discussion of business ethics primarily because it highlights the wider moral obligations that a company should address within its corporate ethos. While the moral bases for a company's objectives and how it operates relate strongly to internal concerns, the moral imperatives regarding the outcomes of business activity cover a much wider field – the impact upon society itself.

Corporate Social Responsibility (CSR)

Christianity has emphasized certain duties towards our fellow human beings. For example the parable of the Good Samaritan encourages a broad interpretation of the obligation to do good to our neighbour. It follows from the principles that we considered in Chapter 8 as putative criteria for the just business that companies cannot disregard the wider role they play in the community. In particular, the criterion of reciprocity demands attention to the impact of business upon the community in which it operates. Of course, many aspects of this issue are addressed through the civic, fiscal and judicial systems. Nevertheless, as we have argued, laws and regulations are never comprehensive and cannot handle those more imprecise matters that demand a moral, not a legal, response. Because in Western Europe there is a strong tradition of state intervention, in that part of the world there is a temptation to argue that business responsibility is discharged entirely through conformity to what the state requires – paying taxes, meeting regulatory requirements and so on. In North America, where there is much greater distrust of the state, a wider field for company discretion in the field of social action has traditionally obtained. This tradition was at its most robust in the last century with the philanthropy of extremely wealthy entrepreneurs such as Rockefeller and Carnegie who endowed foundations with huge funding to carry out socially beneficial work.

In the 1980s, with a renewed enthusiasm for free-market capitalism in Western Europe – and especially in the UK – there was a move to greater participation by the private sector in tackling social problems. This reflected a general reassessment of where the interface lay between public and private sector. In the early 1980s, Business in the Community, a UK organization of which I was a director for some years, was set up specifically to encourage companies to put expertise and resources into tackling social issues. That period saw a major renewal of private sector involvement in what had come to be seen as exclusively the work of government – urban renewal, skills training, environmental conservation and preservation, support for culture and the arts, education and teaching, to name but a few examples.

The debate about the extent to which business should diversify its efforts away from its primary role of making goods or providing services remains open. In 2001 David Henderson, a distinguished economist, wrote a resounding critique of CSR, arguing that it dilutes management concentration upon its job and risks impairing company performance.[2] Against Henderson's viewpoint, it can be seen that many companies engage constructively in social activities and do so to the benefit of both the wider community and themselves. A well-thought-through statement of principles will enable a company to identify those areas where commitment to, say, justice, or respect for human beings may call for a particular response and action.

Here are several examples drawn from my own experience. Esso in the UK had a strong commitment to responsible use of energy and it was therefore quite consistent for the company to support work in that field, helping to install good insulation in poor housing, for example. People for whom proper home insulation was most difficult were those who were relatively poor. Esso's resources were deployed both to address energy conservation and also to ameliorate the condition of people living in poor housing. Again, in high-tech companies, dependent on well-qualified employees to carry out complex technical work, it was a straightforward matter to put into practice a moral commitment to training and educating employees by offering support to technical educa-tion institutions. Similarly, at ARCO Chemical, where we celebrated the diversity of the national and ethnic backgrounds of our employees, it was rational to donate a high-level language teaching laboratory for use by local schools.

It is not difficult for a business organization to examine where the sensitive interfaces lie between its commercial activities and the wider community within which it operates. Just as the code of ethics will emphasize the areas of greatest sensitivity for a business, so thoughtful examination of concerns about proportionality and reciprocity will iden-tify points at which the company interacts with the community in deli-cate areas and where special responsibilities may arise.

In the 1970s and 1980s, when I worked in the middle management of Esso, the oil industry was subject to huge pressure to simplify and to reduce the costs of its operations. Failure to control costs and to ration-alize operations would have put at risk the very survival of the company. Many of these pressures were the consequence of competition within the industry, which in turn was greatly increased by upheavals in the world supply of oil and the effects of the OPEC cartel of oil-producing coun-tries. As part of the Esso response to these pressures many of the storage depots that it operated across the UK were no longer needed (primarily because of improved methods of distribution and changes in demand for the different oil products supplied by the company). Closing work locations is very painful and difficult. Employees are made redundant; there are knock-on effects in the local community; equipment and facilities have to be dismantled and sites restored for other possible uses.

The application of company principles in such situations becomes a matter for serious management consideration. For example, what does 'respect for people' mean in a situation where employees are no longer needed in the jobs they do? At Esso, management sought to reconcile principle with economic necessity. In most instances, when a depot or plant was scheduled for closure a long-term plan was devised, sometimes extending over two years. During that time employees were helped to find other work either within or outside the organization; training schemes were supported for those who wished to acquire new skills; favourable terms were made available for those who chose to take early retirement; support was provided for diversification in communities where local unemployment was high. As a consequence of these measures, the number of employees who experienced redundancy was minimal. The human dimensions were managed with regard to company commitments to the principles it had articulated for treatment of employees and its commitment to the communities in which the company operated.

The critic of business will probably argue that a large, wealthy company such as Esso was so profitable that it could easily afford to act generously and that in doing so it was merely paying 'conscience money'. One can accept the validity of such views. I would argue, however, that if Esso had not managed its business successfully it would have generated insufficient resources to deal with the problem in a humane way. A key duty for a business is to be financially competent. Furthermore, although the term 'conscience money' is used as a term of opprobrium, I would argue – it is one of the themes of this book – that the development of corporate conscience is a desirable goal. Awareness of special responsibility is the mark of conscience and not a sign of moral turpitude.

Considerations such as those mentioned illustrate that the remit for business is not confined, as Milton Friedman contended, simply to the furtherance of immediate business goals. Just as individuals recognize the importance of relationships with other human beings, so businesses must address these relationships and establish a moral framework for dealing with them. At the personal level we cannot relate to the amoral person. Similarly the wider community cannot accept an amoral basis for the behaviour of business. This is one of the points of tension between the processes of wealth creation and the criteria that underpin Christian moral understanding. Just as John Donne, the seventeenth-century dean of St Paul's, observed that no man is an island, so it should be understood that no business can disregard its effect upon the wider community in which it operates.

It is nevertheless important to emphasize the need for balance in the area of corporate responsibility. Companies are not required by the nature of what they do to act philanthropically. If the owners of a business wish to dispense largesse without regard to the company's business objectives, they should do so only under limited circumstances. Whenever a company engages in activities that are not business-related, it should do so only with the prior consent of shareholders, whose resources are being used in this way. The business case for the expenditure should be made clear. If a company's owners wish to set aside resources for addressing social issues which are not business-related, it is generally preferable to do so by the establishment of an independent trust with clear purposes and charitable status. The establishment of a trust or foundation avoids potential for conflicts of interest. It retains the company's clarity of purpose, uncomplicated by considerations of societal benefit that are not related to the business.

International considerations

Because modern business is all-pervasive, the breadth of societal issues that impinge upon a company is bound to increase. The case of Shell's involvement in Nigeria illustrates the point. In the 1990s Shell was obliged to recognize a wider duty to the local community, since the Nigerian government was engaged in unacceptable behaviour that was perceived to have been sustained by Shell.

The international nature of much business activity raises many issues similar to those which faced Shell in Nigeria. As companies locate manufacturing facilities in developing countries they are called upon to address such questions as child labour, comparative wages and working conditions for employees in those countries and employees in the developed world, comparative standards for health and safety, and the treatment of bribery and corruption. The huge disparities in living standards across the world cannot simply be ignored and multinational businesses are obliged to address them and to formulate a response. We shall look at some of the questions raised by the so-called phenomenon of globalization in the next chapter.

As always, the response by a company to these issues will be based on its own operating principles and will also recognize the demands made upon it by public opinion. Experience has repeatedly demonstrated that the behaviour of a company working to its own considered principles will be less vulnerable to criticism than that of a company which conducts itself with no due consideration of moral concerns. Marks & Spencer, the UK retailing chain, offered an interesting example of this when it was accused of selling goods manufactured by child labour. The company had always worked to very high ethical standards. Undoubtedly its standing with customers was high and, at that time, it was consistently identified in public opinion polls as a company commanding public respect in all it did. Nevertheless, when allegations were raised that it was profiting from the exploitation of child labour, the company engaged in a thorough review of its purchasing policies and found it necessary to set out clear guidelines to ensure that such practices were avoided.

Cross-cultural aspects of business ethics, such as relative labour conditions, health and safety standards, and financial probity, will always be sensitive areas for companies that operate internationally. It is not possible to set out rigid rules by which such concerns can be resolved. To pay developed-world wages in developing-world economies is not feasible: a country's economic structure could be put at risk. Likewise, it might be that application of certain rigorous environmental standards in a developing country could compromise the development of a major potential source of wealth for that community. For the international company, each situation must be judged separately in the light of the principles it has established.

The first commitment of a business is to be financially successful. Unless it is, it will not have the resources to enable it to work to its principles. At ARCO Chemical it was judged incompatible with our health and safety policies to apply different standards in different countries. This was a very expensive principle to apply and was only made possible by the financial good health of the company. Similarly, when ICI took the decision in Pakistan that it would not tolerate bribery, it did so in recognition of a potential cost to the company.

The application across different cultures of principles embodied in company policy is never easy, and requires considerable time. Commitment to equal opportunity for all employees may, for example, require patient and sensitive handling in certain cultures where women and men are treated differently as a fundamental feature of the culture. In extreme cases a business may be obliged to cease operation rather than compromise. It might well be argued that pursuit of equal treatment on a gradualist basis might serve the moral imperative more effectively in the long run. History is still unable to reach a clear conclusion on the famous example of companies that operated in South Africa under apartheid. Some companies withdrew; other companies remained and tried to influence conditions. No doubt both courses of action contributed in different ways to the eventual change in attitudes and laws in the country.

At various points in this chapter I have pointed to the benefits that accrue to a company that publicly sets out its principles and puts in place mechanisms to ensure that they are adhered to – establishing and maintaining a good reputation, building trust and acceptance among those who engage with the company, and securing and perpetuating the consent of wider society for the company to go about its business. All these are crucial to the success of a business.

These benefits are intangible: they do not figure as quantified items in the financial accounts of a company. This raises the question whether adherence to ethical standards translates into measurable benefits for a business.

In an ideal world virtue should be its own reward. We pursue what we believe to be good for its own sake. In the world of business, an organization may set out its principles as goals to be pursued for their own sake and a sound company mission and code of ethics reflect that aspiration. As we have seen, many of those principles are shaped by the culture of the communities in which companies operate. We have argued for a more positive consideration of the principles refined within the Western Christian culture to underlie the principles applied in business. Society's permission for a company's licence to operate will be conditional upon adherence to certain accepted and generally recognized standards. Well-embedded codes of ethics undoubtedly contribute to securing that consent.

The purpose of business, however, is not to offer models of behaviour. Companies exist to provide goods and services and, in doing so, to furnish rewards for the owners of the business. If the goods and services are not provided to satisfactory standards, or if the operation fails to provide rewards for its owners, then a company will cease to exist. There is an urgent imperative upon a business organization to perform efficiently. Whereas for individuals in our societies the consequences of misfortune or failure will be mitigated by some kind of social support system (the sick are cared for; the unemployed receive benefits) it is unusual for society to offer such assistance to companies that fall upon hard times. It will occur only in very special circumstances, most commonly where the business concerned is providing goods or services that are essential to society, such as transport or clean water. If society is obliged to offer support, it does so only under certain conditions. In extreme cases, of course, the condition may be transfer of ownership to society by way of nationalization.

Given these imperatives under which a company has to operate, it is legitimate to ask whether awareness of ethical considerations and efforts to integrate them into the business will assist in securing economic success. Does good business ethics pay its way?

Does ethical behaviour pay?

This question illustrates some discontinuity between Christian teaching and the motivations that drive business. For the Christian, the pursuit of virtue is an end in itself: it is done without seeking further reward. Business is not like that. It is carried out in order to gain reward for the effort expended. Is the pursuit of virtue in business in conflict, therefore, with the pursuit of reward?

There are, of course, many factors that will affect the economic performance of a business, some of which are beyond the ability of the company to influence. It is very difficult to isolate the particular effects of any one factor upon performance. If we take the case of ARCO Chemical, for which I worked, it was undoubtedly true that its proprietary ownership of ground-breaking technology for the manufacture of propylene oxide in an environmentally friendly manner and at lower cost than alternative technologies was a critical ingredient for success. Without the ownership of its technology, the company might not have been as successful as it undoubtedly was. On the other hand, a great array of other factors, such as managerial competence, governmental regulation, demand for products, and the skills of employees, all had a critical part to play in economic performance.

It is, therefore, extremely difficult to isolate and to measure with precision the impact of a company's ethical stance and behaviour on its success. In 1998 I contributed to a book that examined this question.[3] My article rehearsed some of what is set out in Chapter 9 of this book. Other contributors reflected upon such considerations as the impact of the ethical investor movement or the regulatory and legal frameworks within which business is conducted. The general conclusion drawn by the editors was that sound business ethics is an important determinant of economic performance and that enlightened self-interest on the part of companies offers good arguments for improving business ethics. One contributor identified a clear link between business ethics and economic performance, correlating superior share price performance and superior business ethics. And there appeared to be no evidence to suggest that economic performance was in any way impaired by the application of business ethics. At about the same period, the Industrial Society conducted a survey which indicated that three-quarters of the business managers believed that maintaining ethical standards would have a positive effect on financial performance.[4]

In the United Kingdom and in the United States the ethical investment movement aims to provide investors with the opportunity to select their portfolios not only on grounds of financial performance, but also of ethical choice. A discriminating investor might, therefore, avoid investment in companies engaged in business of which he or she disapproves. This is a tricky area about which the Christian conscience may have something to say. For many individual Christians, engagement in certain fields of commercial activity can present an unacceptable compromise of principle. Businesses such as the manufacture of cigarettes or of armaments pose very obvious ethical challenges. More subtle, perhaps, are the occasions where business seems to prompt and stimulate undesirable appetites. Where should the line be drawn as to what desires should be prompted and stimulated?

Russell Sparkes, Fund Manager at the Central Board of Finance of the Methodist Church, has suggested that there is a very clear positive selection effect and that it is the actual process of selection rather than concentration on the products excluded that might account for any superior performance.[5] In other words, it is the careful examination of the companies to be included or excluded from ethical portfolios which seems to account for the inclusion of companies that offer superior performance. Consideration of the nature of the business in which a company is engaged is a very special aspect of evaluating its ethical performance. Generally speaking only a relatively small segment of the stock market is subject to such sensitivities, where the particular business activity itself – such as tobacco, armaments, alcohol or gambling – might raise ethical concerns for the investor. These problems are not generally posed by most business activity. It is probably easier to evaluate the economic performance of companies selected on the basis of the nature of the business in which they are engaged than to judge the effect upon economic performance for the majority of companies of the manner in which they conduct business – that is, to say whether ethical principles are articulated and applied. For it is clear that some factors that influence the financial performance of a company are not readily quantifiable in the conventional sense. The adage that if one cannot measure something one cannot manage it is unduly simplistic.

The mode of governance of a company will clearly have a major impact upon its prospects and ultimately upon its operating and financial performance. Corporate governance has been regularly and extensively reviewed and reported in the United Kingdom.[6] In 2000, Standard and Poor's (S&P), an organization engaged primarily in establishing credit ratings for businesses, developed an instrument for the assessment of how a company is governed. *Corporate Governance Evaluations and Scores*, and its accompanying analyses, measure and evaluate the corporate governance standards of companies around the world. The basis of these assessments is the assumption that investors are prepared to pay a significant premium for a company with sound governance practice. S&P assesses corporate practice on the basis of information that goes beyond what is publicly disclosed and includes conclusions drawn from interviews with company directors. For instance, S&P gauge the independence of the company's external audit – a crucial weakness in the Enron case. Careful consideration is given to the transparency and concentration of ownership, ownership rights and takeover defences. Many of the areas examined by S&P relate closely to ethical issues that may arise in the conduct of business.

Another attempt to evaluate the non-financial aspects of business performance in the United Kingdom is provided by Social & Environmental Risk Management (SERM) Rating Agency, which was set up in 1996 to assess the risk involved in the management of the social and environmental factors associated with the industry sector and type of business in which they operate. SERM attempts to provide a consistent quantitative assessment of risk on the 'softer' issues – environment, health and safety, social, ethical. The ratings it provides, based on its own methodology, focus upon two key factors: the inherent risk factor for the company associated with the area in which it operates, historical operational issues, and its reputational profile; and the efforts made by the company to reduce risk. Thus the assessment takes into account such matters as the business and marketing practices adopted by a company, whether it has been involved in bribery and corruption, its degree of community involvement, and so on. SERM is at pains to emphasize that its ratings and assessments do not assume any particular moral stance. The rating is not, however, a measure of financial performance but of the risk to company performance represented by certain social and environmental considerations.

In 2003 the Institute of Business Ethics (IBE) in the UK published a thorough study of the relationship between business ethics and business performance in large companies.[7] Its research was based on the use of four indicators of business success – economic value added (EVA), price/earnings (P/E) ratio volatility, market value added (MVA) and return on capital employed (ROCE) – and compared the performance over five years (1997–2001) of two groups of companies: those who demonstrated commitment to ethical behaviour by having a published code of business ethics, and those who did not.

The IBE research drew upon previous attempts to examine whether there is any link between corporate financial performance and some kind of corporate responsibility. Some studies had looked at financial performance and commitment to environmental conservation and had tentatively drawn the conclusion that 'green' policies appeared to make money.[8] Other studies, principally conducted in the United States, had endeavoured to look at the relationship between financial performance and ethical business and had generally found it to be positive. In particular, Dr Curtis Verschoor of De Paul University, Chicago found that companies publicly committed to following an ethics code as an internal control strategy achieved significantly higher performance measured in both financial and non-financial terms. He found that the average MVA of 87 companies where an ethics code was stated to be part of management's control strategy was 2.5 times that of those that did not mention a code of ethics or conduct. Verschoor noted that the more extensive or explicit the commitment to the ethics code, the higher the MVA.[9]

The IBE adopted a methodology based on that of Dr Verschoor, using the indicators mentioned above. It found that in a sample of between 41 and 86 companies taken from the FTSE 350 over five years, the financial performance of companies with a code of ethics was superior on three of the four measures of corporate value (EVA, MVA and P/E ratio volatility) to a similar-sized group who said they did not have a code. The ROCE indicator revealed a different result. There was no discernible difference for the first two years, but a better performance by companies with a code of ethics for the following three years. On the basis of these findings, the Institute drew the general conclusion that larger UK companies with a code of ethics out-perform in financial and other terms those who say that they do not have a code. Ethical behaviour, it said, is not only right in principle but pays off in financial terms.

The conclusions drawn by the IBE suggest that if companies cannot be persuaded to examine their conduct for reasons of principle, they might nevertheless be so persuaded on business grounds. Since human beings are rarely motivated by simple considerations, at the most basic level it would seem prudent for companies to incorporate business ethics into their mode of operation.

From personal experience I would emphasize one consideration that is identified in the IBE study and lies at the core of the processes described in Chapter 9. The treatment of a code of ethics as a core policy will bear fruit in the management and application of all company policies and procedures. The fact that it may be more difficult to measure and manage the application of a code of business ethics than, say, the application of a policy on credit terms for customers presents a challenge to managerial competence. If a company can successfully rise to that challenge, its management skills will be enhanced and that may be one key element in better financial performance.

As we have examined the formulation, integration and application of codes of business ethics, we have stressed the elements of established Christian practice. An individual Christian who seeks over a lifetime to integrate the virtues with his or her life-style might well be unable to offer any measurable way in which such a life is managed. For those of us who have been fortunate enough to know people who have integrated the virtues into their lives, the result does not necessarily have to be measured – but it is very obvious. And for the individual Christian, the example to be followed is that of Jesus Christ. The virtues and ideals that he represents in his life are the inspiration for individual Christians to follow, however inadequately.

Despite the problems and limitations that this chapter has considered, the pursuit of virtue through its integration into a company's ethos is both valuable in its own right and also rewarding in its outcomes. That is a key insight which the Christian community should seek to sustain.

Notes

1. For a wide-ranging and provocative contribution to the stakeholder debate, see John Plender, *A Stake in the Future: The Stakeholding*

Solution, Nicholas Brealey Publishing, 1997, and also the 'Tomorrow's Company' initiative, a programme set in train by the UK's Royal Society of Arts to integrate a wider agenda of social considerations into the conduct of businesses.

2. David Henderson, *Misguided Virtue: False Notions of Corporate Social Responsibility*, Institute of Economic Affairs, 2001.

3. Ian Jones and Michael Pollitt (eds), *The Role of Business Ethics in Economic Performance*, Cambridge University Press, 1998.

4. *Managing Best Practice no. 26: Managing Business Ethics*, Industrial Society, 1996.

5. Russell Sparkes, 'The Challenge of Ethical Investment: Activism, Assets and Analysis', in Jones and Pollitt (eds), *The Role of Business Ethics in Economic Performance*, p. 166.

6. See, for example, *The Cadbury Report on the Financial Aspects of Corporate Governance*, 1992; *The Greenburg Report on Directors' Remuneration*, 1995; *The Hampel Report on Corporate Governance*, 1998; *The Turnbull Report on Internal Controls*, 1999; *The Higgs Review of the Role and Effectiveness of Non-executive Directors*, 2003; all available from GEE Publishing Ltd.

7. Simon Webley and Elise More, *Does Business Ethics Pay? Ethics and Financial Performance*, Institute of Business Ethics, 2003.

8. N. Wilks, 'Good Behaviour is its Own Reward', *Professional Engineering*, 15:8 (May 2002); K. Christensen, 'Sustainable Investments: An Analysis of the Correlation between Corporate Sustainability and Financial Performance', Master's thesis, Copenhagen Business School Department of Finance, 2002; *The Emerging Relationship between Financial and Environmental Performance*, Business in the Environment, 2002.

9. Curtis C. Verschoor, 'Corporate Performance is Closely Linked to a Strong Ethical Commitment', in Webley and More, *Does Business Ethics Pay?*, appendix 3.

Whither prosperity? Three challenges

The subject of our study has been wealth and its creation. Wealth is a contentious subject on which people hold strong and diverse opinions, and for which there is no universally acceptable definition. That which offers pleasure and well-being to one person may be abhorrent to another. The element of free choice is inescapably linked to any meaningful concept of wealth. To give true meaning to wealth people should be able to choose freely what they want. Some would argue that such freedom of choice must be totally unfettered. In this book I have been careful, I hope, not to take that position. Not all wants are desirable and some limitations are necessary. John Ruskin said, 'There is no wealth but life.' He had a point.

Inevitably the discussion of wealth in this book has put a strong emphasis upon the mechanisms of free-market capitalism as practised in the democratic societies of Western Europe, North America and, increasingly, many countries in Asia and South America. This emphasis is not to be taken as an unqualified endorsement of that system. It derives from the incontestable success of free-market economies in creating wealth and raising the living standards of millions of people in the world. It was the success of market-driven economies that led many countries to adopt this approach in the last years of the twentieth century – a trend that seems set to continue. The effectiveness of the free-market system has not, however, won it universal approval. Even after the collapse of the Soviet communist economies at the end of the twentieth century there remain those who argue that the principles of communism are still valid. Alongside these critics of the market system are many who find aspects of it distasteful and unacceptable – notably the selfish motivations that it exploits, the inequalities in the distribution of the wealth that it creates, the competitive forces upon which it relies for its success, the social and environmental damage that it may provoke. These criticisms of the free market have validity and demand attention. In partial response governments and inter-governmental organizations across the world are continuously devising mechanisms to address and mitigate the adverse consequences of the successful wealth-creation machine that now dominates much of the globe.

It is not the purpose of this book to endorse or to condemn the free-market model. It has had a prominent place in the book because it is a dominant system and our investigations and arguments have been concerned primarily with coming to terms with the world as it is, not as it might be. Our purpose has been to consider a balanced Christian perspective on wealth and its creation and to derive from that a moral framework for the conduct of that activity, based upon Christian virtue ethics. The broad principles that we have considered are sufficiently robust to retain their validity irrespective of any particular economic system that might be adopted.

Within the so-called free-market system there are many variations; the principles we have set out in this book may be applied to any of them. What we might refer to as the Anglo-American system is characterized by loose labour relations, maximization of shareholder value and short-term profitability, emphasis upon free trade and freedom for individual enterprise. Mainland European free-market systems have rigid labour regulation accompanied by good social benefits, a balanced apportionment of benefits to stakeholders, and emphasis on continuity, alongside free and managed trade. The Far Eastern or Asian system has traditionally offered lifetime employment and close links between societal groups, emphasis upon market share and long-term sustainability, and a protectionist view on trade. It is possible to identify other models within the broad category of free-market economies and it is important not to characterize it in a simplistic or monolithic fashion. Different societies can make widely differing choices about the kind of wealth-creation system they adopt.

The case for a sound Christian theology and for moral guidelines based upon Christian understanding remains constant for any market economy model. And it is equally valid for centrally planned and publicly owned economic systems. The fundamentals of Christian thought are universally applicable to human creativity as manifested in economic processes and the attendant goal of creating human well-being.

It is such universality that now has to be addressed at this juncture in human affairs. Human endeavour harnessed to the creation of wealth and the satisfaction of human needs and wants has evolved through the distinct phases of the hunter-gatherer, the agricultural, the industrial and the post-industrial economies. Each phase built upon the creativity of individuals, the power of choice, the shaping of wants and desires. And as the economic process evolved it became clear that certain conditions were important requirements for its success – such as the rule of law, ownership of property, and the existence of an enabling, but not controlling, state within which business might be conducted.

Globalization

The very success of the current model for creating wealth has prompted a giant change in the way that humankind's economic activities are conducted: wealth creation has become a global phenomenon, moving away from the limitations of the older model, which was primarily based on the nation state.

The phenomenon of globalization means many different things to many different people. Globalization is an inescapable consequence of dramatic technological changes in the fields of transport and communication which have greatly reduced travel times throughout the world and enabled virtually instantaneous communication to come within the reach of large sectors of the world's population. Hence the term 'globalization' is used to describe the ever more pervasive economic, political and cultural links that now connect people and places across the world. These global linkages provoke many fears: the apparent loss of local identities; the apparent colonization of the world economy; in brief, the loss of control to anonymous unknown forces that originate somewhere far away.

At the political level, globalization has prompted experiments and initiatives that involve national governments working together in unprecedented ways – the United Nations or the European Union, for example, or transnational bodies like the various UN agencies, the World Bank, or international campaign groups like Amnesty International and Friends of the Earth. Our cultural differences are also melting and re-forming as ideas are exchanged, as great numbers of people migrate and as travel, trade and communication break down old divisions and barriers.

In the sphere of economics, goods, money and even services now develop and move around the world in bewildering complexity. The financial centres of London, New York and Tokyo are home to international banks and finance houses whose shareholders are spread across the Earth. US companies make their cars in Britain. Japanese electronics giants sell their products extensively in North America and Europe.

Beefburgers or soda drinks formulated to meet US tastes are enjoyed in Europe, Asia and Africa. Jobs and pensions depend upon markets in far-away places through interlinking trade and investments. The tastes and fashions that originate in one place create markets, jobs and wealth on the opposite side of the globe.

Globalization – especially economic globalization – arouses much suspicion and hostility. It is portrayed by its opponents as a new form of colonialism, of oppression, of destruction of local culture and local autonomy. The fact that it is largely a free-market capitalist system that dominates world economic activity provokes the opposition of those who are politically opposed to capitalism and seek to prevent its adoption on principle. Opponents of economic globalization decry the unequal distribution of benefits, the exploitation of developing economies by the more developed economies, the destruction of the natural environment, the power wielded across the world by large corporations that possess powerful global brands or enormous financial resources. Globalization, it is argued, erodes the autonomy of national governments, putting poor people at the mercy of financial institutions over which they have no vestige of control and also destroying individual freedoms. The catalogue of accusations against the globalization of business and of economic activity is comprehensive and damning. Is it, therefore, the case that the wealth-creation process we have been considering – when translated to the global level – no longer serves human needs and wants? Is wealth creation as we currently know it unacceptable when conducted at the international level, as distinct from the national or local level?

For the Christian concerned with business these questions have a special urgency. Christianity is a religion rooted in the material world and the incarnation is the theological expression of that truth. Christianity emphasizes the uniqueness of each individual and individual responsibility for our decisions. Freedom to choose between different options lies with the individual and entails a responsibility that cannot be avoided or assigned to others. This freedom of choice is, of course, an integral part of the wealth-creation process and is fundamental to the operation of a free market. The elements of a Christian theology of wealth creation that were considered in Chapter 4 may go some way to explaining why humankind's most successful attempts to create wealth emerged in cultures shaped by centuries of Christian belief. This fact places a special responsibility upon Christians as the Western economic model gains wider acceptance across the globe.

Against this it can be argued that the great leap forward in wealth creation took place only as the process was freed from its religious context and became a secular activity. The link between secularization and the emergence of an effective wealth-creation machine is readily apparent and it is not my intent to dispute it. But secularization occurred within a culture shaped by Christian thought and is underpinned by key tenets derived from it: the autonomy of the individual and his or her responsibility for personal decisions; the awareness that the material conditions of existence in this world are not fixed but can be shaped to improve the standard of living; the creative instinct that can be fostered in each person; the concept of service to others as a special duty upon each member of the community. Secularization does not eliminate these concepts: indeed it integrates them into the economic system. The significant departure represented by secularization is that it no longer seeks to apply theological concepts and principles as direct practical measures to be implemented in economic life. However, since Christian thought shaped the culture that gave birth to our present-day economic model, it follows that a continuing Christian perspective and input is desirable in order to provide the theological and moral bases for the process. This has been the thesis of preceding chapters.

The question we must now consider is whether the globalization process as manifested in the economic sphere is acceptable within a Christian framework. Should the criticisms of globalization be accepted or rejected by the Christian engaged in the world of wealth creation? This is, of course, an immense subject and requires a wider treatment than is possible in this book. I can address it, therefore, only in outline.

Many of the criticisms levelled against economic globalization are the same as those deployed against wealth creation at a local level. Let us consider some of the more vigorous of these complaints.

Fair trade

Poverty in underdeveloped countries is of overwhelming magnitude and the process of alleviating it is far from easy. The straightforward solution is to generate economic growth. The evidence that economic growth is stimulated by trade rather than by protectionism is very clear. Comparisons between countries that liberalize trade and those that do not show very sharp differences in economic performance. Countries such as China, India or Vietnam which have opened their economies to global trade have seen living standards rise: those in closed economies, such as many African countries or Myanmar or Cuba, have witnessed at best static and at worst declining standards over the decades since the 1960s. Economic growth through trade is the only way forward for poorer countries. The alternatives of mass emigration or huge transfers of wealth from richer countries are not viable options. The process of raising living standards through economic growth is painful and difficult. The history of developed countries, as we have noted, demonstrates this fact. For those who live through the painful transition process it is hard to recognize the improvements that will result. The first migrants from agricultural to urban economies did not immediately enjoy the higher living standards that were to be offered to their children and grandchildren. But at least the transition curve may now be rising more sharply. It was more than two centuries before the benefits of wealth creation based on trade rose to current levels in Europe. The same process took about a century in the United States. South Korea grew rich on trade and exports between about 1960 and 2000, a mere forty years.

Trade, it is argued, is unjust and unfair when conducted between rich developed countries such as Britain and France and poorer underdeveloped countries such as many in modern Africa or parts of Asia or South America. The term 'free trade' may sometimes provoke hollow laughter. The richer nations possess greater bargaining power, which is deployed at the expense of the poorer countries. This criticism is valid and has to be addressed within the appropriate international forums. Christian concepts of justice as embodied in the criterion of reciprocity are to be invoked to correct imbalance and abuse. For example, the principle of reciprocal benefit places a very large question mark against the perpetuation of tariff barriers and distorting subsidies employed by the developed economies, which inhibit and distort fair trade with less developed countries. The dilemma is acute because trade is the most effective way out of poverty for communities in the underdeveloped world. The conduct of trade on just and fair terms is an ethical challenge that must be faced. No one would suggest that this is an easy task: it is not. But it is an issue that must be resolved in order that the benefits of wealth may be brought to the underprivileged of the world.

Free choice

The simple fact of economic growth is not, of course, the whole story and anti-globalization critics have a wider range of problems in mind.

Along with more open markets, access to global trade, and rising living standards, it is argued, come significant disadvantages. For example, critics of globalization see it as a Trojan horse which brings greatly reduced choice through the dominance of global brands such as Coca-Cola or McDonald's burgers, and the loss of local autonomy to external forces such as major international companies like Shell or Exxon, or the requirements of agencies like the World Bank or the World Trade Organization. Local and national governments, it might seem, are largely impotent in the face of these threats.

These criticisms do not stand very close scrutiny. The ubiquity and success of global brands and global corporations is not the same as overwhelming power and influence. Global brands are not omnipotent, nor do they generally have monopoly positions. One virulent critic of global brands, Naomi Klein, implies that people are very gullible and very unintelligent in the choices they make as consumers.[1] But the success of 'brand leaders' like Nike or Gucci is not achieved by brainwashing people into buying things they do not want. The argument that someone else knows what the consumer wants better than the consumer does is not sustainable. If we ask our friends, they will all vehemently deny that they are brainwashed into buying things they do not want or do not need. So who, then, are the suckers who so unthinkingly part with their money? This is not to argue that some extreme brand advertising and brand awareness practices are acceptable. As in all human activities there is abuse. There is some evidence that by overemphasis on brand, mass marketing techniques may be self-defeating. People rebel against the norm and seek to assert their individuality by rejecting the popular brands. Brand success is not based on brainwashing or absence of free choice.

Local autonomy

A more serious charge against globalization is that it emasculates local and national governments. The increasing mobility of capital, it is claimed, forces governments to lower taxes and reduce regulations in a 'race to the bottom' in order to preserve economic growth. But this picture portrayed by the critics of globalization is not wholly accurate. Although there has been considerable liberalization of trade in recent decades, national governments can – and do – retain many means of placing restraints upon free trade. Further, the concerns about the damaging effects of global capital mobility upon national autonomy can be exaggerated. Most domestic investment is financed domestically, and foreign investment is the exception rather than the rule. Nation states retain and in certain circumstances should use powers to influence capital flows. Even the much-quoted international competition on tax rates is a misrepresentation of reality. If taxes are well spent, an economy benefits and achieves competitive advantage over other economies that may have lower tax rates. A regime of well-invested tax will ensure a good transport infrastructure and healthy, well-educated workers – elements necessary for a successful economy. The effect of international pressures upon governmental autonomy is not to be disregarded, but some critics of globalization greatly exaggerate its impact.

The victims of trade

Another theme in the critique of the globalization of trade and of business generally is the damaging consequences for workers in developed countries and for the poor in the developing world. The transfer of jobs from workers in the advanced economies (including those who are amongst the lower-paid) to people who will do the same work for less in poor countries is seen as a double offence: it deprives developed-world workers of jobs and also exploits poorer people in underdeveloped countries. There is no doubt that a displacement of work from developed to less developed countries takes place. Jobs are transferred to poorer people who are consequently better off and the increase in demand for labour will tend to put up wages in those countries. For the workers in well-off countries whose employment is lost, there will be mixed consequences: some will lose out; some will gain; some will be as well off as before. In richer countries, however, few displaced workers are likely to be out of work permanently since new jobs are created as trade opens up new opportunities. Inevitably there are losers as well as winners – just as Western Europe experienced painful social consequences when it industrialized – but the technological progress that accompanies trade and industrialization will usually create new employment. It is however broadly true that technological changes benefit the skilled worker, who will enjoy a greater rise in living standard than the unskilled worker. Differentials grow wider, at least in the initial stages of technology-driven change. This effect is overwhelmingly greater than any inequalities arising purely from trade and its globalization.

The argument that the globalization of trade hurts workers in developing countries merits some further comment. Much suspicion is based upon the erroneous assumption that the benefits which a rich country derives from trade are gained at the expense of the poor in the country with which it trades. This assumption is founded on the notion that wealth creation is a zero-sum game – that country A can increase its wealth only at the expense of country B because there is only a finite amount of wealth to go round. This is a false notion: wealth creation, as we have seen, is a positive-sum game. There is solid evidence that economic growth helps the poor, and the developing countries that have achieved sustained and rapid growth have made remarkable progress in reducing poverty. Increase in wealth is gradually accompanied by greater rights for workers, redistributive taxation and other mechanisms that arise from the political pressures that accompany economic freedoms. Nor is the evidence clear-cut that rich country incomes rise faster than poorer country incomes (for example, in 1975 US income per head was 19 times that of China; by 1995 that figure had fallen to six). Admittedly examples chosen from Africa compared with the US show incomes rising more slowly – but then most African states opted out of the global economy after colonialism ended.[2]

It may be argued that I have dealt superficially with these criticisms of the globalization of trade. To some extent this is true, of course, because this book is not about globalization per se. I have offered only summary comments but at this juncture in human affairs, it is impossible to ignore the subject. It has been dealt with at great length by many opponents and proponents of trade globalization, such as Naomi Klein, referred to above, and Philippe Legrain,[3] on whose work I have drawn for some of the comments I have made. The purpose of the foregoing comments on trade globalization is to illustrate that the process of wealth creation as conducted at the world level through trade is, at bottom, not greatly different from when it is carried out locally. There are winners and losers, there are periods of acutely painful social adjustment, inequalities appear to be inherent in the process and the outcomes are far from perfect. Yet despite these deficiencies and our many attempts to correct them, the market-driven model that has evolved in our Western democracies results in increased wealth that is available to ever-larger numbers of people. Therein lies its strength and the reason why so many countries adopt it.

Many of the reservations about the globalization of the successful wealth-creation process are open to challenge, and evidence of the beneficial outcomes is readily available. That does not conclude the argument however. There are indeed concerns about globalization that are not so readily answered and we should take these into account.

Financial markets

'Globalization' is a very elastic term and for the purposes of this chapter I have so far restricted myself to considering the globalization of trade. However, the freedoms that allow trade to grow are generally accompanied by freedoms in financial markets. Global financial markets add greatly to the potential benefits to be derived from domestic financial markets, primarily by allowing a country to borrow more widely in order to invest. Such investment may be part of a prudent growth programme, it might permit recovery from some economic problem such as natural disaster – or it may be part of an unwise overexpansion of an economy beyond its natural capacity for growth. Recent history is full of examples of countries that have overextended their capacity, or have squandered borrowings that could have been safely invested for sound economic growth. The penalties paid by countries shackled by unsustainable debt are well recorded. Furthermore, the exposure of weaker economies to global financial markets makes them extremely vulnerable to the inherent instability that characterizes such markets. Again, there are many examples of developing countries suffering great damage as the consequence of failures in market confidence – and indeed in the 1920s and 1930s it was developed economies that were threatened in this way. While the proper management of debt as a mechanism to aid necessary investments is an inescapable element in the complexity of modern wealth creation, it lies outside the more general purpose of this book. The highly specialized world of expertise that concerns itself with interest rates, exchange rates and open financial markets is an aspect of the wealth-creation process that calls for specialist treatment.[4] It is nevertheless subject to the same disciplines of moral debate that have formed the substance of our arguments. For those whose responsibilities lie in the world of global financial markets, the Christian virtues of prudence and moderation are particularly relevant and their application in reforming the excesses that can occur is essential. The fact remains, however, that the global consequences of instability in financial markets pose threats to the well-being of much of the world's population. Prudent conduct of those markets is of fundamental importance. Until some way is found to guarantee that conduct, governmental caution in exposing frail economies to world financial market fluctuations is necessary.

There remain two further dimensions to the globalization of business that call for consideration: the cultural impact of economic activity, and the threats that economic activity poses to the physical environment.

Cultural imperialism

There seems to be an inescapable link between economic growth, which benefits the many rather than the few, and the individual freedoms that characterize the developed world. The freedom to engage in entrepreneurial risk has been the wellspring of modern prosperity. With rising prosperity comes a demand for increased personal freedoms. This synergy appears to be real and has led to dramatic rises in living standards for billions of people. Respect for the individual and protection of certain basic human rights and freedoms lie at the heart of Christian social attitudes. In the economic sphere the free choices exercised by the many are a key component of the so-called market system. At its most basic level the market is a mechanism whereby free individual consumer choice can be matched by free producer or supplier ingenuity. These freedoms are in direct contrast to controlled economies, where choice for the individual is constrained by economic rules imposed by some kind of bureaucracy. Experience seems to have demonstrated conclusively that freedom to exercise choice is a more reliable way to generate wealth than the imposed views of a small number of people who take all the decisions.

Together with the freedom of individual choice, experience shows that certain other key ingredients are required for economic growth – for example, the rule of law, a degree of private property ownership, governments that enable rather than control, freedom to engage in and to observe contractual undertakings. These features have become the essential elements of so-called democratic, free-market cultures. The benefits that have accrued in the shape of relief from deprivation are impressive. It remains an open question whether these benefits can be secured without the freedoms and other ingredients that have contributed to rising living standards in the developed world.

It is undeniable that the very success of the developed-world model in economic terms is accompanied by what many regard as unwelcome cultural implications. There is a widespread fear that national and local cultures are under threat and that some kind of global uniformity is the price to be paid for rising prosperity. Those who argue against a global cultural imperialism fuelled by economic success predict a world in which everyone drinks Coca-Cola, watches US television programmes, speaks English and wears Levi jeans. The successful model for overcoming poverty is thus a Trojan horse that brings within it the forces that will lead to the destruction of cultural diversity and autonomous ways of life. The opponents of globalization argue that the in-built tendency for competitive market economies to end up with monopolies will have the same outcome in cultural terms. Eventually the whole world will become a gigantic replication of the culture that exists in North America and, to some extent, in Western Europe. Its dynamic is too powerful, its appeal too great for other cultures to withstand it.

This fear is something that a Christian perspective on wealth creation and its outcomes must take seriously. It used to be said, only partially in jest, that the British Empire was conquered through prayer. The missionary, it was claimed, said 'Let us pray' and while people's eyes were shut someone ran the Union Jack up the flagpole. Is a new form of cultural imperialism taking over the world in the name of rising living standards? It can be argued that the outcome of rising prosperity need not be uniformity and that where cultures meet and even clash, the outcomes are not necessarily the total submersion of one culture within the other. But it remains a fact that the impact of increased prosperity will inevitably modify cultures. Of course, local cultures have always been subject to and modified by external influences. War and conquest have historically been the principal agents of such change and frequently the victors rigorously suppressed the cultural traditions of the losers. So cultural conflicts, modification and even destruction are not new phenomena.

For the Christian, respect for the individual person – and by extension respect for the individual's freedom to make choices – is a fundamental principle. The potentially damaging consequences of loss of cultural diversity must be addressed. Respect for local custom, local preference, local taste is to be observed within the moral framework to which companies operate. There is a proper balance to be observed between the inevitability and desirability of change and due recognition of differing cultural traditions and preservation of their integrity.

In his book on globalization Philippe Legrain quotes John Stuart Mill:

The economical benefits of commerce are surpassed in importance by those of its effects which are intellectual and moral. It is hardly possible to overstate the value, for the improvement of human beings, of things which bring them into contact with persons dissimilar to themselves, and with modes of thought and action unlike those with which they are familiar . . . it is indispensable to be perpetually comparing [one's] own notions and customs with the experience and example of persons in different circumstances . . . there is no nation which does not need to borrow from others.[5]

Here Mill states clearly the case both for economic growth and for an accompanying respect for cultural diversity. The benefits of economic progress are by no means the sum total of human well-being. It lies deep within the truth of Christian understanding that man does not live by bread alone and that human beings are not satisfied solely with material well-being – a point to which we shall return. In respecting others, Christians must respect their right to disagree. It is, perhaps, the ultimate test of freedom to allow others freely to choose to reject it. And so, if others freely turn their backs upon the benefits of economic growth because they decide that the disadvantages it brings outweigh them, then the Christian viewpoint should respect that choice.

Critics of globalization will continue to point to what they regard as an unwelcome trinity: the power of a particular economic process that overrides all others as it brings material, consumer-driven benefits; a culture of liberal postmodern values derived from a Christian tradition that affirms individual freedoms; and an apparently incurable trend towards monopolies in the economic, political and cultural spheres. For too long Christians have failed to face up to this challenge, hiding behind the mantra that wealth creation and what comes with it is a secular process about which their faith has but little to say.

In arguing a contrary view, we have established principles whereby Christian input may be integrated into economic activity. Those principles remain as valid at the macro- or global level as they are at the local or national level. The phenomenon of economic globalization is essentially no different from what took place in villages and rural communities at the beginning of the industrial period. Christians must not repeat past error and turn their backs on globalization or content themselves with unthinking condemnation of it. The challenge is to use Christian wisdom to avoid the destruction of cultural bio-diversity. Like Rabbi Jonathan Sacks, we must rejoice in and promote the dignity of difference.[6] And at the same time we may rejoice in some very positive consequences of the globalization of certain ideas. As Professor Michael Howard points out, we now recognize that war is not an inevitable condition for humankind: 'The establishment of a global peaceful order ... depends on the creation of a world community sharing the characteristics that make possible domestic order, and this will require the widest possible diffusion of those characteristics by the societies that already possess them'.[7]

Environmental conservation

Probably the most carefully argued criticisms of globalization relate to conservation of the natural physical environment. The adverse consequences of economic activity at the local level are perceived to be greatly magnified at the global level. They are generally regarded as the most urgent threat to the delicate balances that constitute the miracle of our global environment.

Easter Island in the Pacific Ocean offers a salutary warning to humankind. There is evidence that the island once supported a prosperous and developed community. Yet when the island was first visited by explorers from Europe they found only a few people scratching a living from an impoverished and ravaged environment. Subsequent investigations have indicated that the inhabitants of Easter Island destroyed their own prosperity by wars and by disregard for the natural environment. Eventually, no trees remained on the island and so the remaining inhabitants were not even able to build boats that would enable them to go elsewhere. Easter Island is a stark warning to humankind of the perils we face, unless we come to terms with the fragility of our natural environment and learn to respect it.

To the Christian who engages in business, environmental conservation has to be a supreme challenge. The call to give love and service to fellow human beings is matched by a duty to preserve the fragile ecology within which life itself is sustained and to avoid irreparable and possibly catastrophic damage to it. The whole thrust of the Judaic tradition from which Christianity emerged is resonant with respect and awe for the natural world. It is captured, for example, in Psalm 8, with its exclamation of wonder at the beauty of creation and a recognition of the special responsibility of humankind towards it:

> When I look at thy heavens, the work of thy fingers,
>   the moon and stars which thou hast established;
> what is man that thou art mindful of him?
>   .   .   .   .
> Thou hast given him dominion over the
>   works of thy hands;
>   thou hast put all things under his feet,
> all sheep and oxen,
>   and also the beasts of the field,

the birds of the air, and the fish of the sea,
whatever passes along the paths of the sea.
(Psalm 8.3–4a, 6–8)

The service of human needs and human well-being can never be compatible with destruction of the very ecosystem within which life evolved and is sustained. There are those who argue that the very success and effectiveness of our efforts to achieve the former have put at risk the latter.

Environmental conservation is above all an ethical issue. As we have repeatedly observed, ethical choices are rarely concerned with black and white. In life generally and in business in particular, we are much more likely to be confronted with choices between options all of which contain elements of good and bad. Indeed, we are frequently faced with the choice between two apparent goods. And so it is with wealth creation and conservation of the physical environment. To quote the old Yorkshire adage, we want both the ha'penny and the bun. It is of the highest importance for Christians that those engaged in the activity of wealth creation should recognize the nature of this dilemma and apply a sound moral approach to its resolution.

There are a number of observations that can usefully be made about the challenge of environmental conservation at both local and global levels. First, it is of fundamental importance that the issue be addressed upon the basis of fact, not upon misrepresentation or ignorance. The celebrated issue of the Shell North Sea Brent Spar was portrayed initially by Greenpeace as a major threat to the environment. Subsequently the organization admitted that it had misrepresented the environmental threat. It is doubtful whether in so doing Greenpeace secured a desirable outcome: distortion of facts is not a sound basis for sensible decision-taking. At a more general level the debate on the true state of the environment cannot helpfully be conducted without a serious commitment to truth. In 2002 a Danish environmentalist named Bjørn Lomborg challenged the conventional views on some key environmental issues.[8] For example, he produced evidence to challenge accepted views on species extinction and global warming, arguing that they were exaggerated. He also pointed to what he claimed were errors in statements about pollution levels, resource depletion and waste. In general, other environmentalists rejected Lomborg's arguments. The case is sufficient to make the point. Facts and data, not mere opinions, should be the substance of environmental debate. That said, it remains beyond reasonable dispute that when all the facts are objectively assessed, the ravages of humankind upon the natural environment must be moderated and our behaviour adjusted to minimize that damage. That imperative applies to the activities that support the creation of wealth.

It is unduly simplistic to attribute all environmental degradation to humankind's efforts to improve well-being, that is to create wealth. Much of the worst environmental damage is the result of poverty and ignorance – for example, destruction of natural forests to provide fuel or to clear land for grazing or cultivation. To point this out is not to avoid facing up to the environmental problems posed by economic activity, but rather to avoid oversimplification of very complex issues.

More affluent societies are generally those where awareness of environmental problems is more acute. As we move through the range of human needs, away from subsistence and towards affluence, consideration for the environment emerges with greater urgency together with recognition that critical issues must be addressed. In part, the very nature of effective wealth creation, with its deployment of private ownership and freedom of personal choice, can offer some bases for incentives to conserve. For example, private parks have become centres of conservation, some of them supported by 'eco-tourism'.

Those responsible for the creation of wealth bear a special responsibility where protection of the environment is concerned. The internal disciplines which we have argued should motivate and guide business conduct have a key role to play in shaping conduct. It may be helpful to look at one way in which this is being done.

The international chemical industry has been highlighted as posing major threats to conservation of the natural environment and it has tried to respond to this challenge in an interesting way. In 1988 the Canadian chemical industry adopted the so-called 'Responsible Care' initiative, which was rapidly taken up by the Chemical Manufacturers Association of the United States. It has now become a worldwide programme to which all major chemical industry associations subscribe. 'Responsible Care' requires all participating companies to pledge publicly to adhere to its guiding principles: continuous improvement and upgrading of environmental, health and safety performance year on year, decade on decade. The commitment includes acceptance of the need for open and transparent communication and reporting by chemical companies about their performance to the communities affected by their operations. This declaration of principles is only the start. 'Responsible Care' embodies a number of codes of practice covering all aspects of company operations, which in turn are translated into operating standards.

So the programme entails continuous improvement in performance, which in turn demands careful and transparent monitoring and reporting. It is a self-regulating commitment, whereby increasingly the companies set the targets to be met, rather than have them imposed by external bodies. The programme demands acceptance by the chemical industry of full responsibility for its behaviour in the critical areas of health, safety and environmental protection. Even from this skeleton description, it is possible to identify the elements of ethical concern in the 'Responsible Care' programme. It is an interesting example of ethics in practice within business and illustrates one way in which wealth creation can be made more compatible with conservation of the natural environment.

In addressing the problems caused by humankind in our pursuit of wealth creation we must endeavour to be as objective and factual as possible. The virtue of justice demands no less. And the virtue of tolerance translates into a balanced and proportionate approach to environmental issues, with due consideration of benefits and costs involved. Likewise on a key issue where the very future of existence itself may be at stake, the measured and considered assessment of risk as required by the Christian virtue of prudence must play a critical part.

The Christian perspective is expressed clearly by Michael Mayne:

> To have 'dominion' over the world of nature does not mean to dominate it, but to stand as the Creator's representatives in his creation; to respect and nurture it. Ecological insight not only demands that we closely observe the lives of animals, plants and streams and stones, but use our imaginations to enter into, and learn to empathise with, forms of life quite different from our own: mysteriously other than we are, but not alien to us.[9]

It may well be that the issues around environmental conservation present the greatest moral issues for those responsible for the conduct of our wealth-creation activities. The danger of incorrect choices could hardly be greater: the possible extinction of life itself on our planet. That this is a serious possibility could hardly be more cogently demonstrated than it has been by the Astronomer Royal, Sir Martin Rees.[10] None the less, the seeds of a dramatic solution to the issues of environmental conservation may well be within the grasp of humankind as we embark upon the latest phase of our engagement with the never-ending search for human well-being.

Humankind is not seen in its most attractive light when engaged in economic activity and associated functions. The legitimate pursuit of well-being can be rapidly transformed into greed and voracity. Accepted standards for behaviour in other spheres of human activity are sometimes put aside when we engage in business and commerce. The companies and corporations that conduct much of the wealth-creation activity are perceived as depersonalized and amoral entities to which the usual norms may not apply. It is sometimes difficult to sustain the argument that the end-purpose of seeking human well-being is an adequate justification for much of what is done to achieve that end.

The brief commentary in the first part of this chapter, which considered two major aspects of modern wealth creation – globalization and environmental conservation – serves to illustrate the power and the potential of the forces that have been unleashed. While we must be wary of some critics who are unduly alarmist and distort the situation, the fact remains that a very potent genie has been released from its bottle, capable of both great good and great harm.

Faced with the dynamic of present-day wealth creation, its critics seek to moderate its harmful outcomes in a variety of ways. The construction of national and global regulations and protocols is clearly an essential element in moderating the adverse effects of humankind's selfishness and folly in the search for wealth. Laws and regulations can do a great deal, but they cannot be a total solution because they are not comprehensive, are difficult to enforce and can never take account of the behaviour which their very existence provokes. Much effort has been devoted to trying to change or frustrate the various economic systems that humankind has devised. Since free-market economies appear to have been the most successful and most resilient, they have attracted the most attention and there have been a large number of attempts to modify or replace them. At the present time, their effectiveness in delivering prosperity seems to have cleared the field of most of the alternatives that have been put forward from time to time. The most ferocious and extreme attempts to overcome the problems that accompany wealth creation are represented by the nihilism of terrorist attacks, which damage and destroy with no apparent alternative vision to replace what it assaults with such violence.

The application of moral guidelines derived from the principles of love and service that underlie Christian teaching and as developed in the framework of virtue ethics can make a lasting contribution to directing our endeavour in the field of wealth creation. The application of this moral framework complements and focuses economic activity but does not frustrate its broad, desirable end-purpose – the attainment of human well-being. This is not, however, the sum total of the contribution to be made from Christian understanding in the field of wealth creation.

The hierarchy of needs

In 1943 the US psychologist Abraham Maslow wrote a paper entitled 'A Theory of Human Motivation'.[11] Maslow's theory was that 'Human needs arrange themselves in hierarchies of pre-potency. That is to say, the appearance of one need usually rests on the prior satisfaction of another, more pre-potent need. Man is a perpetually wanting animal.' Maslow identifies as his starting point human physiological needs – for example the salt, sugar and protein contents of the blood stream which amount to the need for food. Until our stomachs are filled we do not conceive of other needs. Equally, at that point we do not realize that satisfying the need for food does not lead to a state of complete satisfaction.

Once hunger needs are satisfied, argued Maslow, 'safety needs' emerge: a need for freedom from pain or fear, the desire for a sense of an orderly and predictable world. After safety needs are met, we have love needs, such as a sense of belonging and security represented in friends and family. When love needs are satisfied, people move on to 'esteem' needs – the demand for a 'stable, firmly based, high evaluation of themselves, for self respect . . . and for the esteem of others'. Finally, after esteem needs are met comes the need for self-actualization, 'to become everything that one is capable of becoming'.

The hierarchy of needs presents a greatly simplified picture of how human beings behave. The implication that self-actualization is attainable only after all other, more material needs and wants have been satisfied does not bear much scrutiny. There are plenty of examples of people who have found that material attachments are an impediment to spiritual development, as Christ himself warned. Meeting bodily wants is not a precondition for spiritual progress.

However, we do not have to subscribe totally to Maslow's theory in order to recognize that his observations contain simple truths, namely the insatiable nature of human needs and wants. When the basic requirements for existence (food, warmth, shelter, etc.) are met, our human nature drives us on to want other things. As one set of needs or wants is met, so we look for something else to satisfy us. And as Maslow observed, when we are at the stage of meeting our need for food, we are unable to recognize that satisfying our hunger will not stop us from wanting something else. It is this very insatiability of human wants that drives the process of wealth creation, of course. As one set of needs or wants is met, a complex series of interactions arise between the person who wants (the consumer) and the person who meets those wants (the supplier). At this point, new wants can be stimulated by the supplier before the consumer has even considered them. This degree of sophistication in the process is attained only when basic needs for existence have been met and when the technical means are available for the ready satisfaction of the new wants that are stimulated. It is because human wants and desires are limitless and insatiable that wealth creation is not a zero-sum game, as we have previously observed. Each individual has his or her own particular wants which are rarely identical to those of anyone else. When something such as the Kohinoor diamond is the object of desire by more than one person then supply is indeed limited, there being only one Kohinoor diamond. But such is human ingenuity that we are capable of creating and satisfying an otherwise limitless range of desires.

Maslow identified in his theory a hierarchy of wants and needs. Our wants begin with basic necessities without which survival is not possible. Maslow's hierarchy is crowned by the desire for self-actualization, with something like an inevitable progression from the basic necessities towards this peak. We respond instinctively to a certain element of truth in Maslow's concept of a hierarchy of needs because we feel, for example, that when we are not preoccupied with finding the next meal, we can better address some of those things which we feel to be less basic and selfish, such as caring for our spouse or children, or concern for the sick or the elderly. Recognition of some kind of hierarchy of human wants is suggested by Jesus for his followers, inverting the normal way in which we put priorities on our desires: 'provide yourselves with purses that do not grow old, with a treasure in the heavens that does not fail, where no thief approaches and no moth destroys. For where your treasure is, there will your heart be also' (Luke 12.33–4).

At the peak of the Christian hierarchy of needs, the perfect expression of Maslow's goal of self-actualization is love of God and union with God. It is no accident that so many Christian seekers have used the imagery of journeys or searches to describe their spiritual quests – for example St John of the Cross or St Teresa of Avila, who write of the ascent of Mount Carmel or the exploration of the many different rooms in a mansion, all leading to a union with the divine. For the individual, life is set out as a journey and also as a progression to be sought. Indeed, Christian exploration of those very virtues that we have been considering has attempted to establish them in some kind of hierarchical order of desirability.

Christian understanding has always been concerned with the duality of the human condition: we are both material and spiritual beings. One of the great mysteries of humankind is how our material and spiritual natures are related and how they interact. Descartes proposed a dualism that we no longer find tenable: the soul and the body, we now recognize, are inextricably linked. But the soul is critically grounded in the material world and the baser needs of human beings, desires that lie towards the lower end of the hierarchy. The more spiritual aspects of our needs are in the higher reaches of the hierarchy, in our sentiments of love for God and for our fellow human beings. The elements of this hierarchy are repeatedly stressed in the writings of St Paul, with his admonitions to master and reject our baser desires and to seek after higher things. And yet the mystery of the incarnation and the life of Christ as a human being in first-century Palestine is an affirmation that the material world is not to be rejected, but to be affirmed and enjoyed. There is value and joy in our material needs, as well as in our higher spiritual desires.

Humankind has reached a juncture at which a new dimension of well-being is within our grasp. For most of the 150,000 years that humankind has existed, life has been an intense struggle for material survival. Our efforts have been directed at finding the basic necessities for sustaining life and discovering the means to protect ourselves from a frightening and often hostile environment. That is the existence of the hunter-gatherer. We do, of course, have evidence that even those shadowy forebears were concerned with non-material aspects of life – we see the drawings and paintings that they left on the walls of caves and we discover artefacts made for decorative purposes, all of which suggests that immediate material needs did not demand their every waking moment. And among those of our fellow human beings today who live by hunting and by feeding upon what nature provides it is clear that physical survival is not their sole preoccupation and that they develop artistic pursuits which appear to serve no strictly utilitarian purpose.

The weightless economy

The emergence of the post-industrial economy, the information age or the 'weightless economy' represents, for the first time in human history, the opportunity to develop unlimited wealth that is uncoupled from material goods and the consumption of natural resources. The implications of this revolution are immense and offer the prospect of resolving the two great challenges that we considered in the first part of this chapter: globalization and environmental conservation. The limitless possibilities opened up by such mechanisms as the Internet make nonsense of the concept of a monochrome world culture. Likewise, the new non-material consumption made possible by new technology presents the way forward for a less environmentally destructive mode of living.

The industrial or capital economy brought enormous material benefits to huge numbers of ordinary people for the first time. Before the nineteenth century material well-being beyond satisfaction of the most basic needs was not available to most people. Affluence and prosperity were the preserve of a small fortunate stratum whose lives were very different from those of the majority. The advent of the capital economy made not only basic necessities widely available but also a plenitude of material goods that added greatly to comfort and choice. Thus domestic appliances have reduced the time devoted to housework; the development of trains, cars and aircraft have brought travel opportunities to people whose grandparents rarely moved more than ten miles from where they were born. Alongside these benefits, the capital economy provided mass education and public health for everyone in the developed world as well as leisure time in abundance for the enjoyment of entertainment and personal interests. For the developed world, representing about a third of the global population, the consumer society has arrived. And this phenomenon, which today benefits up to two billion people, has taken place in less than two hundred years. We have endeavoured, in early parts of this book, to argue that there is no reason to believe that the mechanisms that provided these benefits in Western Europe and North America could not do the same for all humankind.

The capital economy in the developed world has evolved further, beyond the provision of material goods to the so-called 'weightless economy'. What are the characteristics of the new weightless economy? The first feature that characterizes the new paradigm is the fact that it offers well-being which is primarily of a non-material nature. Let us consider some features of 'weightlessness'.

In the industrial capital economy, the bases for wealth creation are primarily static, consisting of factories, machinery, raw materials and stocks of goods. In the information and new-technology paradigm, the sources of wealth are highly mobile – for example people, computer programmes, television programmes, entertainment and music. These are not rooted in physical plant and machinery to anything like the degree that pots and pans, bicycles and furniture are.

The new forms of wealth are inexhaustible. They can meet an infinity of human wants. It is trite to observe that I am able to wear only one set of clothes at a time, that I can eat only so much food in a certain period of time, that I can live only in one house at any given moment. The potential for enjoyment from a portable computer, a video recorder or a compact disc player is infinite. There is literally no limit to how many football matches one may enjoy, or how much music one may listen to. Personally I adore the music of Franz Schubert. My collection of compact discs enables me to enjoy almost every note that he wrote.

The weightless economy consumes relatively little of the finite natural resources of the world. Admittedly the use of computers, television sets or CD players consumes energy but the amount of physical material taken by the continued use of the instruments of the weightless economy is small. If I watch five football matches every day for a week, I have consumed virtually no physical resources in doing so. My passion for the music of Schubert can be indulged for the rest of my life for the physical debit of the batteries used to power my CD player or Walkman when I listen to my collection of discs. Even for the inveterate traveller, the magic screen of television is able to offer the most eco-friendly of ways to visit other places through virtual reality.

The ownership of this new wealth is very widely dispersed. The primary source of the new wealth does not lie in capital-intensive equipment or the employment of a large labour force or the ownership of great tracts of land. These constraints have traditionally led to major concentrations of wealth-creation power in the hands of small numbers of people. The new weightless wealth lies in the creative talent of those who personally own the ideas or skills that can create the wealth to be enjoyed by the new consumer. The infinite freedom of choice for the consumer of the new wealth of computer programmes, TV and radio programmes, leisure activities, or the arts is matched by a corresponding freedom for individuals who are able to offer this new form of weightless wealth.

One of the main critiques of traditional wealth creation has been dissatisfaction with the unfair distribution of this world's goods. Even in modern societies where redistributive social and fiscal policies have addressed the issue, severe inequalities of distribution persist. The new forms of wealth offer renewed opportunity to break away from this condition. Not only is ownership of the means of production of the new wealth more widely dispersed, but also its consumption is potentially available to everyone. The capital economy, through mass production of material goods, made wealth more widely available. But the distribution of material goods suffers from physical constraints which eventually place some kind of limit on equality of access. It is not so with the new forms of wealth. Through the benefits of modern communications technology it has become possible for everyone to enjoy at the same time and in the same way the delights of a concert, a radio programme, a football match. We are no longer dependent upon redistributive mechanisms to ensure equal access and distribution of the new wealth.

The new wealth-creation paradigm is already creating new communities. In the previous cultures of agricultural and industrial activity, communities were centred on villages or factories. These communities engendered feelings of solidarity, often accompanied by rather rigid social stratification. New communities are evolving in the weightless economy based upon commonality of interest which are no longer limited to geographical locations or to mass physical participation in the same activity.

The rigid, materially based nature of the agricultural and industrial wealth-creation models gave enormous power to governments and other authorities. Political processes were closely allied to physical immobility. It was necessary to accept the mores and ideas of the place where you lived because there was no alternative. These bonds have now been greatly loosened. Among the reasons why the Soviet system collapsed was the fact that it was no longer possible to exclude external ideas: the new technologies had broken through the conventional barriers. By the same token the power of governments to establish mass dependency upon centralized authority is challenged by the new mobility and transience of tastes, skills and ideas. My physical location is no longer the sole or even the primary determinant of the influences to which I may be exposed.

The weightless economy and the new paradigms of wealth began to emerge in the 1990s. The final form that these may take is far from clear. At the present time, the new information-based economy is a pipe-dream for the four billion or so people in the developing world whose primary concerns are for food, shelter, education and health care, rather than for fifty TV channels, a new football team or the ability to create animated graphics on a home computer. The gulf is great – but the examples of countries such as South Korea, Singapore, Malaysia and Taiwan show how rapidly it is possible to move from near subsistence to the new model. There is a strong correlation between growth in energy consumption and economic development for those countries whose GDP per head is less than about $15,000. As GDP per capita rises above that level the link becomes less strong and above $25,000 there ceases to be a link. The challenge of raising per capita wealth to these levels is, of course, immense and would demand great creativity and the application of new sources of energy, such as hydrogen, to avoid irreparable damage to the natural environment. At the same time the concepts of what constitutes wealth should be challenged in light of the potential now available through the new economy, bringing down the level at which economic growth is uncoupled from energy consumption. We can say with confidence that there is no unavoidable reason why all the six billion human beings on planet Earth should not have their essential material needs met or why they should not move on to the unlimited wealth offered by the weightless economy.

It is already clear that the new paradigm has characteristics which differentiate it sharply from earlier models. The weightless economy is no longer constrained by material limitations in its ability to satisfy people's wants: we have freedom from materialism within our grasp. The new economy is also closely linked to freedom of personal choice: individuals will have almost unlimited choice of different kinds of well-being in the information-driven economy. The new forms of wealth will be free of the old limitations of traditional supply and demand: the customization of mass markets is possible.

The incarnation, which roots Christianity in the material world, requires Christians to come to terms with that world: escapist other-worldliness is not a permissible option for the Christian believer. Early Christianity was tempted by the Manichaean heresy that the material world is inherently bad but rejected it. Christ himself drew endlessly upon incidents from our daily material life to illustrate his teachings. He certainly enjoyed the material world, eating and drinking with his friends and participating in wedding celebrations. And yet we also know (even without reference to Maslow) that our well-being cannot be satisfied by material things alone. The crassest forms of consumerism ultimately leave the consumer unsatisfied. Herein lies a dilemma, which was perhaps neatly illustrated by the name of a shopping emporium I once noticed in Cambridge: The Shopping Forum in Jesus Lane. Christians affirm the material world and its delights, but recognize its insufficiency even in the midst of material plenty.

A balanced Christian view of wealth and its creation can come to terms with the insatiability of human desires only when it extends to a vision that outstrips the purely material. The warnings against greed and the destructive power of riches that resonate so strongly in the New

Testament take on a new dimension when our desires are channelled into less gross forms. As the Psalmist says, 'Like as the hart desireth the waterbrooks: so longeth my soul after thee, O God' (Psalm 42.1BCP). Higher desires for non-material things are like our longing for material things – but yet different. This duality of desire reflects the dual nature of human beings, material and spiritual: 'We all know that the ability of traditional wealth to create happiness hits diminishing and then negative returns; it is the non-economic dimensions, cultural and spiritual and psychological dimensions, that become the most important areas for individual responsibility and individual creation'.[12] We are now at a point in humankind's economic activities when those different dimensions can be fully addressed.

It was a great strength of early Christian communities that they were able to colonize and Christianize the pagan world in which they found themselves. Examples abound: thus spring fertility rites were Christianized in the feast of Easter; pagan wells were transformed into baptismal fonts; Roman law became the basis for canon law. The sacraments were a paradigm for this process, taking outward, visible and material signs to manifest inward and spiritual meaning. But later Christian generations seem to have lost this genius for colonization. The secular world is so often seen as separate and impregnable, something the Christian community often turns its back upon and with which it wishes to have minimal contact. This posture is very pronounced in traditional Christian attitudes towards the creation of wealth.

The new, weightless economy, with its limitless potential and its ability to free human desires from their grosser, materialistic chains, represents a unique opportunity for Christian colonization. The founder of the Salvation Army, William Booth, once said that the devil should not be allowed to have all the best tunes and Salvation Army bands at the end of the nineteenth century vigorously demonstrated the point. And so it should be with the new forms of wealth. There is no reason why present-day concepts of wealth and well-being should remain outside the embrace of Christian love and understanding. In medieval times games, music, drama, painting, sculpture, were all deployed in the naves of great European churches, both directly and indirectly, to display the glory of God. These riches were embraced and enjoyed and celebrated by the Christian community. It can be so again as the new wealth becomes universally accessible. Christians should confront the challenge that some 80 per cent of Internet activity is said to be related to pornography. It is our mission to change that, not accept it.

For the Christian, looking at this world through the lens of the incarnation, delight is to be found in humankind's creative capacity to promote well-being. The explosion of popular enjoyment in the shape of music, mass entertainment, sport and so on offers an enormous challenge for a new understanding of sacramentalism and the colonization of the secular into the sacred. This should be the vision for the Christian who engages in business. Just as previous generations of business entrepreneurs learned to stimulate wants for material goods, so the Christian engaged in business can now seek to prompt desire for non-material things.

Herein lies the challenge. How do we displace the material objects of our desires from the overriding position that they occupy? Consumption of material things lies at the very heart of the Western concept of wealth and well-being. An alternative vision is now technically within our grasp. Ways have to found to wean people from the material to the non-material. If the essence of wealth is rooted in the satisfaction of wants, then we must endeavour to modify and re-orientate our desires. This is a huge task because the very insatiability of human wants means that people will demand both material *and* non-material well-being to an inordinate degree. This is not a new dilemma. The great economist John Maynard Keynes argued in the 1930s that the human race would, within a century, create enough wealth to satisfy most material wants and he envisaged a new age of leisure.[13] Things have not worked out that way: a world of leisure is still remote for many. The Christian perspective on wealth creation can help to reshape our notions of well-being. It is a task of great magnitude, but not one that can be shirked. For the Christian engaged in business it has to assume priority.

Not only does the new wealth-creation paradigm – the weightless economy – offer an opportunity for reshaping and satisfaction of limitless desire but it also changes fundamentally the opportunities for individual Christians to serve their fellow human beings. The capital economy is now giving way to the economy of individualism. The individual creates his or her own capital: good ideas and creative thinking are sufficient. The potential for individual self-realization, as set out at the peak of Maslow's hierarchy, can come within the reach of all. We shall no longer be dependent upon institutions and corporations for the new well-being. The wheel turns full circle and the ability to create satisfaction and well-being can return again to the individual. It is in helping to shape and fulfil that sense of well-being within the new economy that the Christian community should seek to play a vigorous role. We cannot stand aside.

Notes

1. Naomi Klein, *No Logo*, Flamingo, 2000.
2. See 'A Survey of Globalisation', *The Economist*, 29 September 2001, p. 12.
3. Philippe Legrain, *Open World: The Truth about Globalization*, Abacus, 2002.
4. See Stephen Green, *Serving God? Serving Mammon?*, Marshall Pickering, 1996.
5. John Stuart Mill, *Principles of Political Economy* (1848), quoted in Legrain, *Open World*, p. 312.
6. See Jonathan Sacks, *The Dignity of Difference*, Continuum, 2002.
7. Michael Howard, *The Invention of Peace*, Profile Books, 2000, p. 105.
8. Bjørn Lomborg, *The Skeptical Environmentalist: Measuring the Real State of the World*, Cambridge University Press, 2001.
9. Martin Rees, *Our Final Century: Will the Human Race Survive the Twenty-First Century?*, Heinemann, 2003.
10. Michael Mayne, *Learning To Dance*, Darton, Longman & Todd, 2001, p. 80.
11. Abraham Maslow, 'A Theory of Human Motivation', *Psychological Review*, July 1943.
12. Richard Koch, 'Work and the Individual: The Rise of the Creative Individual', lecture given to the Royal Society of Arts, June 2002. See also his *The 80/20 Revolution: Why the Creative Individual is King*, Nicholas Brealey Publishing, 2002.
13. John Maynard Keynes, 'Economic Possibilities for Our Grandchildren', in *Essays in Persuasion*, Macmillan, 1931.

Select bibliography

Ferguson, Niall, *The Cash Nexus*, Allen Lane, 2001.

Griffiths, Brian, *Morality and the Market Place*, Hodder & Stoughton, 1982.

Griffiths, Brian, *The Creation of Wealth*, Hodder & Stoughton, 1984.

Harries, Richard, *Is There a Gospel for the Rich? The Christian in a Capitalist World*, Mowbray, 1992.

Higginson, Richard, *Called to Account: Adding Value in God's World – Integrating Christianity and Business Effectively*, Eagle, 1993.

Higginson, Richard, *The Purpose and Values of Business: An Annotated Bibliography*, Foundation for Business Responsibilities, Issues Paper No. 5, 2000.

Landes, David, *The Wealth and Poverty of Nations*, Little, Brown, 1998.

MacIntyre, Alasdair, *After Virtue*, Duckworth, 1981.

Schmidt, Thomas E., *Hostility to Wealth Creation in the Synoptic Gospels*, JSOT Press, 1987.

Smith, Adam, *An Inquiry into the Nature and Causes of the Wealth of Nations*, first published 1776.

Vallely, Paul (ed.), *The New Politics: Catholic Social Teaching for the Twenty-First Century*, SCM Press, 1998.

Weber, Max, *The Protestant Ethic and the Spirit of Capitalism*, trans. Talcott Parsons, George Allen & Unwin, 1930.

Index

The Society for Promoting Christian Knowledge (SPCK) was founded in 1698. Its mission statement is:

To promote Christian knowledge by
- **Communicating the Christian faith in its rich diversity;**
- **Helping people to understand the Christian faith and to develop their personal faith; and**
- **Equipping Christians for mission and ministry.**

SPCK Worldwide serves the Church through Christian literature and communication projects in over 100 countries, and provides books for those training for ministry in many parts of the developing world. This worldwide service depends upon the generosity of others and all gifts are spent wholly on ministry programmes, without deductions.

SPCK Bookshops support the life of the Christian community by making available a full range of Christian literature and other resources, providing support for those training for ministry, and assisting bookstalls and book agents throughout the UK.

SPCK Publishing produces Christian books and resources, covering a wide range of inspirational, pastoral, practical and academic subjects. Authors are drawn from many different Christian traditions, and publications aim to meet the needs of a wide variety of readers in the UK and throughout the world.

The Society does not necessarily endorse the individual views contained in its publications, but hopes they stimulate readers to think about and further develop their Christian faith.

For further information about the Society, visit our website at *www.spck.org.uk,* or write to:
SPCK, Holy Trinity Church, Marylebone Road,
London NW1 4DU, United Kingdom.